Financialization of the Economy, Business, and Household Inequality in the United States

This second volume on the political and social economy of financialization in the US focuses on the consequences of the rise of finance for the American macroeconomy, household inequality, and the management of nonfinancial business enterprises.

A historical–institutional balance-sheet approach to long-term trends and recent change in the US reveals a series of anomalies and provisos for critical, heterodox, and mainstream economic approaches and provides new perspectives on debates about political economic change in advanced economies since the 2007–2008 financial crisis.

This book marks a significant contribution to the literature on financialization and studies in social economics, household economics, the structure and management of nonfinancial business enterprises, and American political economy.

Kurt Mettenheim taught at the FGV-EAESP in São Paulo, Brazil, the University of Oxford the University of Pittsburgh, and Columbia University.

Olivier Butzbach is an Associate Professor of Political Economy at the Department of Political Science of the University of Campania 'Luigi Vanvitelli', Italy.

Routledge Frontiers of Political Economy

Political Economy of Financialization in the United States
A Historical-Institutional Balance-Sheet Approach
Kurt Mettenheim

The International Political Economy of the Renminbi
Currency Internationalization and Reactive Currency Statecraft
Hyoung-kyu Chey

Explaining Wealth Inequality
Property, Possession and Policy Reform
Benedict Atkinson

Financialization of the Economy, Business, and Household Inequality in the United States
A Historical–Institutional Balance-Sheet Approach
Kurt Mettenheim with Olivier Butzbach

Economic Ideas, Policy and National Culture
A Comparison of Three Market Economies
Edited by Eelke de Jong

Political Economy of Contemporary Italy
The Economic Crisis and State Intervention
Nicolò Giangrande

For more information about this series, please visit: www.routledge.com/
Routledge-Frontiers-of-Political-Economy/book-series/SE0345

Financialization of the Economy, Business, and Household Inequality in the United States

A Historical–Institutional Balance-Sheet Approach

Kurt Mettenheim
with Olivier Butzbach

LONDON AND NEW YORK

First published 2022
by Routledge
2 Park Square, Milton Park, Abingdon, Oxon OX14 4RN

and by Routledge
605 Third Avenue, New York, NY 10158

Routledge is an imprint of the Taylor & Francis Group, an informa business

© 2022 Kurt Mettenheim and Olivier Butzbach

The right of Kurt Mettenheim and Olivier Butzbach to be identified as authors of this work has been asserted by them in accordance with sections 77 and 78 of the Copyright, Designs and Patents Act 1988.

All rights reserved. No part of this book may be reprinted or reproduced or utilised in any form or by any electronic, mechanical, or other means, now known or hereafter invented, including photocopying and recording, or in any information storage or retrieval system, without permission in writing from the publishers.

Trademark notice: Product or corporate names may be trademarks or registered trademarks, and are used only for identification and explanation without intent to infringe.

British Library Cataloguing-in-Publication Data
A catalogue record for this book is available from the British Library

Library of Congress Cataloging-in-Publication Data
Names: Mettenheim, Kurt von, 1957– author. | Butzbach, Olivier, author.
Title: Financialization of the economy, business, and household
inequality in the United States : a historical-institutional balance-sheet
approach / Kurt Mettenheim, with Olivier Butzbach.
Description: Abingdon, Oxon ; New York, NY : Routledge, 2022. |
Series: Routledge frontiers of political economy |
Includes bibliographical references and index.
Identifiers: LCCN 2021024287 (print) | LCCN 2021024288 (ebook)
Subjects: LCSH: Financialization–United States–History. | Economic
development–United States–History. | Income distribution–
United States–History. | United States–Economic conditions.
Classification: LCC HG181 .M478 2022 (print) |
LCC HG181 (ebook) | DDC 332.04150973–dc23
LC record available at https://lccn.loc.gov/2021024287
LC ebook record available at https://lccn.loc.gov/2021024288

ISBN: 978-1-032-12151-2 (hbk)
ISBN: 978-1-032-12154-3 (pbk)
ISBN: 978-1-003-22332-0 (ebk)

DOI: 10.4324/9781003223320

Typeset in Bembo
by Newgen Publishing UK

Contents

List of figures		vi
List of tables		viii
Introduction		1
1	The financialization of the American economy	13
2	The financialization of American household inequality	55
3	The financialization of American nonfinancial business OLIVIER BUTZBACH	111
Conclusion		135
Index		153

Figures

1.1	Percentage annual change in US wages, prices, and long-term interest rates, 1800–2019	18
1.2	Percentage annual change in prices, M2, the monetary base, and corporate bond interest rates, 1870–2020	21
1.3	New York Stock Exchange monthly and annual percentage change in total capital, 1815–2020	22
1.4	Chicago Board Options Exchange volatility index, 1990–2020	24
1.5	New York Stock Exchange volatility, 1966–2020	24
1.6	Annual percentage change in US real gross domestic product, 1930–2020	26
1.7	Quarterly real GDP change, 1947–2019	26
1.8	Chicago Federal Reserve Bank economic activity index, 1967–2019	27
1.9	US labor productivity: Real per-person business sector output, percentage annual change, 1948–2020	28
1.10	Primary, secondary, and higher education, 1940–2019	29
1.11	Military expenditures as percentage GDP, US, UK, France, and Germany, 1949–2019	29
1.12	Private and government investment as a percentage of US GDP, 1929–2019	30
1.13	Personal consumption, private investment, and government contributions to GDP change, 1929–2019	31
1.14	Goods, services, and structures as percentage of current dollar GDP, 1929–2019	32
1.15	Annual raw price changes for gross domestic purchases, services, and financial services, 1929–2019	32
1.16	Unemployment rate (U-3 measure of labor underutilization), 1949–2020	37
1.17	Employment to population ratio, 1948–2020	38
1.18	Weekly initial unemployment insurance claims, 1967–2019, thousands	39
1.19	US industry capacity utilization, 1967–2020	40

List of figures vii

2.1	Gini coefficients pre-tax and transfers, post-tax, and post-tax and transfers, 1979–2016	62
2.2	Tax burden on US social classes, 1979–2016	64
2.3	Government transfers as percentage total income by social class, 1979–2016	64
2.4	Financialization index by social class, 1989–2019	71
2.5	Leverage index by social class, 1989–2019	71
2.6	The labor share of income: wages and salaries as percentage of US gross income, 1929–2018	85
2.7	The percentage of annual change in real wages, 1930–2019	86
2.8	Personal income receipts as percentage personal income, 1929–2019	93
2.9	The percentage of annual change in US personal consumption, private investment, and government, 1929–2018	94
2.10	Principal US household financial claims; percentage total household financial claims, 1951–2020	99
2.11	US household debt service payments, percentage disposable personal income, 1980–2020	103
2.12	Home equity by social class, 1990–2019, $ trillion	106
3.1	US nonfinancial corporate financial income and financial payout ratios, 1958–2019	115
3.2	Breakdown of financial payout ratios, 1958–2019	116
3.3	Financial payouts as percentage of net operating surplus, 1947–2019	117
3.4	Nonfinancial and financial trade receivable assets, 1946–2019, $billion	118
3.5	The financial assets of nonfinancial corporations, percentage total US assets, 1951–2020	120
3.6	Nonfinancial business debt annualized quarterly percentage growth rate, 1952–2020	124
3.7	US nonfinancial business debt as percentage of GDP and total assets	125
3.8	Composition of US nonfinancial corporation financial debt, 1952–2020	126
3.9	Financialization index for corporate and noncorporate business, 1960–2018	127
3.10	Leverage ratio for US corporate and noncorporate business, 1960–2018	127
3.11	Balance-sheet totals for noncorporate business enterprises, 1960–2018, $trillion	128
3.12	Balance-sheet totals for US corporate business enterprises, 1960–2018, $trillion	128

Tables

1.1	Drivers of US GDP growth: Personal consumption, capital, foreign trade, and government, 1930s–2010s	34
1.2	Decade average composition of US gross domestic product, 1930s–2010s	42
1.3	Decade average savings and investment by sector, 1930s–2010s	48
1.4	Social sector composition of US gross domestic product, five-year averages, 1960–2019	50
2.1	US household balance-sheet portfolios by wealth percentile classes, 1989–2019	67
2.2	The balance sheets of the bottom 50% income percentile of American households, 1989–2019	73
2.3	The balance sheets of the next 40% (top 50–90%) income percentiles of American households, 1989–2019	75
2.4	The balance sheets of the next 9% (top 90–99%) income percentile of American households, 1989–2019	77
2.5	The balance sheets of the top 1% income percentile of American households, 1989–2019	79
2.6	Decade average composition of US personal income and its disposition as percentage GDP, 1930s–2010s	87
2.7	US personal spending on goods and services, 1930s–2010s	91
2.8	US household aggregated balance sheets, decade average percentage total assets, 1960s–2010s	95
2.9	US household disaggregated balance sheets, decade average percentage total assets, 1960s–2010s	96
2.10	Percentage of families with debts 60 days or more past due, 1989–2016	104
2.11	Percentage of families with debt payment ratio greater than 40 percent income, 1989–2016	105
3.1	Decade average value of the financial income ratio for US nonfinancial corporations	115

Introduction

This book is the second volume of a political-economic, historical–institutional, and balance-sheet inquiry into financialization in the United States. The preceding volume presented the theories and concepts of modern pluralist and critical political economy, the techniques of historical–institutional analysis, and the fundamentals of social sector financial portfolios and balance sheets. Conceptual stretching, mis-aggregation, double-counting, loading on the dependent variable, and private sector biases were found to flaw economic approaches to bank change and the rise of finance (Mettenheim, 2021).

The recovery of the original concepts behind US national income accounts enabled the elaboration of alternative approaches to the long-term origins, the changing character, and the limits to the rise of finance. The theory of compounding financialization, and the evidence from the US, suggested that the rise of finance occurred far earlier than assumed in critical political-economy research. Post-Keynesian endogenous money theory (Wray, 1990) helps explain the long-term multiplication of financial claims[1] and liabilities. However, the conceptual stretching of money to include financial claims, the shift away from the private production to the public accommodation of financial claims and liabilities, and the redefinition of banks as financial firms along the lines of contemporary banking theory and financial intermediation theory require revision of endogenous money approaches. Moreover, the evidence from the US since the financial crisis of 2007–2008 indicates both limits to the ascendence of finance and the expansion of the scope of conflict over monetary policy and authority.

To explain these anomalies of longer-term origins, public accommodation, and the limits to the rise of finance in the US, the preceding volume returned to the founding ideas of modern political and social economy, especially as elaborated by Karl Polanyi and E.P. Thompson. The rise and fall of finance in the US are consistent with Karl Polanyi's conception of the two political-economic moments that shaped the origin of our times (Block and Somers, 2014; Polanyi, 1944). According to Polanyi, the first political-economic moment that shaped modern capitalism was the imposition of laissez-faire policies to create markets for land, labor, and money during the 1830s in England. The second moment, decades later, was the emergence of social reactions of self-defense against the

DOI: 10.4324/9781003223320-1

2   *Introduction*

social exclusion, inequalities, and market failures produced by the commodification of land, labor, and money. Polanyi's framework of two moments is especially helpful to explain both the origins of, and limits to, financialization. It is consistent both with theories from critical political economy of the origins of financialization in the late 1970s and, decades later, the emergence of social reactions of self-defense against the commodification of credit, finance, and banking in the US.

The founding work of E.P. Thompson on popular economic moralities also inspires the approach to banking that informs this book (Thompson, 1971). From this perspective, the social orientations of savings banks, cooperative banks, and other financial institutions (and public finance) represent alternative monetary moralities designed, and able, to counter the ideologies of free markets and financial economics. The larger institutional scale of alternative banks and public policies – compared to the subterranean ideas of subaltern peoples and popular revolts that Thompson studied – does not invalidate this parallel.

The founding ideas and concepts of political and social economy help explain the origins of financialization, the consequences of deregulation, and the reregulation of banking and finance during the 2010s in the US. This implies a critique of standard economic approaches, especially to banking, finance, and politics. Part of the historical–institutional method is to recover the original meanings and measures of concepts and categories in political economy. Unexpectedly, the US constitution of national economic accounting (Bureau of Commerce, 1934), provides a series of insights about the composition of core economic aggregates such as money, personal savings, social banking, bank reserves, bank capital, social class, inequality, savings institutions, fiduciary trust, and the differences between both personal income and corporate income, and between financial capital and nonfinancial capital.

This back-to-the-future approach to the definitions and data in the official historical statistics provided by the Department of Commerce Bureau of Economic Analysis in the US National income and product accounts (from 1929–2019) made it possible to increase the number of observations and, equally important, to avoid the biases produced by the financialization of macroeconomic categories that ensued after 1945. A central argument throughout the two volumes of this study is that the concepts of classic modern political economy were stretched, through redefinition, to become economic and financial ideologies. Ideologies of financial economics have caused, and concealed, financialization and the financialization of inequality, while also obscuring the social, political, and economic forces that may (and, indeed, once again during the 2010s in the US *have*), countered the rise of finance and inequality. Although often dressed up as neoliberal theory, the financialization and centralization of monetary authority run counter to the core conceptions and traditions of political liberalism, pluralism, federalism, populism, and the separation of powers that define American political institutions in the US (Jones, 2005; Mettenheim, 1997).

The previous volume elaborated the theory of compounding financialization by building on the contributions of critical political economy, the burgeoning, transdisciplinary international literature on financialization, and post-Keynesian endogenous money approaches (with the provisos that financial claims are not money and banks cannot be viewed simply as financial firms). The preceding volume contained three empirical chapters; one dedicated to the origins and evolution of the US banking system, the second tracing the centralization and financialization of monetary authority in the US, and the third on shadow banking, off-balance-sheet operations, and nonbank financial entities in comparative perspective.

The evidence from the US confirms the core ideas of critical political economy about the origins of financialization in the turn to neoconservatism, monetarism, and high interest rate policies in the late 1970s (Mader et al., 2020; Krippner, 2011; Dúmenil and Lévy, 2004). However, during the four decades since the 1970s, new phenomena and different causal mechanisms shaped financialization. Post-Keynesian approaches to endogenous money help explain the continued rise of finance, despite the fall of interest rates to near zero. However, the conceptual stretching of money to include financial claims, a tendency to ignore the relations between financial claims and liabilities (debt), the public accommodation of private financial claims (and liabilities), and the declining marginal returns to finance during the 2010s in the US suggest the need for alternative explanations.

This second volume extends the analysis in the following chapters to explain, more carefully, how financialization effected the other US social sectors while controlling for broader changes in the US economy. The first volume explored the financialization of banking and monetary authority (the sectors of finance and government in the terms of balance-sheet studies). This volume explores the consequences of financialization for household inequality and the structure of nonfinancial business in the US, while attempting to control for broader macroeconomic trends and, albeit less systematically, the relations between the US and the rest of the world.

The first chapter of this book reviews the macroeconomic evidence about financialization in the traditional source of national income accounts data from 1929–2020 in the US: the Department of Commerce Bureau of Economic Analysis's National income and product accounts (NIPAs). The second chapter explores the implications of the second largest variance (after the rise of finance) in the balance-sheet data from the US from 1945 to 2019: the proportional decline of US households. A historical–institutional approach to the data from the US on the balance-sheet portfolios of households reveals unexpected patterns of continuity, change, and the financial causes of inequality.

However, the evidence from the US also indicates, unexpectedly, that social policies and income transfers were able to counter the rise of inequality in the US since 1980, far more than the literature on the dismantlement of Welfare States and critical political economy approaches suggest. Chapter 3 examines how financialization hollowed out nonfinancial business enterprises in the US.

4 *Introduction*

The evidence also suggests how the financialization of corporate businesses arose from the globalization of American firms, while the data on unincorporated business enterprises provide control for claims about financialization and serve as an alternative paradigm.

A wide variety of phenomena have been associated with financialization. However, the evidence reported in this book from the US National income and product accounts (NIPAs, 1929–2019) and the Integrated macroeconomic accounts (IMAs, 1960–2019) are consistent with only two of the consequences emphasized in the comparative literature on financialization (Hein et al., 2016, 2015), claims that are often shared in comparative studies of advanced capitalist economies. The data from the US confirm substantial increases in both inequality and unused industrial capacity since 1980. However, after increasing the number of observations back in time and disaggregating the data to control for broader macroeconomic changes, the evidence from the US NIPAs, and other data sources, fails to support *any* of the other claims about the deleterious consequences of financialization. This implies that classical Keynesian ideas about demand management remain far more relevant for social inclusion and countercyclical economic policies than the post-Keynesian focus on endogenous monetary phenomena.

The problems of theory and method discussed in the preceding volume require more in-depth discussion than is possible in this second volume. However, a brief synopsis of the critical, pluralist, and classic modern approaches of political economy, the methods of historical–institutional balance-sheet analysis, and the implications of the findings of the first volume are in order. The concepts and categories of classic modern political economy suggest that major literatures in economics about banking and finance in the US are flawed by serious problems of conceptual stretching (Sartori, 1970), mis-aggregation, and loading on the dependent variable (Geddes, 1990).[2]

The conceptual stretching of macroeconomic aggregates to include financial claims and liabilities runs counter to core principles of social science, the categories of classic modern political economy, and the original meanings and measures of US national accounts. Conceptual stretching redefined personal savings from the traditional meaning of other people's money into the financial assets (claims) of banks and financial firms. Bank reserves and bank capital were redefined from being hard assets such as gold, coin, and currency into the very opposite: the most liquid liabilities that arise from capital-market funding. Monetary aggregates were stretched to include increasingly exorbitant, unrealistic, murky, unpriceable, and unmarketable financial claims. The preceding volume traced how errors of concept, theory, and double-counting combined, in the US, to cause, and conceal, the longer-term compounding of financialization and inequality.

The 1934 constitution of US national income accounts provided the conceptual and methodological cornerstones to elaborate this critique (Bureau of Commerce, 1934). Consultation of the original concepts elaborated for US national income and product accounts (NIPAs) suggested how the redefinition of savings into the financial assets of banks and financial firms became an ideological veil of finance capital. This error induced serious, performative fallacies across economic approaches – mainstream, critical, and heterodox alike. However, unexpectedly, the original definitions and classifications of the NIPAs permit a back-to-the-future recovery of the concepts and theories of classic modern political economy, concepts and theories that help counter the ideologies of corporate finance and financial economics that skew academic research, public policy, and regulatory frameworks.

A further word on the main findings in the previous volume about the US banking system is in order. The US banking system is described as a dual system (De Young, 2010). This captures the reality that the US banking system is indeed still, in the third decade of the twenty-first century, composed largely of thousands of small local and regional banks, savings institutions, and credit unions. These institutions stand in stark contrast to the concentration of banking and finance in four large, capital-market-based, bank holding companies. However, the evidence, especially since the financial crisis of 2007–2008, runs against two central ideas normally associated with the concept of a dual banking system in the US.

The first idea at odds with the evidence from the 2010s is that the two sides of US banking arise from dual equilibria. The second idea is that the largest US bank holding companies realize the competitive advantages of scale, scope, and size over the vast number of smaller banks, depository institutions, and financial entities. A historical–institutional approach suggests more specific, path-dependent causes (such as mergers and acquisitions), different competitive advantages (of traditional banking), and new problems, such as brinkmanship, bailouts, and direct government accommodation of the market positions of large banks. The marginalization of small and midsize banks and financial institutions, the concentration of investment banking and wholesale operations in four bank holding companies, the declining marginal returns to concentration, and a back-to-the-future trend away from market-based banking during the 2010s are all phenomena quite different than expected by the ideas of dual equilibria or the competitive advantages of large scale.

Indeed, movement in the very opposite direction appears in the data from the US, especially during the 2010s. The large number of local and regional banks (the other side of the dual US banking system), evolved alongside money-center banking. Moreover, significant evidence from a variety of sources suggests that, during the 2010s, smaller banks in the US realized competitive advantages over the big four (or big six), bank holding companies precisely because of the former's more traditional deposit-taking and loan-making operations and business models. The implications of these developments since the financial crisis of 2007–2008 are considerable. Instead of a transition toward money-center banking, as supposed by mainstream and critical approaches alike (for better or worse), the evidence from the US during the 2010s suggests

6   *Introduction*

the contrary: A back-to-the-future return to traditional deposit-taking and loan-making, even on the part of money-center banks. This belies central expectations about bank change in contemporary banking theory and financial intermediation theory, expectations that are often shared by post-Keynesian and critical political economy approaches to financialization. Instead of convergence toward money-center banking, the reverse obtained in the US during the 2010s.

Comparisons of the structure, performance, and balance-sheet composition of US banks from the nineteenth century through the 2010s confirm the contours of this back-to-the-future movement. Moreover, the classic ideas from modern political and social economy that inform this study (social reactions of self-defense, alternative monetary moralities, and the laws of large assets based on declining marginal returns), imply a different view of financialization. Theory, and the evidence from the US during the 2010s, suggest the end of the rise of finance.

This implies a new political phenomenon; the expansion of the scope of conflict over monetary authority and monetary policymaking. The expansion of the scope of conflict over banking, finance, and monetary policy since the financial crisis of 2007–2008 runs counter to economic theories of central banking. Economic approaches to central banking seek to reduce or eliminate politics. Central bank independence is another economic ideology that helped cause, and conceal, the financialization and centralization of monetary authority in the US. This study adopts an alternative approach from political science that examines central banking as a particular mode of authority: monetary authority (Mettenheim, 2016; Whitehead, 2002). In this respect, the evidence from the US suggests a long history of liberal, pluralist, separationist, federalist, democratic, and populist traditions, all opposed to the concentration of banking, finance, and monetary authority. The policy experiment of deregulation pursued by neoconservative political forces based on neoliberal economic theory thereby diverged, profoundly, from central traditions of philosophy, politics, economics, and public policy in the US. There is nothing liberal about the centralization and financialization of monetary authority. It is at odds with two centuries of the separationist, federalist, pluralist, and democratic traditions that inform American political institutions.

The recovery of classic modern ideas about public finance also helped counter the ideology of fiscal constraints. Since the abandonment of the electoral road to socialism in the 1970s, a perverse consensus has obtained across normally antagonistic theoretical perspectives (Scharpf, 2011; Przeworski, 1985; Wright et al., 1975). The consensus is that fiscal constraints are primordial and fiscal controls are necessary to maintain the confidence of markets and the flow of private investment. However, this emphasis on fiscal constraints conceals, indeed serves to *neutralize*, fundamental ideas in classic modern political economy about the importance of public finance for countercyclical policymaking, social inclusion, and other roles of government. The neutralization of public finance by the imposition of fiscal controls has become especially acute because the central ideas of monetarism (about benchmark interest rates being able to help manage economies with a light touch) have ended. The central ideas of monetary theory and policy ended in the US with the massive measures of government intervention first adopted during the 2007–2008 financial crisis, measures that have since been followed, unabated, by a series of unorthodoxies.

However, the causal forces of fiscal and financial ideologies are not inexorable. Instead, the evidence from the 2010s in the US suggests the emergence of counterforces. In this respect, another new phenomenon in the US, examined in the previous volume, merits mention: Efforts to improve the channels of communication, information, and feedback for monetary policymaking through the expansion of the scope of conflict. Reregulation has captured the attention of observers from a variety of perspectives. However, the preceding volume identified new trends that have yet to be fully considered in studies of financialization, advanced capitalism, central banking, and monetary policymaking.

Since the financial crisis of 2007–2008, organizational change also occurred within the (many) entities and agencies of US monetary authority. New research and new policy strategies have attempted to respond to the mandate in the US, since 2012, to ensure maximum employment and growth within the inflation-targeting framework. The traditional policy roles and channels of the 12 regional Federal Reserve Banks reemerged in opposition to the centralization of policy in the Board of Governors of the Federal Reserve System, the Federal Open Market Committee, the New York Federal Reserve Bank, and the US Department of Treasury. New political imperatives to reduce financial crimes to avert terrorism changed the context for tax evasion. The elaboration of a public review of Federal Reserve policies provided the opportunity to rethink monetary policy and the supervision and regulation of banks and financial markets. These phenomena are at odds with economic theories of central banking, including the approaches of critical political economy that focus, excessively, on policy capture. The evidence from the US during the 2010s suggests the expansion of the scope of conflict rather than the depoliticization or instrumental capture of monetary policy. The expansion of the scope of conflict is a concept from American political science that describes the alternative trajectory of political development and democratization in the country (Burnham, 1970; Schattschneider, 1960; Key, 1955; Weber, 1946).

A separate chapter in the preceding volume was required to consider new claims about shadow banking, off-balance-sheet operations, and nonbank financial entities. However, once again, fallacies of conceptual stretching, loading on the dependent variable, and mis-aggregation of data suggest serious flaws in recent research, and recent policy debates, about shadow banking, off-balance-sheet operations, and nonbank finance (Nesvetailova, 2018). The extreme concentration of financial derivatives at four US bank holding companies also suggests a specific, more limited, political-economic problem rather than a systemic trend. From the perspective of political economy, the concentration of

8   *Introduction*

financial derivatives at four banks (with support from the federal government) stands in stark contrast to the key developments of the 2010s; the expansion of the scope of conflict over monetary policy and the closer, more efficient supervision and regulation of banks. The previous volume explores these developments in the US and their implications for both theories of financialization and change in advanced economies.

This book explores the consequences of financialization for household inequality and the structure and management of nonfinancial business enterprises. A brief look ahead at arguments elaborated in the following chapters is in order. The first chapter examines the effects of financialization on the US macroeconomy. Evidence of long-term trends is drawn from the annual NIPAs from 1929 to 2019, the quarterly IMAs from 1960 to 2018, and new sources both further back in time and since the financial crisis of 2007–2008. Tracing dozens of aggregates and their composite parts over time reveals unexpected patterns of continuity and change in terms of personal and institutional income, savings, capital, investment, consumption, and the production of goods and services.

Evidence from nine decades of historical statistics from the US runs counter to central claims about the macroeconomic consequences of financialization in critical political economy and studies of advanced capitalism, with two important exceptions: A marked increase in inequality and slack (unused) industrial capacity since 1980. Comparisons of the data on the US economy before and after 1980 fail to indicate a slowdown in the pace of economic growth, or a substantial decline of labor income shares due to financialization. Nor does the data from the US evidence an increase in the volatility of financial markets or business cycles, or an increase in the levels of unemployment, or an increase of consumption at the expense of private sector investment. Increasing the number of observations back in time, disaggregating the data to avoid composition effects, and paying attention to the traditional categories of US national accounts averts the conceptual stretching, mis-aggregation, and private sector biases that misrepresent economic change, underestimate political factors, and misconstrue public finance.

Evidence of rising inequality and slack industrial capacity within the framework of inflation targeting (modified in the US to include maximum growth and employment) suggests the existence of significant space for classic strategies of Keynesian demand management. Moreover, the data suggest that both social policy transfers and income policies *increased* in the US over the last decades. This is at odds with generalizations about the dismantlement of Welfare States and the reduction of social policy transfers under neoconservative governments and neoliberal economic policy. Although neoconservative movements, and governments, targeted social policy, the empirical evidence from the US suggests that broader political pressures nonetheless produced increases in the levels of income transfers over the last decades, irrespective of the party composition of government.

Introduction 9

The second chapter of this book turns to the financialization of household inequality in the US. The displacement of households by banks and financial institutions as the largest holders of financial claims is the largest variance in the IMAs financial balance-sheet data on US social sectors from 1960 to 2019. The proportional decline of household financial holdings in the US belies core expectations about the efficiency of financial markets and the virtues of disintermediation in economics, contemporary banking theory, and financial intermediation theory (expectations often shared by critical political economy and post-Keynesian approaches).

The decomposition of US household balance-sheet portfolios by social class became possible in March 2019 with the publication of the Distributional financial accounts of the United States (DFAs) as part of the Enhanced Financial Accounts initiative of the Board of Governors of the Federal Reserve. The disaggregation of US household balance-sheet portfolios by social class indicates how the conceptual stretching of money to include, and double-count, financial claims became an ideological veil of capital that concealed both the compounding of financialization and the financialization of inequality. The accumulation of financial claims by the middle and upper classes in the US has turned, disproportionally, on the compounding of debts for lower social classes. Chapter 2 also goes beyond the financial balance-sheet data to explore further evidence about labor income shares, personal consumption and savings, social policy transfers, and taxation in the US.

The balance-sheet data on US households in the IMAs from 1960 to 2019, and DFAs from 1989 to 2019, also suggest another anomaly about real estate for the literatures on financialization and change in the advanced economies. In historical perspective, real estate holdings and home mortgage finance remain a quite stable proportion of both US household portfolios and national accounts (despite inequalities of social class). This belies claims about the profound increase in real estate as part of advanced economies caused by financialization.

In sum, the evidence from the US helps explain how financial factors, balance-sheet wealth, conceptual stretching, and mis-aggregation of economic data contributed to the displacement of households by finance and the rise of inequality. However, political factors such as taxes, government transfers, and social policy are also found to have countered inequality in the US. This runs counter to studies that emphasize the dismantlement of Welfare States and the social exclusion wrought by neoconservative governments and neoliberal economic policies. Moreover, the deleveraging of household debt during the 2010s (and during 2020 amid the dramatic collapse of the economy during the COVID-19 pandemic), provide further evidence of counterintuitive developments in the US. The data from the US suggest a variety of anomalies for theories of financialization, household debt, and broader conceptions of how each social sector manages their particular financial portfolios.

Chapter 3 turns to the financialization of nonfinancial business enterprises in the US. The literature on financialization emphasizes the increase of financial

10 Introduction

revenue at nonfinancial firms as part of a broader change from Chandlerian and Fordist business corporations into vehicles for the extraction of value to benefit rentier investors. This view seems to be confirmed by a significant number of empirical studies. However, it has also been criticized by recent scholarship for overlooking problems of measurement and misspecification. Chapter 3 examines these claims, first by tracing continuity and change in the US data sources, and then by broadening the focus to consider both the income structure and balance-sheet data on nonfinancial firms in the US. The evidence suggests that the US business sector exhibits strong signs of income and asset financialization. However, this may be driven by long-term trends of indebtedness in the US corporate sector. This provides new perspectives on the financialization as rentier-ialization narrative. The data from the US also reveals significant differences between the financialization of incorporated business enterprises and the less financialized unincorporated business sector.

In sum, this book completes the original scope envisioned for this study of the political economy of financialization across US social sectors. Consideration of the consequences of financialization for the macroeconomy, household inequality, and nonfinancial business in the US helps control for claims about trends shared by advanced economies. The recent publication of the DFAs, and other new data sources, make it possible to reassess claims about social class, social policy, and the political economy of advanced capitalism. A historical–institutional approach to the macroeconomic trends in the US complements the historical–institutional balance-sheet analysis of US social sectors.

The rise and fall of finance, the displacement of households by banks and financial business as the predominant holders of US financial claims, the transition from the private production of financial claims to government accommodation and intervention, the financialization of wealth and household inequality, and the hollowing out of nonfinancial business are phenomena at odds with both the predominant approaches in economics and generalizations about change in advanced economies. Recovery of the classic modern, pluralist, and critical traditions of political economy, the qualitative methods of conceptual and historical–institutional analysis, and the original meanings and measures of US national income and production accounts suggest the existence of serious problems with widely accepted views across the predominant approaches in economics – mainstream, critical, and heterodox alike. This volume provides further evidence that a back-to-the-future approach to the concepts and theories of classic modern political economy may provide urgently needed new perspectives on financialization from a different point of view – the traditional view of comparative political economic analysis.

Notes

1 Instead of the term 'financial assets,' this book uses the term 'financial claims.' This is taken from the Financial Stability Board annual reports on nonbank financial

intermediaries and is necessary to avert confusing financial claims with nonfinancial assets, and a variety of other errors induced by this confusion.

2 The literatures critiqued in the preceding volume include contemporary banking theory, financial intermediation theory, endogenous money approaches, efficient market theory, and financial repression theory.

References

Block, Fred and Margaret R. Somers. (2014). *The power of market fundamentalism: Karl Polanyi's critique*. Cambridge, MA: Harvard University Press.

Bureau of Commerce. (1934). 'National income 1929–1932.' Washington, DC: Government Printing Office.

Burnham, Walter D. (1970). *Critical elections and the mainsprings of American politics*. New York: W. W. Norton.

De Young, Robert. (2010). 'Banking in the United States,' in Allen Berger, Phillip Molyneux, and John Wilson. (eds). *The Oxford handbook of banking*. Oxford: Oxford University Press, pp. 777–806.

Duménil, Gérard and Dominique Lévi. (2004). *Capital resurgent: Roots of the neoliberal revolution*. Cambridge, MA: Harvard University Press.

Geddes, Barbara. (1990). 'How the cases you choose affect the answers you get: Selection bias in comparative politics.' *Political Analysis*, 2: 131–50.

Hein, Eckhard, Daniel Detzer, and Nina Dodig. (eds). (2016a). *The demise of finance-dominated capitalism: Explaining the financial and economic crises*. London: Edward Elgar.

Hein, Eckhard, Daniel Detzer, and Nina Dodig. (eds). (2016). *Financialisation and the financial and economic crises: Country studies*. London: Edward Elgar.

Hein, Eckhard, Daniel Detzer, and Nina Dodig. (eds). (2016a). *The demise of fi nancedominated capitalism: Explaining the fi nancial and economic crises*. London: Edward Elgar .

Jones, Charles O. (2005). *The presidency in a separated system*. Washington, DC: Brookings Institution (1994, 1st edition).

Key, Victor O. (1955). 'A theory of critical elections.' *Journal of Politics*, 17(1): 3–18.

Krippner, Greta. (2011). *Capitalizing on crisis: The political origins of the rise of finance*. Cambridge, MA: Harvard University Press.

Mader, Philip, Daniel Mertens, and Natascha van der Zwan. (eds). (2020). *The Routledge handbook of financialization*. London: Routledge.

Mettenheim, Kurt. (2021). *Political economy of financialization in the United States: A historical-institutional balance-sheet approach*. London: Routledge.

Mettenheim, Kurt. (2016). *Monetary statecraft in Brazil: 1808–2014*. London: Routledge.

Mettenheim, Kurt. (ed). (1997). *Presidential institutions and democratic politics: Comparing regional and national contexts*. Baltimore, MD: Johns Hopkins University Press.

Nesvetailova, Anastasia. (ed). (2018). *Shadow banking: Scope, origins, and theories*. London: Routledge.

Polanyi, Karl. (1944). *The great transformation: Origins of our times*. New York: Farrar & Rinehart.

Przeworski, Adam. (1985). 'Social democracy as a historical phenomenon,' in *Capitalism and social democracy*. Cambridge: Cambridge University Press, pp. 7–41.

Sartori, Giovanni. (1970). 'Concept misformation in comparative politics.' *American Political Science Review*, 64(4): 1033–53.

12 *Introduction*

Scharpf, Fritz. (2011). 'Monetary union, fiscal crisis, and the pre-emption of democracy.' *Zeitschrift fur Staats- und Europawissenschaften*, 9(2): 163–98.

Schattschneider, Elmer E. (1960). *The semi-sovereign people*. New York: Dryden Press.

Thompson, Edward P. (1971). 'The moral economy of the English crowd in the eighteenth century.' *Past & Present*, 50: 76–136.

Weber, Max. (1946). 'Politics as a vocation,' in Hans Gerth and C.W. Mills. (eds). *From Max Weber: Essays in sociology*. New York: Macmillan, pp. 77–128 (1917, 1st edition).

Whitehead, Laurence. (2002). *Democratization: Theory and experience*. Oxford: Oxford University Press.

Wray, Randall. (1990). *Money and credit in capitalist economies: The endogenous money approach*. Aldershot: Edward Elgar.

Wright, Erik O., David Gold, and Y.H. Lo. (1975). 'Recent developments in Marxist theories of the capitalist state.' *Monthly Review*, 27(5): 29–51.

1 The financialization of the American economy

Introduction

It has become common for economists to assert that a golden age of capitalism existed from the 1930s (or 1945) to the 1970s (Temin, 2002). This begs fundamental questions about politics and skews the evidence toward two recoveries; either from the 1929 crash in the US, or from the devastation caused by World War II abroad. Both imply low baselines that overstate the pace of economic growth before 1980. The evidence from the US is also inconsistent with almost every claim about the perverse macroeconomic effects of financialization, except inequality and unused industrial capacity (Hein et al., 2016, 2015). Many structural changes appear in the historical statistics on the US economy. However, the evidence runs counter to claims that, after 1980, financialization produced slower growth, higher unemployment, lower investment, a decline in personal savings, falling labor income shares, an increase in consumption, and greater volatility in financial markets and business cycles (Evans, 2016; Kotz, 2015). The US may be exceptional. Many changes appear in the balance-sheet data on US social sectors, especially for US banks and financial institutions. However, the historical statistics from the US Department of Commerce Bureau of Economic Analysis National income and product accounts (NIPAs) from 1929 to 2019 and Integrated macroeconomic accounts (IMAs) from 1960 to 2019 are not consistent with central claims in the critical political economy literature about the deleterious consequences of financialization. With two exceptions: increased inequality and unused industrial capacity.

These two exceptions suggest that significant space exists in the US for policies of redistribution based on classical Keynesian demand management strategies (Foley et al., 2019; Taylor et al., 2019; Carvalho and Rezai, 2016; Rezai, 2013). Indeed, the evidence from the US indicates that income transfers and government spending on social policies increased from the 1980s through the 2010s. Moreover, the fiscal character of income policies designed to counter the COVID-19 pandemic in 2020 and 2021 also suggest that pragmatic use of classical Keynesian policies continue to be at the center of American political economy.

DOI: 10.4324/9781003223320-2

14 *Finance and the American economy*

There was no golden age. Financialization is not a monolithic cause of capitalism gone wrong. Not all bad things go together. Discounting the effects of recovery from depression in the 1930s and mobilization for war in the 1940s, the levels of gross domestic product (GDP) growth, unemployment, savings, investment, and the volatility of business cycles and financial markets do not deteriorate after 1980 in the US. To the contrary – notwithstanding the financial crisis of 2007–2008 and the great recession that followed from 2008–2009. The problem with financialization is the same problem that was noted by Simon Kuznets about inequality in 1934: It is structural (Bureau of Commerce, 1934). The financialization of the US economy occurred without deterioration in the fundamental indicators used in macroeconomics. This may be evidence of the inadequacy of the indicators, or of American exceptionalism, or of the benefit that the US reaps from center-periphery relations at the expense of other nations. Or a combination of these explanations. However, a historical–institutional approach to the macroeconomic indicators from the US runs counter to the central claims in critical political economy about how financialization caused change across the advanced economies (claims that are often shared in mainstream and heterodox research).

Comparison of the US data before and after 1980 suggests smoother and more durable periods of economic growth, lower inflation, and less severe bouts of unemployment during recessions after 1980, even considering the sharp decline and slow recovery after the 2007–2008 financial crisis. The exception of inequality has been noted and is addressed in the following chapter. The exception of unused industrial capacity suggests that traditional Keynesian views of demand management are more relevant, and more promising, for the promotion of social inclusion than post-Keynesian endogenous money theory.

This chapter explores these anomalies and provisos for theories of financialization that appear in the traditional, *non*financial measures of aggregate income and production from the US: of finance as part of the long-term shift away from manufacturing to services; of sustained increases in government social benefits (contrary to claims about the dismantlement of Welfare States); of recoveries after 1980 that may be slower but are sustained far longer; of the low cost of US government debt that belies views of fiscal constraints; and of the sustained periods of economic growth after 1980. The sustained decline of US federal government defense production over the last decades (as a proportion of GDP) also differs from both standard views of demand management and claims about declining labor income shares in advanced economies.

In short, US GDP growth after 1980 becomes more stable and business cycles become smoother and sustained for longer periods (despite the slow recovery 2009–2013 and the sharp decline of 2020). The slowdown of growth in the US is slight, typical of mature economies, related to the transition from the manufacturing of goods to the provision of services, does not coincide with the period of high financialization (i.e. after 1980), and is overstated by inflation before 1980 and biased samples that begin with past recoveries. In the US, volatility does not increase over time, neither in terms of the standard macroeconomic aggregates, nor in terms of the capitalization of the New York Stock Exchange (NYSE), nor as measured by other indicators such as prices in financial futures markets. The general tendency of unemployment neither increases after 1980, nor becomes worse during economic downturns, even after considering the large number of jobs lost during the great recession from 2007 to 2009, the unprecedented collapse of the US economy in 2020, and increasing inequality. Consumption has not increased over time as a proportion of GDP in terms of national income, or personal income, or personal expenditures. Savings rates have not declined. Public investment has indeed declined. However, the far larger share of private investment in the US remained, after 1980, within the parameters of past business cycles. And, after 1980, the cost of government debt fell below historic levels because of low interest rates and the countercyclical flights to quality enjoyed by the US during financial crises and periods of economic uncertainty.

It bears repeating that two indicators are indeed consistent with the causal claims of the critical political economy literature about financialization: an increase in inequality and a decline in the use of industrial capacity. This implies that significant opportunities exist to reverse social exclusion through traditional fiscal, monetary, income, and tax policies. Moreover, the data on income transfers in the US also differs from claims about the dismantlement of Welfare States and persistent cuts to social policies by neoconservative governments after 1980 (Castles et al., 2010; Pierson, 1993). And during 2020 and 2021, large-scale fiscal and income policies were used alongside monetary policies to counter the collapse of the economy caused by the COVID-19 pandemic. Crisis, once again, produced enabling constraints (Gourevitch, 1982) for the pragmatic elaboration and implementation of public policy. This belies the economic determinism of theories of crisis in critical political economy.

This chapter uses the methods of historical–institutional analysis to explore these anomalies and provisos. The following section taps new sources of long-term data to compare wages, prices, and benchmark interest rates in the US from *1800 to 2020*. The trends in the raw data counter claims about the inexorability of long-term determinants. Instead, historical perspective indicates how inflation in the 1970s and adjustment in the 1980s were fundamentally different from the 16 decades before and three decades since. Updating the data compiled by Friedman and Schwartz (1963) and Cagan (1965) on US monetary history through 2020 suggests both the profound disjuncture caused by the financial crisis of 2007–2008 and the end of the traditional parameters for monetary theory and policy in the US.

Tracing stock prices on the NYSE from *1815 to 2020* suggests that the volatility of American capital markets *has not* increased over time. Further data from futures markets and shorter time spans confirm this finding in the long-term data from the NYSE. The data suggest the contrary. The boom-and-bust cycles on American capital markets before 1980 were more frequent and more volatile than after 1980.

The same holds for GDP growth. The great moderation from 2003–2007 before the financial crisis, the prolonged recession from 2008 to 2009, and the

16 *Finance and the American economy*

sustained recovery during the 2010s all differed from the shorter and steeper business cycles that predominated in the US before 1980. Tracing the annual percentage change in real gross domestic product in the US from 1930 to 2020 indicates change in the reverse direction than suggested in comparative studies of financialization and critical political economy accounts of advanced capitalism. After 1980, US GDP growth is sustained for longer periods. And a slight decline in the pace of economic growth over the last decades is due to the distorted baselines of recovery from the great depression in the 1930s and the massive mobilization for World War II during the 1940s.

This chapter focuses on the US financial sector as it appears, not in the financial balance-sheet data, but, instead, as banks and financial phenomena appear in the traditional economic aggregates of national income and production accounts. As measured in the traditional macroeconomic data of the NIPAs, the provision of financial services accompanies, quite closely, the trends of the US service sector generally. Since 1929, the prices charged for financial services follow, quite closely, both service sector prices as a whole and the aggregate prices of gross domestic purchases (until 2014, which is another anomaly). Indeed, other nonfinancial service sectors (especially health care), outpace the financial sector, both in terms of expanded shares of US GDP and in terms of price increases over the last decades.

The size of the financial sector in the US is far smaller if the sector is measured in terms of the traditional categories of income, production, and long-term patterns of price changes. From this perspective, increases in newer aggregates such as gross value-added are basically a function of conceptual stretching; of revising the traditional categories of political economy and macroeconomics to include financial claims and liabilities. After controlling for the transition from manufacturing to service provision, the rise of finance in the traditional economic aggregates of the NIPAs is far lower than indicated in the financial balance-sheet data. The traditional data help put banking and finance in context and avert loading on the dependent variables (Geddes, 1990) of financial claims and liabilities.

The third section of this chapter takes a closer look at the trends of investment, consumption, manufacturing, and service industries in the US from 1929 to 2019. The historical–institutional method explores these anomalies and provisos by increasing the number of observations back in time, disaggregating the data to control for composition effects, and paying attention to the original meanings of measures. The fourth section explores the data in the NIPAs from 1929 to 2019 on the net savings of households, business enterprises, and the public sector.

The fifth section suggests that a slight decline of labor income shares in the US economy during the 1980s is due to biased baselines and stretching the concept of income to include, and double-count, the changing values reported for financial claims. Moreover, the sharp increases of labor income shares recorded during World War II, the Korean War, the Vietnam War (and during stock market crashes that temporarily reduce non-labor income), belie claims about a golden age of capitalism, the advances of labor unionization during peacetime, and nondefense-driven growth. Decomposition of the data, historical perspective, and the secondary literature suggest that claims about the decline of labor shares in the US since 1980 are overstated (Autor et al., 2017a, 2017b). Declines in labor income appear in the historical statistics if, and only if, income aggregates are redefined to double-count financial claims. This implies an increase in the denominator, not the numerator.

The sixth section traces the historical data on unemployment, employment, and the use of industrial capacity in the US from 1948 to 2020. After 1980, unemployment continued to rise substantially during recessions. And the prolonged recession from 2007 to 2009 is noted. However, the general tendency and the number, level, and distance between peaks of unemployment (and trends in employment), all suggest that the post-1980 period compares favorably with the pre-1980 data. Before 1980, higher levels of unemployment and lower levels of employment recurred during shorter and steeper business cycles. This is the very opposite of both claims in the literature on financialization and generalizations about advanced capitalism in critical political economy.

The seventh section disaggregates the data on personal income to check, once again, the evidence behind these counterintuitive inferences and findings. Decomposition of personal income and its disposition in the NIPAs data from 1929 to 2019 confirms that labor income shares remain between 52 and 56 percent of total income in the US, unless one accepts the redefinition and conceptual stretching of income that double-counts changes in the value of financial claims and liabilities (Mettenheim, 2021). Another anomaly for comparative studies of advanced capitalism, critical political economy, and studies of Welfare States is the following: the value of social benefits provided by the US government *increases* after 1980; proportionally, nominally, and in real terms (alongside the steady, long-term increase of private pension fund income). The latter is consistent with theories of financialization. However, the variance is small in comparison to other sources of income and reflects the gradual accumulation of private pensions over decades, rather than disjuncture around 1980.

The eighth section disaggregates the NIPAs data on the structure and pace of growth in US GDP from 1929 to 2019. This produces further evidence consistent with the above findings and helps control for composition effects. The variance in investment and consumption is found to be primarily due to long-term gradual declines in the public sector. Both the general tendency and cyclical patterns of private investment during business cycles belie claims of fundamental declines. Three additional measures of savings and investment in the NIPAs also fail to indicate substantial decline after 1980.

This chapter draws out the implications of so many anomalies and provisos for theories of financialization and comparative studies of advanced capitalism. The conclusion returns to Simon Kuznets' observation in 1934: that economic aggregates tend to conceal inequality (Bureau of Commerce, 1934). Inequality does not necessarily produce stagnation.[1] Nor does financialization. This is the second broad finding of the chapter: The data from the US fail to confirm theories about how financialization slows growth, increases volatility, and produces other symptoms that are seen to beset advanced economies. At least in the case of the US. The third broad finding is methodological. Historical–institutional analysis disaggregates the data, increases the number of observations back in time, and turns on the conceptual analysis of economic aggregates. In this respect, the nonfinancial data help avert loading on the dependent variables of financial balance-sheet data that has come to skew, so terribly, the terms of economic analysis and public policy debate.

Long-term perspectives on American political economy

Before turning to the official data in the NIPAs (1929–2019) and IMAs (1960–2019), a broader view of US economic history may be obtained in three sets of historical statistics. The first long-term view is to trace the annual percentage change in the hourly wages of labor, consumer prices, and benchmark long-term interest rates for corporate bond issues from 1800 to 2019. The second long-term view is provided by updating the historical statistics compiled by Friedman and Schwartz (1963) and Cagan (1965) on US monetary aggregates (extending their data from 1870 to 1960 through 2019). Considering the broad sweep of monetary history in the US helps clarify the new political conundrums for economic policy in the 2010s. A third long-term view of US economic history may be obtained by tracing the average monthly percent change in the total capitalization of the NYSE from 1815 to 2020. All three data sets provide a significantly different picture than readers will find in both recent studies of financialization and debates about advanced capitalism. The raw data on prices, wages, and benchmark interest rates also belie generalizations about the linearity or constancy of capital and/or capital returns over long periods of time (Schmelzing, 2020; Piketty, 2014).

The first long-term overview of American political economy is displayed in Figure 1.1. The three lines in Figure 1.1 are the annual percentage change

Figure 1.1 Percentage annual change in US wages, prices, and long-term interest rates, 1800–2019.

Source: Officer and Williamson (2020).

in the wages paid for labor, the annual percentage change in prices, and the nominal long-term interest rates for corporate bonds from 1800–2019. The data compiled from diverse sources over 229 years may involve errors (Officer and Williams, 2020). Analysis of historical statistics on prices and production in the US suggest that the older data are usually overestimated (Romer, 1986). Figure 1.1 therefore leaves annual increases in prices and wages over 15 percent and declines over 10 percent off the chart. And instead of discounting wages and interest rates by price changes, the original values for all three measures are retained. The annual percentage change in prices, wages, and nominal interest rates for corporate bond issues exhibit considerable variance; variance that would be concealed by aggregating wages and prices to measure inflation, or by discounting interest rates with volatile price changes to measure, after the fact, supposed real returns on capital over long periods of time.

Significant differences obtain between the trends of prices, wages, and benchmark interest rates on corporate bonds in the US during the 16 decades from 1800 to 1960 and the six decades since 1960. Both the gradual increase of all three variables from 1960 to 1982 and the sustained decline of all three measures from 1982 to 2019 differ from the far greater volatility of prices and wages and the far greater stability of long-term interest rates before 1960. Both the Great Inflation of the 1960s and 1970s and the turning point of 1980 are unlike previous experiences. Prior to 1960, the rise and fall of prices were far greater, but lasted far shorter in time. And persistent *deflation* was recorded during much of the nineteenth century. The same holds for wages. The trajectory of annual wage increases during the 1960s and 1970s, and the decline in wages after 1981 differ from the more volatile trajectory of wages from 1800 through the 1950s.

From the perspective of political economy, it is also of note that prices and wages peaked during or just after wars (in 1814, 1864, 1918, 1946, and 1974). However, after the end of the Vietnam War, prices continued to increase at twice the pace of wages, reaching 14 percent in 1982. The political adage of avoiding wars on two fronts seems to apply: President Johnson waged war on Vietnam and poverty at the same time to overheat the economy. However, the effects were structural and gradual, not conjunctural. From 1800 to 1860, the five peaks and troughs of annual price changes were far greater than the second set of five bouts of deflation and inflation experienced between the Civil War and WWI (1865–1914). And, from the perspective of political economy, it is of note that sustained annual increases in wages surpass price increases only twice; once during the 1980s and once, previously, during the New Deal from 1935 to 1939.

Interest rates also changed fundamentally. During the 160 years 1800–1960, interest rates remained remarkably stable amid the repeated short-term rise and fall of prices and wages. For 160 years, capital markets and the cost of finance remained a nominal anchor for expectations. The interest rates of corporate bonds remained a benchmark amid large changes in prices and wages (mostly related to the massive efforts of wartime mobilization and demobilization). War

20 *Finance and the American economy*

may have disrupted economic activities, however after the conclusion of hostilities, prices appear to have served as effective signals for the reorganization of trade and commerce.

Prices and wages thereby remained signals for entry and exit into markets during periods of large-scale political-economic change. These trends disappear if the data on wages and prices are combined. These trends also disappear if the large, distinctive nominal changes in prices and wages are used to discount nominal interest rates in the interests of estimating, retrospectively, constant returns to capital. There is nothing constant in the raw data.

In sum, the historical–institutional method traces the data on prices, wages, and interest rates over time to highlight the variance, avoid composition effects, and avert the retrospective imposition of concepts and theories implied by composite indices of inflation, or the discounting of prices, wages, or interest rates in the interests of producing, retrospectively, real values.

This helps clarify how American political economy changed after 1960. Until 1960, wars produced sharp increases in prices and wages followed by equally sharp declines. The war of 1812, war on Mexico from 1846 to 1848, the Civil War of 1861–1865, and participation in world wars from 1914 to 1918 and 1939 to 1945 all produced steep increases in prices and wages. However, equally steep declines ensued after the end of war. Moreover, amid the volatility of prices and wages, the interest rates of corporate bond issues remained on a gradual trajectory of decline, albeit with slight increases during years of war. The American wars in Korea (1951–1953) and Vietnam (1965–1975) produced similar price and wage increases. However, unlike previous experiences, prices and wages continue to decline after 1980. The differences before and after 1980 are consistent with the structural explanation of the political origins of the rise of finance in the US (Krippner, 2011). Specifically, the data are consistent with two influential debates that inform Krippner's analysis: about the Great Inflation that began in the 1960s and about the fiscal crises and stagflation that beset the US and other advanced economies during the 1970s.

A second data set sheds further light on how American political economy changed after 1980. Figure 1.2 displays the percent annual change in prices, the M2 monetary aggregate, the monetary base, and the interest rates of corporate bonds in the US across the 15 decades from 1870 to 2020. The data from 1870 to 1960 are taken from the original data compiled by Friedman and Schwartz (1963) and revised by Cagan (1965). This classic time series on US monetary history is updated with data from 1961 to 2020, as provided by the St Louis Federal Reserve Bank statistics division.

Recent claims about long-term historical statistics are beyond the scope of this book (Schmelzing, 2020). However, Figure 1.2 replicates the original measures of prices, M2, the monetary base, and corporate bond interest rates as defined in the classic works of American monetary history. Figure 1.2 also updates these four variables from 1961 through the first quarter of 2020. This illustrates both the wedge of financialization and the disjuncture of 2007–2008. Several observations are in order. First, the covariance after 1950 differs,

Finance and the American economy 21

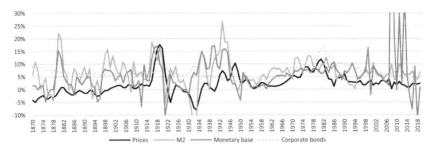

Figure 1.2 Percentage annual change in prices, M2, the monetary base, and corporate bond interest rates, 1870–2020.
Sources: Friedman and Schwartz (1963) and Cagan (1965) for 1870–1960. St Louis Federal Reserve statistics for 1961–2020.

fundamentally, from the relations between the core monetary aggregates before 1950. Second, the cost of capital as measured by the nominal interest rates of corporate bond issues remains remarkably stable at around 5 percent from 1870 to 1965 (except for 1921 and 1932). This is consistent with the data above. Third, the nominal interest rate price of corporate bond issues increases gradually after 1965 to peak at 16.4 percent in 1982; then declines to 4.6 percent in 2019. This is consistent with the discontinuities emphasized in critical political economy accounts of financialization, debates about fiscal crisis and stagflation during the 1970s, and traditional histories of money and monetary policy in the US.

However, fundamental changes occur in 2007. The traditional relations between prices, the M2 monetary aggregate, corporate bond interest rates, and the monetary base change abruptly in 2007. Karl Brunner's description of finance as a wedge between the money supply and the monetary base informs this study (Brunner, 2018). While this idea is valid for the previous decades, the wedge of finance splits, definitively, the traditional relations between the core monetary aggregates in the US in 2007. Gaps exist between the monetary base and the other variables from 1870 to 1981. From 1982 to 2007 the gap between the monetary base and the three other variables declines. However, the traditional relations end in 2007. Thereafter, the variance goes off the chart, first as unprecedented increases, then as unprecedented declines in the percentage annual change of the monetary base. The conceptual stretching of money to include financial claims and liabilities expands the denominator and dilutes the numerator (the traditional aggregates of wages, salaries, and savings).

The traditional relations between money and the real economy emphasized in the class works of monetarism *end* in 2007. Concepts such as hot money implied that monetary policies could fine-tune business cycles (Brunner, 2018; Cagan, 1965). The appeal of monetary theory and policy was that management of the money supply provided efficient and effective countercyclical control over business cycles with a light touch (Rache and Johannes, 1987). However,

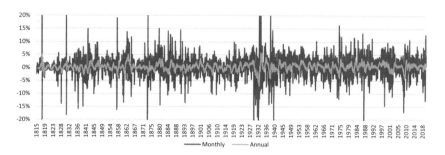

Figure 1.3 New York Stock Exchange monthly and annual percentage change in total capital, 1815–2020.

Source: Cowles data, Yale School of Management, for 1815–1925. New York Stock Exchange historical statistics for 1926–2020.

after 2007, monetary policies became blunt instruments requiring massive amounts of public funds that produced a sequence of unexpected consequences, distortions, and wealth effects.

A third long-term perspective may be obtained in the historical statistics provided by the NYSE. Figure 1.3 reports the average percent monthly volatility in the capitalization of the NYSE from 1815 to 2020 (total closing value). Estimates of volatility vary according to the unit of time. This is an observation that has remained at the center of debates about stock markets since Bachelier (1900). The mathematical properties of stock market data are beyond the scope of this book. However, one observation about the limits of cognate disciplines is in order: The use of numbers in the study of stock markets also has limits.

The average percent change of the NYSE over 15 decades is just above zero. If one calculates decade averages, greater variance appears. If one calculates running five-year averages, more variance appears. The same holds, as one shortens the sample, for annual averages, monthly averages (as reported in Figure 1.3), and so on as the time spans are reduced. The problem is that time is infinitely divisible. And investors buy and sell stocks at a specific moment on a specific day and time, not in average time periods. It follows that stock market trends, like risk measurement and the realization of investments, turn on the categories of time. Stocks are not liquid like money. This is not a question of probability. Nor is it a question about fat tails, or outliers, or standard errors, or other categories of statistics. It is a problem that remits the limits to the use of numbers and mathematics to explain financial phenomena.

The data from the NYSE run counter to the idea that financialization increased stock market volatility. The US may be exceptional. Since Andrew Shonfield's landmark comparison of the US and the UK with Continental Europe from 1945 to 1965, the greater volatility of financial markets and business cycles in the US (and UK) is widely recognized (Shonfield, 1965). Indeed, this is a central tenet about the varieties of capitalism (Hall and Soskice,

Finance and the American economy 23

2001). However, comparison of financialization in the US and abroad suggests further anomalies for debates about advanced capitalism. The data from the 2010s suggest that the rise of finance was halted and, indeed, reversed in the US, notwithstanding the continued pace of financialization abroad (Mettenheim, 2021). The traditional, bank-centered financial systems, coordinated capitalisms, and Welfare States of Europe may indeed have experienced more dramatic changes because of financialization. However, this does not invalidate the findings from the US; many indicators taken to be evidence of financialization since 1980 in actuality reflect continuity or a return to levels observed in the US during the 1950s and 1960s. This should not be surprising. After all, concepts and theories about financialization today, in the tradition of critical political economy approaches since the work of Antonio Gramsci in the 1920s, describe important dimensions of change in Europe, and other countries abroad, as a process of *Americanization.*[2]

However, this book is the second volume of a case study of the US. And the evidence suggests that financial market volatility in the US has *declined* since 1980, not increased. This can be seen in three measures. First, the average monthly and annual percentage change in the total capitalization of stocks listed on the NYSE from 1815 to 2019 are displayed in Figure 1.3. The data do not seem to indicate fundamental change after 1980, despite the large declines of 1987, 2000, and 2007. A period of greater stability does appear in the data from 1948 to 1972. However, thereafter, the number of sharp monthly declines and equally sharp monthly increases occur with a fair amount of regularity through 2020. Even the collapse and recovery of the NYSE in the first semester of 2020 caused by the COVID-19 pandemic remains below the levels recorded in 1973, 1987, 1998, and 2008, not to mention the declines produced by market crashes, financial crises, and runs on banks during the nineteenth century.

The second measure is the Chicago Board Options Exchange volatility index from 1990–2020. Trading options for NYSE stock prices began on Chicago futures markets for commodities in 1990. The Chicago Board Options Exchange volatility index is based on 30-day futures prices for the Standard & Poors stock index of the largest 500 companies listed on the NYSE. The general tendency from 1990 through September 2020 is negative, as indicated by the dotted line drawn through the 1040 weekly observations over this period (see Figure 1.4). The volatility of prices on stock exchange futures markets does increase substantially during 2009 and 2020, with further significant peaks during 2010 and 2011. However, the sustained periods of lower volatility that appear in the more recent periods of the NYSE historical statistics above (i.e. during the 1990s, again from 2003 to 2007, and once again from 2012 to March 2020), also appear in the more recent data on the Chicago Board Options Exchange volatility index.

Given the counterintuitive character of this finding, examination of a third measure of stock market volatility is in order (see Figure 1.5). The volatility of US capital markets over time may also be traced by comparing the percent change, up or down, in the total capitalization of the NYSE during each

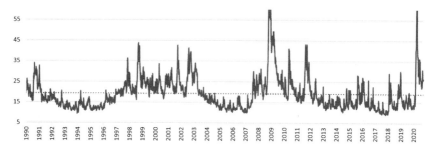

Figure 1.4 Chicago Board Options Exchange volatility index, 1990–2020.
Source: Chicago Board Options Exchange (CBOE).
Note: Volatility index = 30-day futures price for S&P 500 stock index. Dotted line = general tendency.

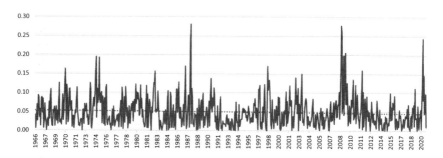

Figure 1.5 New York Stock Exchange volatility, 1966–2020.
Source: NYSE historical statistics.
Note: Volatility is quarterly ratio of change in total capitalization of the NYSE. Dotted line = general tendency.

quarter from 1966 to 2020. Volatility is measured here by simply converting the negative numbers of (percent) declines in the total capitalization of the NYSE into positive numbers. The general tendency of the line drawn through the 224 quarterly observations is negative. Volatility does indeed increase during 1987, 2008, and once again in 2020. However, both the number and duration of periods of volatility decline from 1988 to 1997, 2004 to 2007, and 2010 to 2019. The periods of lower volatility (periods of greater stability in US financial markets), appear to last longer after 1980.

In sum, the aggregation of historical statistics on the capitalization of stock markets also produces composition effects. The average long-term change in the stock market is roughly 2 percent – not discounting inflation. The average decade change in the NYSE is roughly 5 percent – not discounting inflation.

The average monthly changes in the NYSE are displayed in Figure 1.3. The average weekly change in the NYSE is largely the same but with standard deviations and outliers far higher. The same holds for daily and hourly averages. The problem is not mathematical or statistical. The problem is that investments are made in a particular moment, not on average. Standard deviations increase geometrically, to infinity, as zero is approached.

The relevance of the data here is that the evidence from the US is not consistent with a core claim about financialization. The volatility of American financial markets does not appear to increase over time in a simple, or singular, or fundamental way after 1980, despite the financial crisis of 2007–2008 and the collapse of financial markets in 2020 that will be examined in due course.

The political economy of financialization and growth in the US

Another claim about financialization is that the rise of finance since 1980 has slowed the pace of economic growth. This is at odds with both traditional theories of economic growth and the evidence from the US (Gordon, 2016; Barro, 1990; Denison, 1974; Solow, 1970; North, 1961). A slowdown of growth experienced in the US and other mature economies was first noted in the 1950s (Kaldor, 1957, 1966; Kuznets, 1966; Steindl, 1952). However, this observation was based on comparisons to the high baselines of growth during westward expansion and industrialization in the US during the nineteenth century, and the mobilization for two world wars in the early twentieth century. Decades have passed since the first debates about the slowdown of economic growth in the US. Nonetheless, many of the concepts, theories, and empirical observations from the 1950s and 1960s still apply to the political-economic realities of the US in the early twenty-first century. Of the four major factors explaining the reduced pace of GDP growth in the US (the large but declining marginal gains to the democratization of education, the transition away from manufacturing to the provision of services, the incorporation of new technologies, fundamental changes in work, and increasing inequality), only the last (inequality) can be associated with financialization. The financialization of inequality is a central concern of this book. However, the claim that financialization slows GDP growth requires caution. Not all bad things go together. Recent debates about slow growth in the US emphasize wage repression, monopoly power, and the emergence of superstar firms (Taylor, 2020; Eggertsson et al., 2018; Wu, 2018). However, the relations between these factors and financialization are not clear.

Consideration of three traditional measures of the pace of growth indicates the importance of historical perspective and the continued relevance of past debates about the slowdown of mature economies. The first measure is the annual percentage change in the real GDP of the US from 1930 to 2020.[3] The trend in the pace of annual real changes in US GDP from 1930 to 2019 is displayed in Figure 1.6. Several observations are in order. First, the steep recoveries related to New Deal policies in the early 1930s, the mobilization for

Figure 1.6 Annual percentage change in US real gross domestic product, 1930–2020.
Source: BEA NIPAs, Table 1.1.1.
Note: Percentage change from preceding period in real gross domestic product.

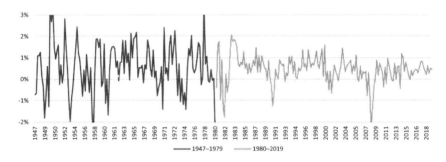

Figure 1.7 Quarterly real GDP change, 1947–2019.
Source: NIPAs.

World War II in the late 1930s and early 1940s, and the sharp recovery from 1946 to 1948 (from the steep decline in GDP caused by demobilization) stand out from the less volatile peaks and valleys of business cycles thereafter.

Second, business cycles are shorter and steeper from the 1950s to the 1970s compared to the decades after 1980, notwithstanding the downturn produced by the 2007–2008 financial crisis. Statistical analysis may reveal further particularities and better control for underlying factors. However, both the general tendency of real GDP growth and the stabilization of business cycles after 1980 run counter to two core claims in critical political economy: That financialization causes stagnation and increases the volatility of business cycles.

A closer look at the data on GDP change in the US may be obtained by comparing the quarterly percent increases and declines recorded in the NIPAs from 1947 to 2019 (see Figure 1.7). Separating the sample from 1947 to 1979, and 1980 to 2019, presents results consistent with the inferences from the annual data on the pace and variance of real GDP change above. The variance

Figure 1.8 Chicago Federal Reserve Bank economic activity index, 1967–2019.
Source: Federal Reserve Bank of Chicago.

in quarterly GDP growth in the US appears to decline substantially after 1980. The decline of the US GDP recorded during 2008 (the first full year after the financial crisis that began in 2007), goes off the chart. However, so, too, do the downturns in 1953, 1957, and 1980; and the periods of sustained growth after 1980 differ from the shorter, steeper, and more frequent quarterly increases and decreases in US GDP recorded from 1947 to 1979.

A still closer look at the pace of economic growth in the US is available in the monthly levels as reported in the Chicago Federal Reserve Bank national activity index (CFNAI), (Chicago Federal Reserve Bank, 2020; Stock and Watson, 1999). The monthly variation in the CFNAI from 1967 to 2019 is displayed in Figure 1.8. The CFNAI is composed of 23 measures of production and income; 24 indicators of employment, unemployment, and hours worked; 15 measures of consumption and housing; and 23 measures of sales, orders, and inventories. Many of the 85 variables used to compile the CFNAI index of economic activity are considered separately in the following sections. A core argument of historical–institutional analysis is that indices often suffer from composition effects because they conceal underlying sources of variance. However, to introduce the anomalies and provisos about economic growth in the US, the monthly CFNAI index from 1967 to 2019 provides another check on the data. The trends in the CFNAI from 1967 to 2019 are consistent with the differences observed above between the data on US GDP before and after 1980. The steep declines and recoveries recorded during 1970, 1974, and 1980 suggest that, after 1980, the US economy sustained growth for longer periods with fewer interruptions, despite the sharp declines recorded during 2008 and the slow recovery thereafter.

Before turning to further data from the NIPAs and IMAs to control for composition effects, tracing a final indicator of economic growth is in order: The productivity of labor (Ryan, 2020). The productivity of labor as measured in terms of output per hour (an index of real output divided by an index of hours worked for employees, proprietors, and unpaid family workers) is displayed in Figure 1.9. The aggregate productivity of labor *decreases* from 1948 to 1980.

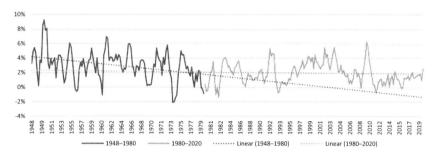

Figure 1.9 US labor productivity: Real per-person business sector output, percentage annual change, 1948–2020.

Source: St Louis Federal Reserve statistics.

Note: Labor productivity (output per hour) = index of real output divided by an index of hours worked of employees, proprietors, and unpaid family workers.

However, after 1980, the aggregate productivity of labor in the US remains largely stable. Like all aggregates, these trends require disaggregation to avert composition effects. Studies of labor productivity include classic contributions from a variety of theoretical perspectives to complex recent debates (Sichel, 2019) that remain beyond the scope of this chapter. However, comparison of the pace of labor productivity gains before and after 1980 fails to indicate sustained declines. To the contrary, productivity in the US economy declines before 1980 at a far greater pace than after 1980, as can be seen by comparing the two best-fitting lines drawn through the data: the black line for the 1948–1980 period and the gray line for the 1980–2020 period.

Two further drivers of growth are education and military expenditures. The democratization of public education is also under assault by neoconservative movements and liberal economic ideologies. However, historical perspective suggests both the large-scale of gains in the past and, in comparison, the marginal scale of recent reversals in primary, secondary, and higher education (see Figure 1.10). The price of higher education has increased geometrically, the privatization of schools threatens long-standing gains of social inclusion, the quality of education may have suffered, and student debt is a large problem for many younger Americans.

If financialization is defined broadly as a transition to shareholding private business models, the rise of private, for-profit education may be considered as part of the problem. However, a central argument in qualitative methods is that minimal definitions are required to avoid conceptual stretching (Mettenheim, 2021). Another argument is that not all bad things go together. The neoconservative assault on public education is a part of political reaction in the US and abroad. However, as a structural cause of declining growth in the US, the far greater variance of long-term advances in education suggests that recent reversals are not likely to be causes of economic slowdown (see Figure 1.10).

Finance and the American economy   29

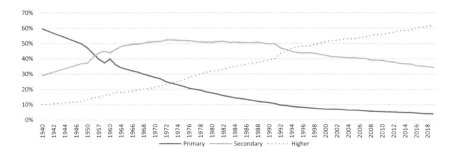

Figure 1.10 Primary, secondary, and higher education, 1940–2019.

Source: US Census Bureau. CPS Historical Time Series Tables.

Note: Data = highest level of education attended as percentage of noninstitutionalized population (level attended, not level graduated).

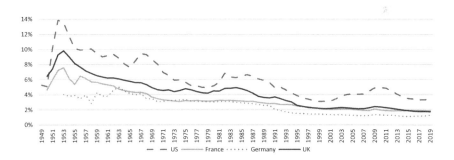

Figure 1.11 Military expenditures as percentage GDP, US, UK, France, and Germany, 1949–2019.

Source: Stockholm International Peace Research Institute. SIPRI military expenditure database.

Another anomaly for theories of stagnation in the US (and other advanced economies) is the consistent decline in the share of military expenditures in the domestic economy since the 1940s. Figure 1.11 displays military expenditures as a percentage of GDP for the US, UK, France, and Germany from 1949 to 2019. The increase of military spending in the US from 3 to 5 percent of GDP from 2000 to 2010 does indeed indicate that this political factor may explain an important part of the variation in GDP growth recorded during this period. However, this does not coincide with the period of high financialization (from 1980 to 2000). And, in longer-term perspective, the share of military expenditures in the US economy declines in far greater proportion: from peaks of 14 percent of GDP in 1952 during the Korean War and 9 percent of GDP in 1968 during the Vietnam War.

30 *Finance and the American economy*

In sum, claims about a slowdown in the pace of GDP growth in the US fail to consider the high baselines, in historical perspective, of rapid industrialization and Western expansion in the nineteenth century, and the effects of the New Deal and economic mobilization for war in the early twentieth century. Moreover, claims about how financialization causes economic slowdown are inconsistent with traditional theories of growth. Traditionally, economic theory suggests that finance is, at best, a small and marginal determinant of growth compared to education, population growth, and gains in labor productivity. The problems of inequality and slack industrial capacity are considered in due course.

Investment and consumption in the NIPAs 1929–2019 and IMAs 1960–2019

Research in critical political economy also claims that financialization contributes to a decline in investment and an increase in consumption (Hein et al., 2015). The vast literatures on mass consumption in the US and other advanced economies are beyond the scope of this chapter. So, too, are the traditional differences between consumerism, and consumer-driven growth, in the US as compared to the greater propensities to save of other countries. The corollary question of investment has also remained at the center of political economy since the beginning of the discipline. This chapter cannot do justice to the complexity and diversity of research on consumption and investment in mainstream, heterodox, and critical political economy research. However, the evidence from the NIPAs is incompatible with claims that consumption in the US has increased at the expense of investment. Figure 1.12 displays the value of private and government investment as shares of US GDP from 1929 to 2019. Private investment does fall substantially after 1929, in the late 1940s, and after 2008. However, the decline after the peak level of the share of private investment (20 percent) in 1984 is reversed in 1991, while the decline after 2008 is

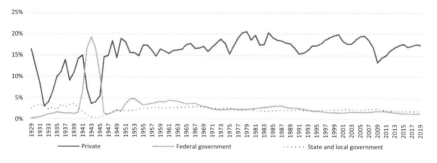

Figure 1.12 Private and government investment as a percentage of US GDP, 1929–2019.
Source: BEA NIPAs, Table 1.5.5.
Note: GDP expanded detail.

Figure 1.13 Personal consumption, private investment, and government contributions to GDP change, 1929–2019.
Source: BEA NIPAs, Table 1.1.2.
Note: Contributions to percentage change in Real Gross Domestic Product.

reversed in 2009. The investments for the samples of the federal and subnational governments both decline gradually after 1953 and 1968 respectively. However, this does not coincide with the turn to monetarism and involves declines of just 1 and 2 percent that are far too small to support broader theoretical claims.

The corollary to claims about the decline in private investment is that financialization produces an increase in consumption. The NIPAs include calculations of the weighted contribution to GDP change that may be attributed to changes in the levels of personal consumption, private investment, and government (consumption and investment are combined in the data on government) from 1934 to 2019 (see Figure 1.13). The tendency of personal consumption to contribute to the pace of annual GDP change declines from 1934 to 2019. The contribution to GDP growth from personal consumption does indeed increase from 1.69 to 3.25 from 1961 to 1966 (and once again from 1.3 to 2.95 percent 1981 to 1987, and in two further peaks in 2000 and 2019). However, the cyclical and aggregate tendencies fail to suggest a profound increase in levels of personal consumption in the US.

The aggregate measures of consumption in the US NIPAs also suffer from composition effects that conceal underlying variance in specific indicators, especially the rise of service provision and the decline of the manufacture of goods. Figure 1.14 displays this variance. From 1929 to 2019, the provision of services increases from below 40 percent of GDP in the late 1940s to 62 percent in 2019. In comparison, after 1950, both nondurable goods and durable goods decrease, from 30 to 17 percent and 20 to 13 percent of GDP respectively. Meanwhile the percentage share of the production of structures (homes and buildings), remains stable at near 10 percent until 2007 before declining to 8.0 percent of GDP in 2019.

To control for the broader shift away from the industrial manufacturing of goods (durable and nondurable) toward service industries, another comparison is in order. Figure 1.15 displays the annual raw price changes from 1929 to 2019

32 *Finance and the American economy*

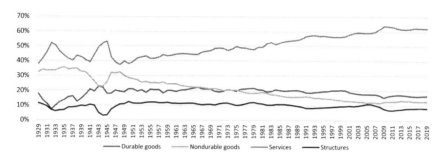

Figure 1.14 Goods, services, and structures as percentage of current dollar GDP, 1929–2019.
Source: BEA NIPAs, Table 1.2.5.
Note: Gross Domestic Product by major type of product.

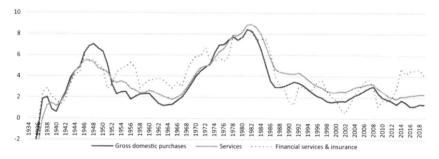

Figure 1.15 Annual raw price changes for gross domestic purchases, services, and financial services, 1929–2019.
Source: BEA NIPAs, Table 1.6.7.
Note: Percentage change from preceding period in prices for Gross Domestic Purchases.

for (1) domestic purchases, (2) the provision of services generally, and (3) the provision of financial services. The data on the service sector is disaggregated below. However, an initial comparison of annual price changes for financial services with the annual price changes for the service sector generally (and gross domestic purchases as a whole) is suggestive. The price increases that obtain for financial services (including insurance) remain above those recorded for services generally and domestic purchases from 1952 to 1974. However, thereafter, the pace of price increases for financial services falls *below* these two broader indicators used here for control, with two brief exceptions (1997 and 2007), and one significant anomaly: after 2013. The price of financial services and insurance do indeed outpace other service sectors and domestic prices generally after 2013. However, the trends before 2013 are an anomaly for theories of financialization.

In sum, the prices of financial services in the US from 1929 to 2019 follow a path quite close to both the prices of service provision generally and the average prices of gross domestic purchases. Neither the data on the pace of GDP growth, nor the data on price changes from 1934 to 2019 are consistent with the claims about the macroeconomic consequences of financialization. In terms of the gross domestic product, the financial sector does not appear to be dominant as a driver of growth. Nor does growth in the US appear to decline or become more volatile after 1980 because of financialization. Indeed, the US financial sector retains a small part of the national economy in the traditional indicators of macroeconomics. Financialization also cannot be associated, in the US, with increases in consumption or declines in the level of private investment since 1980. Tracing the traditional macroeconomic measures of the US from 1929 to 2019 fails to provide evidence in support of central claims about the perverse macroeconomic consequences of financialization. Economic growth in the US has declined slightly. However, the volatility of growth has also declined. Periods of economic growth after 1980 were sustained far longer than before 1980. No evidence of a real increase in personal consumption appears in the NIPAs from 1929 to 2019. Nor is there evidence of a decline in private sector investment.

Decomposition of drivers of GDP growth in the US

These anomalies, provisos, and counterintuitive findings may be checked by decomposing the data explored above into the underlying measures that are used to compile economic aggregates in the NIPAs. Table 1.1 disaggregates the NIPAs data on personal consumption, capital, foreign trade, and government in terms of their respective contributions to the annual percentage change in the US gross domestic product. Decade averages are displayed from the 1930s to the 2010s for personal consumption (split into personal goods and personal services); capital (split into structures, equipment, intellectual property, residential, and inventories); foreign trade (split into goods and services exported and imported); and government (split into federal defense and nondefense, and state and local separately from federal).

Several observations are in order. First, the percentage of US GDP growth based on personal goods declines from 47.8 percent in the 1930s to 21.4 percent in the 1940s. This reflects the shift from the New Deal to the economic mobilization for World War II. The tendency thereafter is a gradual but persistent increase, reaching 32.8 percent in the 2000s to remain at 32.5 percent of GDP growth during the 2010s. This may seem to confirm the importance of consumption. However, a far greater variance obtains in the share of GDP growth due to personal services. Measured as a percentage of the variance in GDP growth, personal services increase from 16.4 percent in the 1930s to peak at *52.1 percent* in the 2000s. Moreover, the contribution of the consumption of personal services to the growth of US GDP declines, substantially, during the 2010s, from 52.1 percent in the 2000s to 39.0 percent for the average during the 2010s.

Table 1.1 Drivers of US GDP growth: Personal consumption, capital, foreign trade, and government, 1930s–2010s

Sector	1930s	1940s	1950s	1960s	1970s	1980s	1990s	2000s	2010s
Personal consumption									
Personal Goods	47.8%	21.4%	21.4%	28.9%	27.5%	26.5%	27.6%	32.8%	32.5%
Personal Services	16.4%	18.1%	26.9%	29.8%	38.3%	39.9%	40.6%	52.1%	39.0%
Capital									
Structures	-23.1%	2.0%	3.3%	4.0%	3.4%	1.3%	0.6%	-1.0%	0.9%
Equipment	-6.0%	5.3%	3.8%	10.2%	13.3%	7.7%	16.7%	3.6%	16.7%
Intellectual property	3.0%	0.5%	2.1%	2.6%	2.8%	5.8%	8.0%	7.8%	10.1%
Residential	-3.7%	4.0%	6.4%	2.2%	6.5%	1.0%	4.3%	-8.9%	5.7%
Inventories	9.7%	-1.0%	5.7%	1.8%	0.6%	0.6%	1.5%	-7.8%	7.0%
Foreign trade									
Exported goods	-4.5%	3.0%	1.2%	5.7%	12.7%	10.2%	17.0%	10.4%	15.4%
Imported goods	3.7%	-0.8%	-4.0%	-5.5%	-9.9%	-14.4%	-26.9%	-14.6%	-26.8%
Exported services	0.0%	0.7%	1.9%	1.5%	2.5%	4.2%	5.0%	7.3%	4.8%
Imported services	3.0%	-1.3%	-3.1%	-1.3%	-0.9%	-3.8%	-2.5%	-5.2%	-3.9%
Government									
Federal govt defense	5.2%	47.8%	19.1%	6.0%	-8.3%	10.9%	-4.3%	9.9%	-1.8%
Federal govt nondefense	35.8%	-0.3%	0.5%	3.5%	3.7%	1.6%	1.9%	5.2%	1.3%
State and local	13.4%	0.8%	9.2%	11.0%	8.3%	8.0%	10.2%	8.3%	-0.4%
Total sector contributions	100.0%	100.0%	100.0%	100.0%	100.0%	100.0%	100.0%	100.0%	100.0%
Average % annual GDP change	1.34	6.02	4.24	4.53	3.24	3.13	3.23	1.92	2.28

Source: Table 1.2.2. Contributions to percentage change in real gross domestic product by major type of product.

The NIPAs data on capital as a driver of growth of US GDP sums the values reported for structures, equipment, intellectual property, residential property, and inventories. Comparing the decade average trends for these five indicators from the 1930s to 2010s suggests further anomalies and provisos for theories of financialization and stagnation (and assertions that historical returns on capital are constant). Disaggregation of the underlying measures of capital suggest large composition effects. The underlying variance in the different types of capital as drivers of GDP growth suggests a far more dynamic process than appears in aggregate measures. Once again, the 1930s stand out with 23.1 percent of the decline in the pace of US GDP growth during this decade due to the decline in the production of structures, with large declines reported for equipment and also residential capital.

However, trends from the 1940s through the 2010s indicate neither a broader decline in the accumulation of capital as implied by critical political economy accounts of financialization, nor constant returns to capital, as argued by Piketty (2014) and other revisionist studies of long-term economic trends (Schmelzing, 2020).

Further anomalies arise for research on economic sectors. For example, the weight of real estate as a driver of economic growth (as measured in terms of the income and production generated by residential property classified as capital in the NIPAs), does indeed increase from a -3.4 percent drag on growth during the 1930s, to a 4.0 percent contribution (i.e. 4 percent of total GDP growth) during the 1940s, increasing to 6.4 percent of GDP growth in the 1950s. However, the decline thereafter to 2.2 percent in the 1960s, 1 percent during the 1980s, and drag of -8.9 percent during the 2000s (and recovery to 5.7 percent of GDP growth during the 2010s) all temper the idea of a structural trend toward economic growth based on real estate valuation in the US. The importance of real estate as a driver of growth before the 1980s belies claims that financialization produced a turn toward real estate-based growth in the US. In terms of the decade averages reported in Table 1.1, residential real estate contributes more to GDP growth during the 1950s and 1970s in the US than any of the decades thereafter.

Although not central to the focus of this book on the domestic US economy, the decomposition of foreign trade data in Table 1.1 illustrates the importance of disaggregation, increasing the number of observations back in time, and paying attention to the underlying categories of economic aggregates. In this case, the decomposition of foreign trade data suggests the existence of substantial differences between the sums reported in domestic accounts and the sums reported in national accounts. On aggregate, international accounts appear to be responsible for a large share of GDP variance. However, considered as drivers of growth, the net balance between imports and exports of goods and services, and the economic effects of imports and exports on the domestic aggregates of US GDP suggest a more complex picture. This remits to complex questions about international political economy, the costs and benefits of manufacturing, the respective tradeoffs that arise from the production of services, commodities,

36 *Finance and the American economy*

and goods, and deeply contested theories and concepts about international trade and finance.

However, given the focus of this book on the domestic US economy, one observation is in order. The decomposition of net foreign trade balances into the four underlying measures (of imported and exported goods and of imported and exported services) indicate large-scale variance in all four trends; variance that is poorly captured by the simple technique of netting out of imports and exports that is used to calculate national accounts.

Finally, the data on the drivers of GDP growth indicate the profound differences that obtain both between federal government defense and nondefense activities, and in the variance in the data on federal, state, and local governments. These differences are also concealed by aggregate measures. The period of the New Deal once again stands out. This can be seen in the far greater role of the nondefense sector of governments that explains 35.8 percent of US GDP growth during the 1930s. However, defense production reaches *47.8 of GDP growth* during the 1940s. The variance thereafter suggests a more complex picture. The large role of defense in the 1950s, the 1970s, and the 2000s, and the more stable contribution of state and local governments to growth until the 2010s, suggest that the political economy of growth in the US is far from linear.

In sum, disaggregation of the macroeconomic data from the US suggests that composition effects belie claims about aggregate trends in growth. The data on unemployment in the US also differs from claims in critical political economy about financialization and unemployment abroad.

Unemployment, 1948–2020

Another central argument in critical political economy about financialization is that it caused unemployment to increase over time across advanced economies, both as a general tendency and because financial crises caused more jobs to be lost during recessions. However, both the terms of academic debates about employment in the US (Abraham and Kearney, 2018; Bertola and Ichino, 1995; Bhaduri and Marglin, 1990) and historical perspective on three measures of unemployment in the US are inconsistent with this claim. The first measure is the rate of unemployment as calculated by the US Bureau of Labor since 1949. The rate of unemployment is defined by the US Bureau of Labor as 'the number of unemployed as a percent of the labor force 16 years of age or older, not including active-duty military personnel, nor those residing in penal and mental facilities, and homes for the aged' (Bureau of Labor, 2020). Mass incarceration, mental health, and age differences are beyond the scope of this book. So, too, are the dramatic differences that obtain between social classes, rural and urban areas, geographical regions, or further differences in accord with gender, ethnicity, and identity. The point here is that the original meaning and measure of the rate of unemployment in the US provides 71 years of monthly data. In

Finance and the American economy 37

historical perspective, several anomalies and provisos arise in the data on unemployment in the US.

Moreover, it is of note that the question of unemployment has taken a central place in the subfields of monetary economics, the research departments of the Federal Reserve System, and debates about monetary policymaking. In 2012, the adoption of *maximum employment* as a goal alongside inflation targets in the mandate of the Federal Reserve System is also of note (Mettenheim, 2021). However, before turning to unemployment and public policy, discussion of the empirical evidence is in order. In this sense, the aggregate data from the US is inconsistent with the causal claim that financialization produced higher levels of unemployment after 1980. Three traditional measures of unemployment in the US suggests otherwise.

Figure 1.16 displays the U-3 measure of labor underutilization (the unemployment rate), as reported by the US Department of Labor from 1949 to 2020. In reverse chronological order, the unprecedented spike of unemployment to 15 percent caused by the COVID-19 pandemic in May 2020 stands out. Purposive gaming of the data and difficulties in the realization of the traditional surveys used by the Department of Labor during the exceptional circumstances of the pandemic appear to have underestimated levels of unemployment during 2020. The abuse of unemployment data during an election year is not unexpected from the perspective of political economy. However, a historical–institutional approach traces the data further back in time while paying attention to the meaning of measures. From this perspective, the data from the US do not support claims about the perverse consequences of financialization in terms of unemployment since 1980.

Proceeding backward in time, the next anomaly is the sustained reduction of unemployment from the peak of 10 percent in April 2010 to 4 percent in

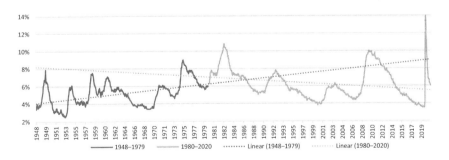

Figure 1.16 Unemployment rate (U-3 measure of labor underutilization), 1949–2020.
Source: St Louis Federal Reserve statistics.

Note: Unemployment rate, percentage, monthly. Seasonally adjusted. The unemployment rate (U-3 measure of labor underutilization) = number of unemployed as percentage of labor force 16 years and older, not including active-duty military personnel and those 'residing in penal and mental facilities, and homes for the aged.'

October 2019, a level not seen since 1969. The sustained decline of unemployment levels from 2010 to 2019 begs important questions about inequality, job quality, wage differentials, the segmentation of labor markets, and the profound regional, demographic, and social-class differences that underlie the data from the US. As mentioned, these themes have emerged as central concerns in both academic research and the research departments of federal government agencies, think tanks, and international institutions. The point here is that recent research on unemployment and historical perspective raise far different problems than the critical political economy literature. The claim that financialization caused an inexorable increase of unemployment since 1980 is not supported in the data from the US.

From this perspective, continuing the reverse chronological order, the peak of 11 percent unemployment in October 1982 is indeed consistent with a central claim about financialization: That a critical juncture of change occurred in the US around 1980. The two-year lag of unemployment behind the record high interest rates that were used to adjust the economy in the late 1970s is consistent with the traditional lag between adjustment, recovery, and unemployment. However, the substantial increases in unemployment recorded from 1953 to 1961, and from 1969 to 1982, suggest that the pre- and post-1980 periods fail to demonstrate a fundamental deterioration as claimed in theories of financialization across advanced economies in critical political economy.

The data on the corollary measure of the number of employed in the US is also inconsistent with the claims of critical political economy. Once again, a single measure of employment here tends to conceal underlying variance between different social classes and groups. However, the macroeconomic trend in the US data is clear, and in the opposite direction of claims about the deleterious structural consequences of financialization. Figure 1.17 displays the employment-population ratio (the number of employed people over 16 years of age (non-military and not institutionalized) as a percentage of the US population), monthly from 1948 through 2020.

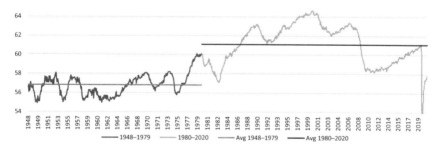

Figure 1.17 Employment to population ratio, 1948–2020.

Source: St Louis Fed statistics, from Bureau of Labor Current population survey.

Note: Monthly number of nonmilitary, noninstitutionalized people over 16 years of age employed as percentage of total US population. Seasonally adjusted.

Finance and the American economy 39

The average employment to population ratio from the period before high financialization (from 1948 through 1979) is 56.83 percent. The average employment to population ratio from 1980 through 2020 is 61.08 percent. Statistical analysis, disaggregation of the data, and control for other explanations are beyond the scope of this chapter. However, the five peaks and six troughs over the 32 years 1948–1979, compared to the four, far more spaced peaks and five troughs over the 41 years 1980–2020, are consistent with the data above on the greater volatility in US business cycles *before* the turning point of 1980. The higher average levels of unemployment before 1980 (noted above), and the higher levels of Americans employed after 1980 are significant anomalies for causal claims that financialization has reduced levels of employment in advanced economies.

Given the importance of these anomalies, consideration of another measure of unemployment is in order. Since 1967, the US Bureau of Labor also measures unemployment as the number of initial unemployment insurance claims. Figure 1.18 displays the number of initial unemployment claims from 1967 through 14 March 2020. Given the nonfinancial phenomena of the COVID-19 pandemic, the data after 14 March 2020 are omitted. The average trend and peaks of unemployment claims clearly increase from 1969 to 1982. Thereafter, the variation is low on average, as indicated by the general tendency, and in terms of a reduction in variance during business cycles, during both recoveries and downturns. Like the other macroeconomic aggregates explored in this chapter, disaggregation of unemployment claims indicates the presence of significant composition effects. Again, although the differences in levels of employment by region, demography, income, gender, race, and age are beyond the scope of this book, the following chapter does examine how financialization contributed to rising inequality in the US.

However, the focus here is on the macroeconomic trends of unemployment and employment. In this respect, the data on (1) unemployment from the US Department of Labor from 1949 to 2020, (2) unemployment claims from 1967 to 2020, and (3) employment–population ratios are consistent with the findings explored so far in this chapter. The data indicate steeper, more serious bouts

Figure 1.18 Weekly initial unemployment insurance claims, 1967–2019, thousands.
Source: Bureau of Labor Statistics.

40 Finance and the American economy

Figure 1.19 US industry capacity utilization, 1967–2020.
Source: St Louis Federal Reserve statistics.
Note: Total industry capacity utilization. Percentage of capacity, monthly. Seasonally adjusted.

of unemployment before 1980 than after 1980, and the generation of greater numbers of jobs since 1980 compared to before 1980. This may beg central questions about multiple employment and deteriorating working conditions. However, the data present further anomalies for theories about the macroeconomic consequences of financialization in critical political economy.

Before disaggregating the data further, discussion of the second tendency in the NIPAs data from the US – a decline in the use of industrial capacity – which is indeed consistent with theories of critical political economy (in addition to inequality) is in order (see Figure 1.19). Contrary to the other macroeconomic indicators explored in this chapter, the downward trend in the use of industrial capacity in the US since 1967 is consistent with the critical political economy literature on financialization in advanced economies. The data is also consistent with the classic modern observations of Kuznets, Keynes, Kalecki, and other twentieth-century economists about the structural consequences of inequality.

Evidence of increasing inequality and a decline in the use of industrial capacity suggest that the core message of classic Keynesianism still applies. Given the structural context of the dollar as international currency, the comparative advantages of cheap finance, and the flexible regulatory frameworks of the US political economy, the opportunities to stimulate economic activity through income policies and demand management are considerable. Indeed, the data on US public policy after 1980 suggest that income transfers and social policy funds *increase*, rather than decline, especially during the 2010s (Mettenheim, 2021).

In sum, the combination of rising inequality and slack industrial capacity in the US provided significant policy space for traditional strategies of macroeconomic demand management. The combination of deflation, dormant industry, and inequality imply that the classic modern insights of Keynes, Kalecki, and others still obtain. The effect of financialization on inequality is not inexorable or irreversible, as will be seen in the following chapter, which explores evidence on US federal government income transfers and taxes. Instead, the two indicators consistent with theories of financialization (inequality and unused

Finance and the American economy 41

industrial capacity), suggest that the traditional policy instruments of demand management still provide the most promising levers for social inclusion in the twenty-first century, along the very same lines emphasized for most of the twentieth century.

Decomposition of consumption and production in the NIPAs, 1929–2019

To further check the above findings, this section disaggregates the evidence from the NIPAs from 1929 to 2019 into the underlying measures used to compile the principal components of US GDP. Hundreds of underlying aggregates are combined to measure gross domestic product. The NIPAs data on US GDP is composed of aggregates that measure the personal consumption of goods and services, the types of private domestic investment, the level and type of government activity, and the gross and net values of the import and export of goods and services. The classifications of industrial production in the NIPAs are still based on the 1934 constitution of national income accounts, with four categories of durable goods and four categories of nondurable goods over the nine decades from 1929 to 2019. The production of services is divided into seven categories (the sixth of which is financial services, including banking and insurance). The gross output and operational receipts of nonprofits serving households is reported separately from the data on households. This differs from the inclusion of nonprofit activities within the data for households in the Z1 Reports and IMAs (implying an overestimation of households due to a composition effect that conceals the rise of nonprofit entities in the US). Personal consumption expenditures are divided into the production of goods and the provision of services.

The NIPAs include data on gross private domestic investment from 1929 to 2019 in terms of fixed investment in ten categories of nonresidential goods: structures, equipment for information processing, computers and peripheral equipment, equipment for industry and transportation, software and other intellectual property products, and entertainment, literature, and art. Residential goods and the level of change in private inventories are reported separately. The annual gross consumption expenditures and investments of the public sector are also compiled separately for the US federal, state and governments, with defense spending reported separately from nondefense spending.

Once again, the nine decades of traditional data on national income and production in the US provide significant opportunities for historical–institutional comparisons. Disaggregation of the data on personal consumption expenditures, private and public domestic investments, and the net exports and imports of goods and services, provides further evidence at odds with claims about the economic consequences of financialization. The NIPAs separate the aggregate values of personal consumption expenditures into four categories of durable goods, four categories of nondurable goods, and seven categories of services. Table 1.2 displays personal consumption expenditures according to the specific contribution of two categories (durable goods and nondurable goods)

Table 1.2 Decade average composition of US gross domestic product, 1930s–2010s

Sector	1930s	1940s	1950s	1960s	1970s	1980s	1990s	2000s	2010s
Personal consumption expenditures	76.0%	59.3%	60.9%	59.8%	60.5%	62.4%	64.7%	67.2%	67.9%
Goods	41.5%	34.8%	34.8%	31.0%	29.0%	26.4%	23.9%	23.4%	21.8%
Durable goods	7.4%	6.7%	9.0%	8.6%	8.8%	8.5%	8.3%	8.4%	7.1%
Motor vehicles and parts	2.3%	1.8%	3.6%	3.6%	3.6%	3.5%	3.4%	3.1%	2.5%
Furnishings and household equipment	3.3%	3.0%	3.3%	2.8%	2.6%	2.2%	1.9%	2.0%	1.6%
Recreational goods and vehicles	0.9%	0.9%	1.2%	1.4%	1.8%	1.7%	1.9%	2.3%	1.9%
Other durable goods	0.9%	1.0%	0.9%	0.8%	0.9%	1.0%	1.1%	1.1%	1.1%
Nondurable goods	34.1%	28.1%	25.8%	22.4%	20.2%	18.0%	15.6%	15.0%	14.7%
Food and beverages takeout	16.7%	14.0%	12.6%	10.2%	8.9%	7.3%	5.9%	5.2%	5.1%
Clothing and footwear	7.9%	6.8%	5.4%	4.5%	4.0%	3.5%	3.1%	2.4%	2.0%
Gasoline and other energy goods	4.0%	2.6%	2.9%	2.6%	2.6%	2.6%	1.8%	2.0%	2.0%
Other nondurable goods	5.5%	4.7%	4.8%	5.0%	4.6%	4.6%	4.9%	5.4%	5.5%
Services	34.5%	24.5%	26.0%	28.8%	31.4%	36.0%	40.7%	43.7%	46.1%
Household service expenditures	33.1%	23.7%	25.2%	27.9%	30.4%	34.9%	39.4%	42.0%	44.0%
Housing and utilities	13.5%	7.8%	9.2%	10.3%	10.3%	11.5%	11.8%	12.2%	12.5%
Health care	2.4%	1.8%	2.4%	3.5%	5.1%	7.0%	9.2%	10.1%	11.3%
Transportation services	2.1%	1.8%	1.7%	1.7%	1.9%	2.0%	2.3%	2.2%	2.2%
Recreation services	1.7%	1.3%	1.1%	1.2%	1.4%	1.7%	2.3%	2.6%	2.7%
Food services and accommodations	4.0%	4.7%	4.1%	3.7%	4.0%	4.2%	4.2%	4.1%	4.5%
Financial services and insurance	2.8%	1.7%	2.1%	2.5%	3.0%	3.7%	4.5%	5.0%	5.2%
Other services	6.6%	4.6%	4.6%	5.0%	4.8%	4.7%	5.1%	5.8%	5.6%
Gross output of nonprofits	0.0%	0.0%	0.3%	3.0%	3.9%	4.9%	6.0%	6.8%	7.7%
Operational receipts of nonprofits	0.0%	0.0%	0.2%	2.1%	2.9%	3.8%	4.6%	5.0%	5.6%

Gross private domestic investment	8.9%	11.2%	16.5%	16.6%	18.0%	18.5%	17.3%	18.0%	16.7%
Fixed investment	9.3%	10.3%	15.6%	15.6%	17.3%	18.1%	16.9%	17.9%	16.3%
Nonresidential	7.1%	7.3%	10.2%	11.0%	12.2%	13.6%	12.6%	12.9%	13.1%
Structures	2.6%	2.3%	3.6%	3.6%	3.8%	4.3%	2.9%	3.0%	2.9%
Equipment	3.8%	4.2%	5.6%	5.9%	6.7%	7.0%	6.6%	6.1%	5.9%
Information processing equipment	0.0%	0.2%	0.7%	1.0%	1.5%	2.3%	2.4%	2.2%	2.0%
Computers and peripheral equipment	0.0%	0.0%	0.0%	0.1%	0.3%	0.7%	0.8%	0.7%	0.6%
Other	0.0%	0.2%	0.7%	0.9%	1.2%	1.6%	1.6%	1.5%	1.4%
Industrial equipment	0.0%	0.6%	1.7%	1.8%	1.9%	1.8%	1.6%	1.3%	1.2%
Transportation equipment	0.0%	0.7%	1.7%	1.7%	1.7%	1.5%	1.4%	1.3%	1.4%
Other equipment	0.0%	0.6%	1.5%	1.4%	1.6%	1.5%	1.3%	1.3%	1.3%
Intellectual property products	0.7%	0.7%	1.0%	1.5%	1.7%	2.3%	3.1%	3.8%	4.2%
Software*	0.0%	0.0%	0.0%	0.1%	0.3%	0.5%	0.9%	1.4%	1.7%
Research and development**	0.3%	0.3%	0.6%	1.0%	1.0%	1.4%	1.6%	1.8%	2.1%
Entertainment, literature, and art	0.4%	0.4%	0.4%	0.4%	0.4%	0.4%	0.5%	0.5%	0.4%
Residential	2.2%	3.0%	5.4%	4.6%	5.0%	4.5%	4.3%	5.0%	3.2%
Change in private inventories	-0.4%	0.9%	0.9%	1.0%	0.7%	0.4%	0.5%	0.1%	0.4%
Net exports of goods and services	0.3%	1.1%	0.3%	0.6%	-0.2%	-1.8%	-1.3%	-4.4%	-3.1%
Exports	3.9%	4.3%	4.4%	5.0%	7.2%	8.2%	10.1%	10.4%	12.7%
Goods	3.4%	3.6%	3.6%	3.8%	5.7%	6.3%	7.3%	7.3%	8.5%
Services	0.5%	0.8%	0.8%	1.2%	1.5%	1.9%	2.8%	3.1%	4.1%
Imports	3.7%	3.2%	4.1%	4.4%	7.4%	9.9%	11.4%	14.8%	15.8%
Goods	2.8%	2.2%	2.9%	3.1%	6.0%	8.2%	9.4%	12.4%	13.0%
Services	0.8%	1.0%	1.3%	1.3%	1.4%	1.7%	2.0%	2.4%	2.8%

(continued)

Table 1.2 Cont.

Sector	1930s	1940s	1950s	1960s	1970s	1980s	1990s	2000s	2010s
Government	14.8%	28.4%	22.4%	23.1%	21.8%	20.8%	19.3%	19.3%	18.5%
Federal	4.8%	22.8%	14.8%	13.4%	10.4%	10.1%	7.9%	7.2%	7.2%
National defense	1.6%	20.7%	12.7%	10.7%	7.2%	7.2%	5.3%	4.6%	4.4%
Consumption expenditures	1.3%	13.4%	9.4%	8.0%	5.9%	5.3%	4.0%	3.6%	3.5%
Gross investment	0.2%	7.3%	3.3%	2.7%	1.4%	1.9%	1.2%	1.0%	0.9%
Nondefense	3.3%	2.1%	2.1%	2.8%	3.1%	2.9%	2.6%	2.6%	2.8%
Consumption expenditures	2.4%	1.7%	1.6%	1.7%	2.1%	2.0%	1.8%	1.9%	2.1%
Gross investment	0.9%	0.5%	0.5%	1.1%	1.0%	0.9%	0.8%	0.7%	0.7%
State and local	10.0%	5.6%	7.6%	9.6%	11.4%	10.7%	11.4%	12.1%	11.3%
Consumption expenditures	7.0%	4.4%	5.2%	6.8%	8.9%	8.7%	9.3%	9.7%	9.3%
Gross investment	3.0%	1.2%	2.4%	2.8%	2.4%	2.1%	2.1%	2.3%	2.0%

Source: BEA NIPAs, Table 1.5.5. Gross domestic product expanded detail.

Notes: *Excludes software embedded, or bundled, in computers and other equipment. **Research and development investment exclude expenditures for software development. Software development expenditures are included in software investment.

with four subcategories: Durable goods consumption (motor vehicles and parts; furnishings and household equipment; recreational goods and services; and others), and four subcategories of personal expenditures on nondurable goods (food and beverage takeout; clothing and footwear; gasoline and other energy goods; and others).

The total value of personal consumption expenditures decreases from 76.0 percent of US GDP in the 1930s to remain at near 60 percent through the 1970s; increasing thereafter to 67.9 percent in the 2010s. However, the bulk of the variance is due to the increase of health care services – from 5.1 to 11.3 percent of GDP from the 1970s to the 2010s. The production of goods in the US declines from over 40 percent in the 1930s to 21.8 percent in the 2010s, while services increase from 34.5 to 46.1 percent. However, decomposition of the data suggests that the consumption of durable goods remains comparatively stable, while substantial declines obtain in the share of nondurable goods production. The consumption of nondurable goods declines from 34.1 to 14.7 percent of US GDP from the 1930s to the 2010s, with basic products such as food and beverage takeout, clothing and footwear, and gasoline and other energy products sharing substantial proportional declines.

Moreover, as suggested above, the gross output of nonprofit organizations increases from zero to 7.7 *percent* of US GDP from the 1930s to the 2010s. This helps explain the marginal declines in other economic sectors. In a broader sense, the rise of nonprofits may be associated with a general process of channeling corporate profits into nonprofit entities to avoid taxes. However, this indirect channel involves other questions of political economy and must remain beyond the scope of this chapter.

The provision of services as a percentage of US GDP increases from 24.5 to 46.1 percent from the 1940s to the 2010s. Financial services and insurance do increase from the postwar level of 1.4 percent during the 1940s to 5.2 percent of US GDP in the 2010s. However, as indicated above, the broader variance in the transition from manufacturing to services in the NIPAs suggests that other sectors (especially the provision of health care services), are a far greater source of change than the financial sector (Cutler and Ly, 2011). The provision of health care services increases from 1.8 to 11.3 percent of US GDP from the 1940s to the 2010s.

The tendencies in gross private domestic investment as measured in the NIPAs also belie the deleterious consequences emphasized in critical political economy accounts of financialization. To avoid the variance produced by government mobilization for World War II, the trend in private investment after the 1950s provides a better point of comparison. Since the 1950s, private domestic investment has increased as a percentage of US GDP from 6.5 percent to reach 18.0 percent, on average, during the 2000s, declining to 16.7 percent during the 2010s. This is at odds with claims that private investment declines over time, or since the 1980s, in the US.

Disaggregation of the data on private investment in the NIPAs also fails to support the idea of a fundamental change toward real estate or a decline

46 *Finance and the American economy*

in fixed investments. Postwar nonresidential investment increased from 10.2 to 13.1 percent from the 1950s to 2010s. Moreover, residential investments declined from 5.4 to 3.2 percent over these decades. This is incompatible with claims about how financialization shifted the US economy toward housing and the private residential sector increasing since 1980.

The bulk of variance in nonresidential investment is due to the increase in new technologies of information and communication. This is reported in the NIPAs categories of equipment and intellectual property products. The share of information-processing equipment increases from 0.7 to 2.0 percent from the 1950s to the 2010s, while the share of industrial equipment production declines from 1.7 to 1.2 percent. Transportation and the residual category of other equipment also decline slightly.

In sum, neither the increase in consumption nor the rise of finance stand out as the greatest variance in the broader structural indicators of the US economy in the NIPAs from the 1950s through the 2010s.

The complexities of international political economy and foreign accounts are beyond the scope of this book, as noted. Two further observations are nonetheless in order. First, the net value of exports minus imports becomes negative in the 1970s. However, this tendency is reversed in the 2010s. Second, as argued above, the disaggregation of the net calculation of a single measure of trade balances into the four component parts of imports and exports of goods, and imports and exports of services, suggests a more complex picture. The standard procedure in the calculation of gross *national* product (not to be confused with gross *domestic* product), is to simply subtract the total value of imports from the total value of exports. This conceals the underlying variance in the four categories of the NIPAs and begs the question of the different weightings, elasticities, externalities, and other considerations for each of the four measures.

Disaggregation of the NIPAs data on US government accounts suggests further anomalies for theories of financialization. The massive increases of the government sector in the 1930s and 1940s stand out from trends thereafter. However, the aggregate trends in the public sector accounts of the NIPAs also conceal underlying trends at odds with standard views of the rise and fall of government in the US economy. First, the federal government share of US GDP does indeed decline from 14.8 to 7.2 percent from the 1950s to the 2010s. However, this decline is largely due to the 8.3 percent decline in defense production (from 14.8 to 7.2 percent). The share of nondefense government production did increase from 2.1 to 3.1 percent from the 1950s to the 1970s. However, the share of nondefense government production thereafter remains largely stable at 2.8 percent through the 2010s. Moreover, the shares of state and local government consumption and investment in US GDP also increased from 7.6 to 11.4 percent from the 1950s to the 1970s, and remained at near peak levels of 11.3 percent of US GDP through the 2010s. The following chapter explores further data on US government accounts that confirm these anomalies and provisos for claims about the dismantlement of Welfare States, inequality, and public policy.

Finance and the American economy   47

Further evidence about long-term trends in the American economy may be obtained by comparing the decade average levels of savings and investment by social sector from the 1930s through the 2010s. Table 1.3 displays data from the NIPAs on the value of gross savings, net savings, consumption of fixed capital, gross domestic investment, net lending or borrowing, and the net investment of the federal, state, and local governments. The data confirm the inferences from annual trends from 1929 to 2019 above. Although the value of gross savings declines from the peak of 23.7 percent of US GDP in the 1960s to 17.8 percent in the 2000s, both the recovery to 18.4 percent in the 2010s and the greater variance in federal government savings compared to private and subnational government savings suggest a more complex picture than causal claims about private savings in theories of financialization. Gross private savings does indeed peak at 22.2 percent of US GDP in the 1970s. This is consistent with theories of financialization. However, the value of gross private savings returns to 22.1 percent in the 2010s. And federal government savings continue to run negative after the 1970s to reach –3.6 percent of GDP in the 2010s.

The data on net savings also indicate a reversal of the tendencies that obtained from the 1970s to the 2000s. During the 2010s, private net savings increased from 6.3 to 9.1 percent of GDP, while the net private savings of domestic business increased from 2.7 to 3.6 percent of GDP, and households increased aggregate net savings from 3.6 to 5.5 percent of GDP. The declines obtain not for the private sector, but, instead, in the public sector: The negative net savings of federal and subnational governments fell to –5.1 and –1.5 percent of GDP respectively during the 2010s.

The consumption of fixed capital also increased after the 1950s, from 11.8 to 16.0 percent of US GDP from the 1950s to the 2010s nationally and, for domestic businesses and households, from 7.1 to 10.4 and 1.4 to 2.7 percent, respectively.

Gross domestic investment declined, but only slightly from the peak of 23.3 percent in the 1960s to the lowest level of 20.2 percent of GDP in the 2010s (22.0 percent in the 2000s). Likewise, gross private domestic investment peaks at 18.5 percent in the 1980s and returned to 18.0 percent in the 2000s, while the federal government declined from 3.8 percent in the 1950s and 1960s to 1.6 percent in the 2010s, and state governments declined from 2.8 percent of US GDP in the 1960s to 2.0 percent in the 2010s.

Both the return of levels of investment in the 2010s and the larger variance of the public sector suggest that the long-term changes in the US economy turn more on declines in public sector investment than variance in private sector investments. This is consistent with the inference above that private sector investment in the US has remained within historical levels and is contrary to claims that financialization produces declining private sector investment. Further data on *net* government investment is consistent with this observation. The net investment of the federal government peaks at 8.1 percent of GDP in the 1960s, then declines to 3.6 percent in the 2010s, while the net investment of state and

Table 1.3 Decade average savings and investment by sector, 1930s–2010s

Sector	1930s	1940s	1950s	1960s	1970s	1980s	1990s	2000s	2010s
Gross savings	13,0%	20,3%	22,4%	23,7%	22,1%	20,7%	19,1%	17,8%	18,4%
Private	12,5%	21,2%	19,1%	20,6%	22,2%	21,7%	19,3%	18,9%	22,1%
Federal government	-2,0%	-2,2%	2,0%	1,7%	-1,2%	-1,8%	-0,6%	-1,1%	-3,6%
State and local government	2,5%	1,3%	1,2%	1,3%	1,1%	0,9%	0,4%	0,0%	-0,1%
Net savings	1,1%	10,0%	10,6%	11,6%	8,7%	5,6%	4,4%	2,4%	2,5%
Private	2,1%	14,3%	10,6%	12,1%	12,2%	9,9%	7,8%	6,3%	9,1%
Domestic business	-0,8%	3,0%	3,3%	4,3%	3,5%	2,8%	2,5%	2,7%	3,6%
Undistributed corporate profits	-0,9%	4,4%	3,9%	3,7%	4,5%	2,5%	2,0%	3,0%	4,1%
Inventory adjustment, corporate	0,3%	-0,8%	-0,3%	-0,2%	-1,0%	-0,4%	0,0%	-0,1%	-0,1%
Capital consumption, corporate	-0,2%	-0,5%	-0,3%	0,8%	0,1%	0,6%	0,5%	-0,1%	-0,4%
Households and NGOs	2,9%	11,2%	7,3%	7,8%	8,6%	7,1%	5,3%	3,6%	5,5%
Federal government	-2,4%	-4,8%	-0,5%	-1,0%	-3,5%	-4,0%	-2,6%	-2,6%	-5,1%
State and local government	1,4%	0,6%	0,5%	0,5%	0,0%	-0,3%	-0,7%	-1,2%	-1,5%
Consumption of fixed capital	11,9%	10,3%	11,8%	12,1%	13,4%	15,1%	14,7%	15,3%	16,0%
Domestic business	8,9%	5,8%	7,1%	7,1%	8,3%	9,7%	9,4%	10,0%	10,4%
Households and NGOs	1,5%	1,1%	1,4%	1,5%	1,8%	2,1%	2,1%	2,6%	2,7%
Federal government	0,4%	2,6%	2,5%	2,7%	2,3%	2,2%	2,0%	1,5%	1,5%
State and local government	1,1%	0,8%	0,8%	0,9%	1,1%	1,1%	1,1%	1,2%	1,4%
Gross domestic investment	13,1%	20,1%	22,6%	23,3%	22,8%	23,4%	21,5%	22,0%	20,2%
Private domestic	8,9%	11,2%	16,4%	16,6%	18,0%	18,5%	17,3%	18,0%	16,6%
Federal government	1,1%	7,8%	3,8%	3,8%	2,4%	2,8%	2,0%	1,7%	1,6%
State and local government	3,0%	1,2%	2,4%	2,8%	2,4%	2,1%	2,1%	2,3%	2,0%
Net lending or net borrowing	0,5%	0,7%	0,2%	0,6%	0,1%	-1,6%	-1,4%	-4,4%	-2,5%
Net federal government investment	-1,4%	4,3%	7,9%	8,1%	7,9%	6,8%	5,8%	5,4%	3,6%
Net state & local gov't investment	0,7%	5,1%	1,3%	1,1%	0,1%	0,6%	0,1%	0,2%	0,1%

Source: BEA NIPAs, Table 5.1. Saving and Investment by Sector.

Finance and the American economy   49

local governments peak at 5.1 percent in the 1940s and decline to 0.1 percent in the 2010s.

Before concluding this chapter, these findings in the annual (and decade average) data from 1929 to 2019 may be checked with the quarterly data in the IMAs from 1960 to 2019. Disaggregating the data on the domestic production of goods and services in the US suggests the importance of the anomalies and provisos explored so far. Table 1.4 displays three categories of household consumption (services, nondurable goods, and durable goods), two categories of business investment (nonresidential and residential), and three categories of government expenditures (federal defense, other federal, and state and local) that may be obtained in the IMAs data. Several observations are in order.

First, the greatest variance in the IMAs data is an increase of household *services* from 28.8 to 46.7 percent of US GDP, 1960 to 2019. This confirms the greater importance of the transition from industrial manufacturing to the provision of services (and belies claims about real estate bubbles). The far smaller share of residential business production (from 5.0 to 3.7 percent, 1960 to 2019, with a peak in the early 2000s at 5.3 percent) in comparison to nonresidential business (that increases from 10.3 to 15.4 percent, 1960 to 2019) also appears to counter strong claims about the role of real estate in financialization. Finally, by separating the public sector share of US GDP into federal government defense and nondefense production, and the contribution of state and local government production to US GDP, the importance of the separation and diffusion of government through federalism also come into perspective.

In sum, the evidence from the NIPAs and IMAs suggest that the broader claims about the structural consequences of financialization are overstated or misleading in the case of the US. The following chapters return to the data from the NIPAs and IMAs to explore the financialization of household inequality and nonfinancial business enterprises in the US. However, a historical–institutional approach to personal income and its disposition in the US from the 1930s to the 2010s, and the data on the changing composition of US GDP from 1929 to 2019 explored in this section, are consistent with numerous trends in the US macroeconomy before and after 1980, reported above. The rise of inequality and the decline in the use of industrial capacity are consistent with theories of financialization and comparative studies of advanced capitalist economies. However, *none* of the other perverse consequences expected by critical political economy theories of financialization, and similar claims in comparative studies of advanced economies, appear to hold in the data from the US.

Conclusion

The problems of financialization are not as endemic or systemic as claimed in debates about advanced capitalism. Comparison of decade averages from the 1930s through the 2010s; decomposition of the historical statistics on the structures and drivers of economic growth in the US; tracing the changing levels of consumption, investment, savings, goods and services; focusing

Table 1.4 Social sector composition of US gross domestic product, five-year averages, 1960–2019

Sector	1960–1964	1965–1969	1970–1974	1975–1979	1980–1984	1985–1989	1990–1994	1995–1999	2000–2004	2005–2009	2010–2014	2015–2019
Household												
Services	28,8%	28,8%	30,7%	32,2%	34,6%	37,4%	40,2%	41,3%	43,1%	44,4%	45,6%	46,7%
Nondurables	23,2%	21,5%	20,6%	19,8%	19,1%	16,8%	16,2%	15,1%	14,9%	15,1%	15,2%	14,1%
Durables	8,3%	8,9%	8,8%	8,9%	7,9%	9,0%	8,1%	8,5%	8,9%	7,9%	7,1%	7,2%
Business												
Nonresidential	10,3%	11,6%	11,8%	12,7%	14,1%	13,1%	11,8%	13,4%	13,0%	12,8%	12,8%	13,4%
Residential	5,0%	4,3%	4,9%	5,1%	4,2%	4,9%	4,0%	4,5%	5,3%	4,7%	2,8%	3,7%
Government												
Federal defense	11,1%	10,3%	8,0%	6,5%	7,1%	7,4%	6,1%	4,4%	4,2%	4,9%	4,9%	3,9%
Other federal	2,6%	2,9%	3,1%	3,2%	3,1%	2,7%	2,7%	2,5%	2,5%	2,7%	2,9%	2,7%
State and local	9,2%	10,1%	11,4%	11,4%	10,7%	10,8%	11,5%	11,4%	12,0%	12,2%	11,6%	11,0%
GDP %	100%	100%	100%	100%	100%	100%	100%	100%	100%	100%	100%	100%
GDP $billion	606	875	1.298	2.124	3.416	4.930	6.557	8.257	11.089	14.093	16.209	19.693

Source: BEA National income and product accounts, Table 1.1.5.

on the long-term trends within the private and public sectors; and evidence of the far greater importance of nonfinancial capital in the traditional, classic-modern nonfinancial data in the US national accounts, all belie claims of slower growth, increased unemployment, greater volatility in business cycles and capital markets, and other downsides that are seen to be caused by financialization. The traditional macroeconomic data from the US do not support the broader causal claims about financialization in the critical political economy literature. The predominant nonfinancial drivers of growth, the sources and direction of change, and the unexpected evidence of continuity in core indicators, all belie generalizations about the deleterious consequences of financialization in the US.

To uncover the causal logic of financialization, it is necessary to go beyond the traditional indicators of macroeconomics and national income and production accounts. In this sense, the traditional macroeconomic data in the US NIPAs and IMAs cast doubt on a central idea in endogenous money theory and post-Keynesian monetary economics: That finance and money shape the political economy of advanced capitalist economies. From this perspective, both post-Keynesian research and mainstream monetarist economics appear to have overestimated the financial and monetary dimensions of American political economy. The following chapters turn to the evidence from the financial balance sheets of US households and nonfinancial business enterprises to check these findings and trace, more carefully, the accumulation of financial claims and liabilities and its consequences.

However, this chapter has focused on the traditional economic aggregates as measured in the NIPAs data from 1929 to 2019. A historical–institutional and political-economic approach reveals a series of provisos and anomalies for claims about the deleterious consequences of financialization and the syndromes of stagnation in advanced capitalism. Moreover, the exceptions of increasing inequality and unused industrial capacity imply that the perverse consequences of compounding financialization may be countered through the classic modern Keynesian policies of demand management. Income policies may counter the economic factors responsible for inequality by increasing aggregate demand while monitoring inflationary pressures. The large volume of unused industrial capacity and the severe shortfalls of indebted households imply a large space for traditional policies of social inclusion. However, before pursuing the implications of these findings on broader trends in the American political economy, the following chapters focus on the financialization of two further social sectors in balance-sheet studies: households and nonfinancial business enterprises.

Notes

1 Although slack industrial capacity and inequality are precisely the factors emphasized by Kalecki, Keynes, and recent studies of inequality, the argument of this book, elaborated in Chapter 2, argues that the financialization of inequality turns on conceptual stretching, misaggregation, and loading on the dependent variable.

52 *Finance and the American economy*

2 Since Antonio Gramsci's description of Fordism and Americanism in *The Prison Notebooks* (1928), this dimension has informed analyses of European political economy. The regulation school (Aglietta, 1976) in France continues this tradition. The argument of this book focuses on other aspects of the American experience and unexpected trends since the financial crisis of 2007–2008.

3 Because of the complexities of foreign trade, the aggregate measure of gross domestic product is favored over gross national product. The simple addition and subtraction of the large and changing volumes and values of imports and exports used to measure the latter are best avoided in favor of the more limited, but more accurate, aggregate of gross domestic product.

References

Abraham, Katharine G., and Melissa S. Kearney. (2018). 'Explaining the decline in the US employment-to-population ratio: A review of the evidence.' NBER Working Paper No. 24333.

Aglietta, Michel. (1976). *A theory of capitalist regulation: The US experience.* London: Verso Books.

Autor, David H., David Dorn, Lawrence F. Katz, Christina Patterson, and John Van Reenan. (2017a). 'Superstar firms and the falling labor share.' *American Economic Review: Papers and Proceedings*, 107(5): 180–5.

Autor, David H., David Dorn, Lawrence F. Katz, Christina Patterson, and John Van Reenen. (2017b). 'Concentrating on the fall of the labor share.' *American Economic Review*, 107(5): 180–5.

Bachelier, Louis. (1900). *Théorie de la spéculation.* Paris: Gauthier-Villars.

Barro, Richard. (1990). 'Government spending in a simple model of endogenous growth.' *Journal of Political Economy*, 98(5): 103–26.

Bertola, Giuseppi and Anrea Ichino. (1995). 'Wage inequality and unemployment: United States versus Europe.' *NBER Macroeconomics Annual*, 10: 13–66.

Bhaduri, Amit and Stephen A. Marglin. (1990). 'Unemployment and the real wage: The economic basis for contesting political ideologies.' *Cambridge Journal of Economics*, 14: 375–93.

Brunner, Karl. (2018). 'High powered money and the monetary base,' in Steven Durlauf and Lawrence Blume (eds) *The new Palgrave dictionary of economics.* London: Palgrave, pp. 5845–7.

Bureau of Commerce. (1934). *National income 1929–1932.* Washington, DC: Government Printing Office.

Bureau of Labor. (2020). *Bureau of Labor Statistics, Unemployment rate.* Federal Reserve Bank of St. Louis. Available at: https://fred.stlouisfed.org/series/UNRATE.

Cagan, Philip. (1965). *Determinants and effects of changes in the stock of money, 1875–1960.* Ann Arbor, MI: University of Michigan Press.

Carvalho, Laura and Armon Rezai. (2016). 'Personal income inequality and aggregate demand.' *Cambridge Journal of Economics*, 40: 491–505.

Castles, Francis G., Stephan Leibfried, Jane Lewis, Herbert Obinger, and Christopher Pierson (eds). (2010). *The Oxford handbook of welfare states.* Oxford: Oxford University Press.

Chicago Federal Reserve Bank. (2020). 'Background on the Chicago Fed National Activity Index.' Economic Research Department.

Finance and the American economy 53

Cutler, David M. and Dan P. Ly. (2011). 'The (paper) work of medicine: Understanding international medical costs.' *Journal of Economic Perspectives*, 30(6): 1174–87.

Denison, Edward F. (1974). *Accounting for U.S. economic growth*. Washington, DC: Brookings Institution.

Eggertsson, Gauti, Jacob A. Robbins, and Ella Getz Wold. (2018). 'Kaldor and Piketty's facts: The rise of monopoly power in the United States.' NBER Working Paper No. 24287.

Evans, Trevor. (2016). 'The crisis of finance-led capitalism in the United States,' in Eckhard Hein, Daniel Detzer, and Nina Dodig (eds) *Financialisation and the financial and economic crises: Country studies*. London: Edward Elgar, pp. 42–67.

Foley, Duncan K., Thomas R. Michl, and Daniele Tavani. (2019). *Growth and distribution*. Cambridge, MA: Harvard University Press.

Friedman, Milton and Anna J. Schwartz. (1963). *A monetary history of the United States, 1867–1960*. Princeton, NJ: Princeton University Press.

Geddes, Barbara. (1990). 'How the cases you choose affect the answers you get: Selection bias in comparative politics.' *Political Analysis*, 2: 131–50.

Gordon, Robert J. (2016). *The rise and fall of American growth: The U.S. standard of living since the Civil War*. Princeton, NJ: Princeton University Press.

Gourevitch, Peter. (1982). *Politics in hard times: Comparative responses to international economic crises*. Cornell, NY: Cornell University Press.

Hall, Peter and David Soskice (eds). (2001). *Varieties of capitalism: The institutional foundations of comparative advantage*. Cambridge: Cambridge University Press.

Hein, Eckhard, Daniel Detzer, and Nina Dodig. (eds). (2016). *Financialisation and the financial and economic crises: Country studies*. London: Edward Elgar.

Hein, Eckhard, Daniel Detzer, and Nina Dodig. (eds). (2015). *The demise of finance dominated capitalism: Explaining the financial and economic crises*. London: Edward Elgar.

Kaldor, Nicholas. (1966). Causes of the slow rate of economic growth of the United Kingdom: an inaugural lecture. Cambridge: Cambridge University Press.

Kaldor, Nicholas. (1957). 'A model of economic growth.' *The Economic Journal*, 67(268): 591–624.

Kotz, David M. (2015). *The rise and fall of neoliberal capitalism*. Cambridge, MA: Harvard University Press.

Krippner, Greta. (2011). *Capitalizing on crisis: The political origins of the rise of finance*. Cambridge, MA: Harvard University Press.

Kuznets, Simon. (1966). *Modern economic growth*. New Haven, CT: Yale University Press.

Mettenheim, Kurt. (2021). *Political economy, banking, and financialization in the United States: A historical-institutional balance-sheet approach*. London: Routledge.

North, Douglas C. (1961). *The economic growth of the United States, 1790–1860*. Upper Saddle River, NJ: Prentice-Hall.

Officer, Lawrence and Samuel Williamson. (2020). 'Annual wages in the United States, 1774–present,' 'The annual consumer price index for the United States, 1774–present,' 'What was the interest rate then?' Measuring Worth website. Available at: www.measuringworth.com/datasets.

Pierson, Paul. (1993). 'When effect becomes cause: Policy feedback and political change.' *World Politics*, 45(4): 595–628.

Piketty, Thomas. (2014). *Capital and ideology*. Cambridge, MA: Harvard University Press.

Rache, Robert and James Johannes. (1987). *Controlling the money supply*. Boston, MA: Kluwer.

54 *Finance and the American economy*

Rezai, Armon. (2013). 'Cycles of demand and distribution and monetary policy in the US economy.' *Journal of Post-Keynesian Economics*, 36: 231–50.

Romer, Christina D. (1986). 'Is the stabilization of the postwar economy a figment of the data?' *American Economic Review*, 76(3): 14–34.

Ryan, Mary M. (ed). (2020). *Handbook of US labor statistics 2020: Employment, earnings, prices, productivity, and other labor data*. London: Rowman & Littlefield.

Schmelzing, Paul. (2020). 'Eight centuries of global real interest rates, R–G, and the "suprasecular" decline.' Bank of England Staff, Working Paper No. 845.

Shonfield, Andrew. (1965). *Modern capitalism: The changing balance of public and private power*. Oxford: Oxford University Press.

Sichel, Daniel E. (2019). 'Productivity measurement: Racing to keep up.' Chicago, IL. NBER Working Paper No. 25558.

Solow, Robert. (1970). *Growth theory: An exposition*. Oxford: Oxford University Press.

Steindl, Josef. (1952). *Maturity and stagnation in American capitalism*. Oxford: Basil Blackwell (1976, 2nd edition).

Stock, James H. and Mark W. Watson. (1999). 'Inflation forecasting.' *Journal of Monetary Economics*, 44(2): 293–335.

Taylor, Lance. (2020). *Macroeconomic inequality from Reagan to Trump: Market power, wage repression, asset price inflation, and industrial decline*. Cambridge: Cambridge University Press.

Taylor, Lance., Duncan K. Foley, and Armon Rezai. (2019). 'Demand drives growth all the way.' *Cambridge Journal of Economics*, 43: 1333–5.

Temin, Peter. (2002). 'The golden age of economic growth reconsidered.' *European Review of Economic History*, 6: 3–22.

US Bureau of the Census. (1976). *Historical statistics of the United States: Colonial times to 1970*. Washington, DC: Bureau of the Census, 2 vols.

Wu, Tim. (2018). *The curse of bigness: Antitrust in the new gilded age*. New York: Columbia Global Reports.

2 The financialization of American household inequality

Introduction

Having controlled for the macroeconomic consequences of financialization in the preceding chapter, this chapter returns to the central goal of this study: to combine pluralist and critical political economy, the qualitative methods of historical–institutionalism, and the basic principles of financial balance-sheets and portfolio strategy to better explain how financialization has affected each American social sector. The preceding volume focused on the financialization of US banks, the centralization and financialization of monetary authority, and the new ideologies, and realities, of shadow banking, off-balance-sheet operations, and nonbank financial entities. The theory of compounding financialization and the critique of standard economic approaches, especially contemporary banking theory, financial intermediation theory, and endogenous money approaches, helped reveal the long-term causal logic, changing character, and limits to the rise of finance. Comparison of the changing proportional social sector shares of US financial claims from 1960 to 2019 (households, banks and financial institutions, nonfinancial business, the federal, state, and local governments, and the rest of the world), began with an overview of the Integrated macroeconomic accounts (IMAs) data provided by the US Department of Commerce Bureau of Economic Analysis. Tracing social sector shares of US national accounts from 1960 to 2019 suggested that the rise of finance in the US came largely at the expense of households (Mettenheim, 2021). The displacement of households by banks and financial industries as the predominant holders of US financial claims belies central ideas in contemporary banking theory, financial intermediation theory, and the standard approaches in economics; indicating serious errors of conceptual stretching, loading on the dependent variable, and mis-aggregation.

This chapter therefore elaborates a more in-depth historical–institutional balance-sheet analysis of two problems: the proportional decline of household control over US financial assets and the rise of household inequality. The primary sources for this chapter, once again, are the National income and product accounts (NIPAs) from 1929 to 2019, the IMAs from 1960 to 2018, and the Distributional financial accounts (DFAs) from 1989 to 2019. Chapter 1 identified several anomalies and provisos about the political and social economy of

DOI: 10.4324/9781003223320-3

56 *Finance and American household inequality*

US households from the data on labor income, personal income, consumption, and savings in the NIPAs from 1929 to 2019. This chapter disaggregates the data and checks further sources to explore the implications of these anomalies and provisos for theories of financialization and generalizations about economic change and social policy reversals in advanced economies. The decomposition of balance-sheet data by social class in the DFAs from 1989–2019 provides further evidence of (1) the conceptual stretching of money to include financial claims, (2) the mis-aggregation of income data, (3) the double-counting of value changes in assets and liabilities, and (4) the netting out of other people's money (household savings) that is held by banks and financial institutions. The decomposition of household balance-sheet data from 1989 to 2019 by wealth percentiles helps explain how core misconceptions about finance, banking, and money became ideological veils of capital that caused, and concealed, the financialization of household inequality in the US.

Concerns about inequality have been at the center of American political economy since the disputes between the founding fathers and the generation of federalists and populists that followed. William Gouge was an advocate of an independent treasury during the terms of Presidents Andrew Jackson (1829–1837) and Martin van Buren (1837–1841). However, in 1833, Gouge also stressed the connection between inequality and the accumulation of wealth in ways that ring true today and anticipate the theory of compounding financialization:

> If two women start in life at the same time, and the one gets, at the commencement, but a small advantage over the other, and retains the advantage for twenty or thirty years, their fortunes will, at the end of that period, be very unequal.
>
> (Gouge, 1833: 90)

The history of American thought on finance and inequality is beyond the scope of this book (Nell, 2019). However, consulting the classics provides secure points of departure for the elaboration of historical–institutional balance-sheet analysis. Another reference to Simon Kuznets' 1934 constitution of US national income accounts is therefore in order (Bureau of Commerce, 1934). This time to help clarify how a political-economic approach is required to explain both the decline of households as the top holder of financial claims in the US and how financialization exacerbated inequalities.

In 1934, Kuznets argued that the extreme inequality of the US in the early 1930s was structural, notwithstanding the record levels of unemployment and economic collapse during the Great Depression (Bureau of Commerce, 1934). For Kuznets, the inequality of early twentieth-century America was structural in the sense of being sustained by the vast economic forces of demand and supply that had skewed 'upmarket' toward a small number of elite households. Two decades later, in his landmark article of 1955, Kuznets provided an addendum about the relations between politics and economics. He warned that *political factors*, not economic factors, were the most important means of 'counteracting the cumulative effect of concentration of savings upon upper-income shares' (Kuznets, 1955: 8). This chapter returns to Kuznets' challenge to social scientists in 1955: To explain both the economic causes of inequality and how political forces may reverse it (Foley et al., 2019).

Recent approaches to inequality in economics largely ignore the political side of Kuznets' challenge in 1955 (Bartscher et al., 2020; Gordon and Dew-Becker, 2008). Economic approaches to inequality are also marred by conceptual stretching, loading on the dependent variable, and mis-aggregation. A central argument of this book, and the volume that precedes it, is that the official US sectoral and national financial balance-sheet accounts (the Financial Accounts of the United States Z1 Reports), launched by the Federal Reserve in 1946, and the IMAs, launched by the Department of Commerce Bureau of Economic Analysis in 1965), present a series of complex analytic challenges. These challenges arise from replacing or augmenting the traditional aggregates designed to measure income, production, and nonfinancial assets with new aggregates designed to measure the value of financial claims and liabilities. The confusion caused by the mixing together of aggregates compiled according to the concepts and categories of national income and production accounts, with the far different aggregates that compose the two sides of financial balance-sheet portfolios (that are based on principles of financial accounting), compromises central claims of contemporary banking theory, financial intermediation theory, and recent approaches to the endogenous creation of money (Mettenheim, 2021).

The conceptual stretching of categories of national and sectoral income and production accounts to include, and double-count, categories of financial accounts was especially pernicious for the financialization of household inequality in the US. Two consequences followed from the redefinition of the traditional measures of income, property, and wealth to include financial claims and liabilities. The first consequence was the overestimation of financial income and, therefore, the size of the financial sector. The second consequence was the creation of an ideological veil that conceals both the compounding logic of financialization and the financialization of inequality. Promising new research has emerged on the distributional effects, positive and negative, of monetary policies (Auclert, 2019; Gornemann et al., 2016; Luetticke, 2015). However, before turning to debates about public policy, it is necessary to understand the causal mechanisms and ideological veils behind the financialization of household inequality in the US.

Analysis of this problem is possible because of a remarkable new data set. The disaggregation, by social class, of US social sector financial balance-sheet data became available in March 2019 in the DFAs (Batty et al., 2019). The DFAs were elaborated as part of the Federal Reserve's Enhanced Financial Accounts Initiative (Piketty et al., 2018). To compile the DFAs, the balance-sheet data from Z1 Reports were split according to the distributions of financial claims and liabilities as captured by the Federal Deposit Insurance Company (FDIC)

58 *Finance and American household inequality*

triennial Consumer Finance Surveys. This implies that the criteria for the percentile categories of social classes are *not* the traditional categories of income. Instead, the definition of social classes turns on percentile ranks according to the value of financial claims and liabilities above and beyond the traditional measure of household *non*financial assets (the sum of real estate and consumer durables owned by households).

The triennial estimates for the 12 variables obtained from the FDIC triennial surveys were then interpolated for the intervening years and quarters. The DFAs data therefore include two measures of non-financial assets (real estate and consumer durable goods) and nine measures of financial claims (checkable deposits and currency, money market fund shares, treasuries and municipal securities, corporate and foreign bonds, corporate equities and mutual fund shares, life insurance reserves, pension entitlements, equity in noncorporate business, and a residual category for other assets). Five measures of liabilities were also interpolated (home mortgages, consumer credit, depository institution loans, other loans, and life insurance premiums). For the first time since the constitution of US national income accounts in 1934, the DFAs make it possible to disaggregate household balance sheets according to social class over time, measured by wealth (i.e. not just income) percentiles.

The DFAs split US households into the top 1 percent, next 9 percent, next 40 percent, and bottom 50 percent of American citizens and residents by total wealth (capitalized wealth, which is precisely the problem). To elaborate the theory of compounding financialization, the value of nonfinancial assets, financial claims, liabilities, and net worth of each of these social classes was compared from 1989 to 2019 (Mettenheim, 2021). This informed the elaboration of the theory of compounding financialization and the following claims. Financialization was caused, and concealed by: (1) the conceptual stretching of money to include the financial claims of banks and financial firms; (2) the composition effects that arise from the aggregation of social sector balance-sheet data; (3) the double-counting of financial claims and liabilities; and (4) the tendency of research in economics (and financialization studies) to focus on the accumulation of financial claims by the rich that tends to draw attention away from, and underestimate, both the variance experienced by other social classes *and* the other side of the balance sheets, that is, the compounding of liabilities (debt) that occurs disproportionally among those with less income and capital.

These problems also mar studies of inequality. Recent studies of inequality argue that the capitalization of income is responsible for much of the rise of inequality since the 1970s, in the US and abroad (Saez and Zucman, 2016; Piketty, 2014). This is consistent with core claims in comparative political economy about financialization. However, the concept of the capitalization of income is problematic. Since Aristotle, money has been defined as the measure of all wealth (Barnes and Kenney, 2014: 279). It follows that, just as in the case of money, stretching the concept of wealth (the dependent variable at hand here), to include financial claims makes it difficult to evaluate the causal weight of independent variables (i.e. the various factors, financial and nonfinancial,

Finance and American household inequality   59

economic and political, that caused inequality). This chapter therefore separates, by social class, the traditional sources of income and the traditional types of nonfinancial assets from the newer, financial claims of income and wealth in the DFAs from 1989 to 2019, and pays attention to both the different financial portfolios of social classes and the distribution of liabilities (debts) on the other side of financial balance sheets.

The redefinition of wealth as capital also ignores Kuznets' warning not to double-count earnings on assets (Mettenheim, 2021; Bureau of Commerce, 1934: ix). Redefining the traditional measures of wealth in national income accounts to include financial claims conceals both the double-counting of financial claims for the rich, and the double-counting of liabilities for the poor (once in income accounts and once again in balance-sheet accounts). This is a central idea behind the theory of compounding financialization. It also helps explain how financialization compounded inequality in the US.

The following sections disaggregate the data on US households[1] to elaborate these arguments. The first section recovers the basic theories and concepts about inequality in classic modern political economy. The second section reviews evidence from the Congressional Budget Office and Executive Office of Management and Budget on the effect of taxes and social policy transfers in the US from 1979 to 2016. The third section disaggregates data on US household balance sheets from 1989 to 2019 in the DFAs. The fourth section takes a step back to further disaggregate the historical statistics from 1929 to 2019 explored in the preceding chapter on labor income, personal consumption and savings, and further data on labor and households in the NIPAs. The fifth section presents evidence of the *re*-intermediation of US household financial portfolios at odds with core ideas about efficient markets, contemporary banking theory, and financial intermediation theory. Before concluding, the sixth section presents evidence from the FDIC Consumer Finance Surveys about the unequal burdens, and costs, of debt management by US social classes from 1989 to 2016.

Inequality in classic modern political economy

In 1955, Simon Kuznets summarized both the economic determinants of inequality and the autonomy of political factors that may reverse inequality. Kuznets' clarity about the political and economic factors of public finance provides a secure starting point for this chapter:

> One group of factors counteracting the cumulative effect of concentration of savings upon upper-income shares is legislative interference and 'political' decisions. These may be aimed at limiting the cumulation of property directly through inheritance taxes and other explicit capital levies. They may produce similar effects indirectly, e.g., by government-permitted or - induced inflation which reduces the economic value of accumulated wealth stored in fixed-price securities or other properties not fully responsive to

60 *Finance and American household inequality*

price changes; or by legal restriction of the *yield* on accumulated property, as happened recently in the form of rent controls or of artificially low long-term interest rates maintained by the government to protect the market for its own bonds.

(Kuznets, 1955: 8–9)

In this passage, Kuznets calls attention to both the economic logic of compounding financialization (the 'cumulative effect of savings upon upper-income shares'), and the factors related to politics and public policy, such as taxes, policy strategies designed to manage inflation that may pressure fixed income markets, and the use of low interest rates to 'protect the market' for public debt.[2] Attention to both economic factors and political factors provides a different picture than recent debates about inequality in advanced economies.

Adequate consideration of the vast literature about inequality is beyond the scope of this book (Benhabib et al., 2017; Atkinson, 2015; Atkinson and Bourguignon, 2015; Stiglitz, 2015; Atkinson et al., 2011; Champernowne, 1953). So, too, is the vast debate about inequality in the US (Bowles and Gintis, 2002; Stiglitz, 1969). However, one observation is in order. The focus on the *capitalization of wealth* in recent studies of inequality by the top 1 percent of Americans risks committing two mistakes emphasized in this study: The conceptual stretching of money to include financial claims and loading on the dependent variable. The problem with financialization is that the unequal accumulation of wealth is shaped less by gaps in the wages and salaries between social classes, and more by the inequalities that arise from the accumulation of financial claims by the rich, and the accumulation of liabilities (debt) by the poor.

From this perspective, the methodological problem with recent research on the capitalization of wealth is that the causal logic of financialization is inserted into the dependent variable. Precise measurement of the dependent variable (inequality) is essential. This is a major contribution of research on inequality (Saez and Zucman, 2016). Better data, such as that available in the DFAs, permits more careful analysis of the causal relations between financialization and inequality. However, wealth, as with all important concepts that are used in the social sciences, is essentially contested (Collier et al., 2006; Gallie, 1956). And redefining wealth to include capitalization (of financial claims and nonfinancial assets) places together what must be kept apart: The income shares of labor and the income shares of property.

This involves two closely related problems: The overestimation of the rise of inequality since 1980 and the underestimation of financialization, both as a determinant of inequality and as an ideological veil of capital. This chapter therefore elaborates four arguments. The first empirical argument is that broader indices, such as the Gini coefficient, differ profoundly after consideration of the distributional effect of taxes and the income transfers of social policy. This provides counterintuitive evidence of how political factors, since 1980, have countered the economic forces of inequality in the US. The second argument is that a tendency to focus on the richest 1 percent (or the poorest Americans) conceals the

Finance and American household inequality   61

variance in the remaining social classes that compose a vast majority of citizens and residents. The gains and losses of each of the four social classes as defined in the DFAs are not linear, nor monocausal, nor indeed amenable to aggregation without serious composition effects. The third argument is that the endogenous multiplication of financial claims and liabilities is a far more important cause of household inequality than gaps between wages and salaries or the valuation of real estate. Moreover, the financial causes of inequality obtain only if one accepts the conceptual stretching of the 'financialized' indicators of wealth and poverty. The fourth argument is that a lack of clarity about the differences between financial and nonfinancial sources of inequality tends to conceal the large variance produced by the double-counting of financial claims and liabilities. The ideological veil of financial capital thereby threatens to conceal, rather than reveal, both the economic forces that produce inequality and the political measures that may counter it. Among the political factors are taxes and government transfers, as the traditional fiscal data from the US suggest in the following section.

In sum, serious methodological problems arise in recent studies of inequality. Recent debates about inequality are also marred by the pursuit of natural laws and the estimation of fixed relations between economic aggregates, an excessive reliance on mathematics at the expense of conceptual analysis, and a lack of more focused qualitative comparisons of similarities and differences. Ironically, an excessive concern with the precise measurement of inequality produces selection bias by loading on the dependent variable. Focusing on the very top and very bottom percentile categories also comes at the expense of accurately accounting for the changes experienced by the other social classes, classes that comprise a vast majority of US citizens and residents. Finally, unless the financial determinants of inequality are controlled for, research on the traditional sources of 'real' wealth such as wages and salaries also, ironically, becomes performative. Either traditional theories and concepts about labor and surplus value fail to explain the accumulation of far larger volumes of financial claims and liabilities, or the latter, if accepted at face value, dilute the traditional concepts of income and wealth by inserting, and double-counting, changes in the value of financial claims and liabilities. In any case, confusion arises from conceptual stretching and the mis-aggregation of data from financial balance sheets into the traditional measures of social sector and national income. To elaborate these arguments, this chapter returns to the traditional, classic modern concepts of political economy, explores the historical and contemporary data from the US, and further elaborates the theory of compounding financialization to explain both how economic factors increased inequality and, more unexpectedly, how political factors countered, at least partially, the rise of inequality since 1980 in the US.

Gini coefficients, taxes, and transfers, 1979–2016

Before turning to the evidence from the DFAs, NIPAs, and IMAs, this section focuses on the question of how political factors may counter inequality. The

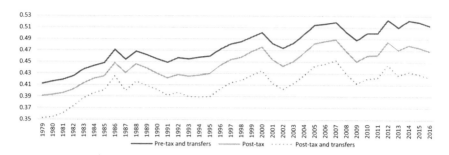

Figure 2.1 Gini coefficients pre-tax and transfers, post-tax, and post-tax and transfers, 1979–2016.

Source: Congressional Budget Office (2019).

Note: 'Projected changes in the distribution of household income. Data underlying figures.'

evidence from the US suggests that traditional measures such as taxes and social policy transfers appear to have ameliorated the rise of inequality. Figure 2.1 provides the first view of how taxes and transfers countered the rise of inequality in the US from 1979 to 2016. The Gini coefficient for the US increased from 0.41 in 1979 to peak at 0.52 in 2014.[3] However, income inequality, as measured *after* taxes and *after* social policy transfers, increased at a far lower pace. This suggests that politics and public policy in the US did indeed counter the economic forces that increase inequality along the lines that Kuznets suggested in 1955. From this perspective, the contribution of Kuznets to studies of inequality is not the hypothetical estimation of an inexorable 'U' shaped curve over long time spans. Instead, his contribution is a political-economic challenge to explain both the economic logics of inequality and the types of politics and public policy that may reverse the economic forces that produce inequality.

The reduction of inequality produced by taxes and government social policy transfers in the US appears to be considerable. Moreover, these effects of public policy appear to *increase after 1980*, rather than decline. This runs counter to research on the dismantlement of Welfare States that is seen to obtain across advanced economies since the turn to monetarism, the rise of neoconservative politics, the deregulation of industries, and financialization, all of which are dated to, or near, 1980 (Barnes, 2020; Klein, 2020; Greve, 2018). The pre-tax and pre-transfer Gini coefficients for the US did, in fact, increase from 4.1 in 1979 to peak at 0.52 in 2012. However, in comparison, the after-tax Gini coefficient increased from a lower base and at a slower rate – from 0.39 in 1979 to peak at 0.49 in 2007.

And the Gini coefficient for the US after taxes and transfers increased from 0.35 in 1979 to peak at 4.5 in 2007. Disaggregation of the effect of taxes and government transfers, and other particularities in the time series data on the US, follows. Comparison of the US data with other countries is beyond the scope of

Finance and American household inequality   63

this book, especially because of the difficulty to compile accurate cross-national indicators of taxes and transfers. However, the gap that obtains, and increases over time, between Gini coefficients for the US based on pre- and post-tax, and pre- and post- government social policy transfers, are the first proviso for strong claims that inequality has increased inexorably in the US since 1980.

The evidence from the beginning of the 1989–2016 time series is consistent with theories of financialization and claims about the dismantling of social policies by neoconservative governments. The gaps between both the pre-tax and pre-transfer Gini coefficients, and the post-tax and post-transfer coefficients, *narrowed* from 6.2 percent to 4.6 percent from 1980 to 1986. This indicates a decline in both the distributive weight of taxes and the volume of federal government social policy transfers – *until 1986.* The distributive effects of the 1986 tax reform in the US are beyond the scope of this book. Distortions may also arise from the effects of disinflation, the severe economic downturn, and the social consequences of adjustment through the imposition of high interest rates from 1979 to 1986. However, the empirical trends in the data from the US change after 1986. After 1986, the percent reduction of the rises in the US Gini coefficient produced by government transfers *increases* to remain at *9 percent* from 2014 to 2016 (the gap between the top and bottom lines in Figure 2.1).

The effect of taxation is much smaller. However, the reduction of the Gini coefficient caused by taxation also does not appear to be profoundly regressive. Nor does taxation appear to be increasingly regressive since 1980. To the contrary, composition effects and omissions may be present here. However, the spreads between the three Gini coefficients from 1979 to 2016 increase, numerically and proportionally. It may, therefore, be inferred from the US household income data reported by the Congressional Budget Office that political factors such as government taxes and government social policy transfers *increased* over most of the period since 1980. This runs counter to the idea that neoconservative politics and neoliberal policies have unilaterally and inexorably downsized government and reduced social transfers in the US since 1980.

As will be seen shortly, inequality in the US does indeed increase during the period of high financialization after 1980. However, the political factors emphasized by Kuznets and classic modern theories of political economy continue to obtain as well. Taxes and government transfer policies appear to continue to reduce inequalities. Indeed, the data suggest that the reduction of inequality produced by these two political factors *increases* since 1979, albeit not enough to fully counter the advance of the economic factors that drive inequality.

Before turning to the data from the DFAs, disaggregation of further data provided by the Congressional Budget Office on taxation and social policy transfers by social class is in order. The Congressional Budget Office disaggregates the data on income taxes paid and government transfers received as a percentage of total income by social class from 1979 to 2016. Figure 2.2 displays further evidence indicating that, since 1980, political factors have countered the economic tendencies that are seen, correctly, to have increased inequality in the

64 *Finance and American household inequality*

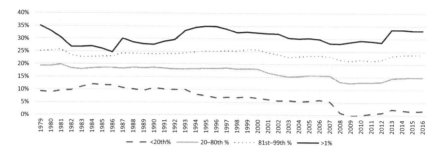

Figure 2.2 Tax burden on US social classes, 1979–2016.
Source: Congressional Budget Office (2019).
Note: 'Projected changes in the distribution of household income. Data underlying figures.'

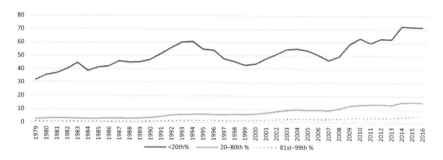

Figure 2.3 Government transfers as percentage total income by social class, 1979–2016.
Source: Congressional Budget Office (2019).
Note: 'Projected changes in the distribution of household income. Data underlying figures.'

US. The tax burden on the lowest 20 percent of taxpayers in the US increased from 1979–1985. However, thereafter, the tax burden of the lowest 20 percent of taxpayers declines. It reached zero in 2009 and remained at 2 percent in 2016. In comparison, the tax burden of the top 1 percent declines from 35 to 25 percent from 1979 to 1986, then increases to 35 percent in 1995 before declining to remain around 30 percent until 2013. A more stable trajectory obtains for the next 19 percent (the 81st to the 99th percentiles), while the tax burden for the middle classes (the 20th to the 80th percentiles) remains around 18 percent until declining after 2000.

Further evidence from the Congressional Budget Office (2019) is also consistent with these inferences from the above data (i.e. that social policy transfers to lower-class Americans did not decline systematically after 1980). Figure 2.3 displays the percentage of total income by social class from 1979

Finance and American household inequality   65

to 2016. The share of government transfers as a percentage of total income for the lowest 20th percentile of US taxpayers increases from 31.8 percent in 1979 to 72.3 percent in 2014. Declines do indeed obtain after 1994 and 2004. The variance may indeed be due to losses of income from lost wages due to unemployment during recessions. However, the periods with lower shares of income transfers to the lowest 20 percent of US taxpayers coincides neither with the period of high financialization (the 1980s), nor with changes in partisan government. Government transfers to the middle and upper classes (20th to the 80th and 81st to the 99th percentiles) increase from 0.9 to 15.3 percent and 0.8 to 4.8 percent respectively. Further comparison of the nominal, proportional, and real changes may reveal disproportions given the lower denominator of lower-income percentiles. Increasing inequality implies a greater reliance on social policy transfers.

In sum, the data from the US Congressional Budget Office on the tax burdens and the social policy transfers received by different social classes (measured here in terms of income percentiles, not capitalized wealth percentiles) are inconsistent with generalizations about increasingly perverse taxation and cuts in government social policy transfers since 1980. Decomposition of trends and comparison of changes in taxation and transfers under Democratic and Republican administrations (and during periods of legislative majorities or divided government) are beyond the scope of this chapter. Nonetheless, the aggregate data on US government transfer payments appears to present several anomalies and provisos for claims about the dismantlement of the social policies of Welfare States. The evidence suggests that the increases in inequality in the US since 1980 turn less on the variance produced by political reaction, regressive taxes, and a reduction in government transfers, and more on the economic factors as emphasized in the theory of compounding financialization. The following section turns to the evidence about social classes, compounding financialization, and inequality in the DFAs.

Financialization and inequality in the US DFAs, 1989–2019

This section compares the accumulation of nonfinancial assets, financial claims, and liabilities by the four social classes in the US from 1989 to 2019 as defined in the DFAs. The DFAs report the total value of nonfinancial assets, financial claims, and liabilities for the bottom 50 percent, next 40 percent, next 9 percent, and top 1 percent of American citizens and residents in terms of (capitalized) wealth percentiles. The preceding volume introduced the marked differences, and markedly different trends over time, in the balance-sheet data on each of these four social classes in terms of the aggregate categories of financial portfolio analysis and balance sheets; financial claims, nonfinancial assets, and liabilities (Mettenheim, 2021). This section disaggregates the data. The annual trends in the disaggregated data from the DFAs from 1989 to 2019 are displayed by social class in Table 2.1. The data are the annual current dollar values of nonfinancial assets, financial claims, and liabilities from 1979 to 2019 for each

66 Finance and American household inequality

Table 2.1 US household balance-sheet portfolios by wealth percentile classes, 1989–2019, percentage GDP and $trillion

	Nonfinancial assets				Total		Financial claims		
	<50%	51–11%	10–2%	>1%	%GDP	$tri	<50%	51–11%	10–2%
1989	21.0%	74.6%	45.1%	17.5%	158.1%	8.92	9.9%	84.4%	100.9%
1990	20.9%	73.1%	42.9%	17.5%	154.5%	9.21	9.9%	84.9%	99.0%
1991	23.2%	71.0%	42.1%	17.5%	153.7%	9.47	10.3%	90.1%	100.9%
1992	23.4%	69.5%	40.1%	17.9%	150.9%	9.84	10.1%	90.3%	100.8%
1993	24.0%	69.0%	38.8%	17.3%	149.1%	10.22	10.1%	90.9%	98.2%
1994	23.5%	68.5%	36.6%	17.3%	145.9%	10.63	10.4%	86.2%	96.5%
1995	26.4%	66.4%	35.6%	15.8%	144.2%	11.02	10.9%	88.6%	98.5%
1996	24.5%	65.9%	35.7%	16.4%	142.6%	11.51	11.0%	92.7%	102.5%
1997	24.1%	64.2%	36.3%	15.9%	140.5%	12.05	11.1%	96.3%	108.5%
1998	23.8%	66.2%	37.2%	16.8%	144.0%	13.05	11.1%	100.8%	115.1%
1999	24.6%	66.9%	37.5%	18.6%	147.5%	14.21	11.2%	103.7%	120.6%
2000	25.0%	71.2%	40.1%	20.4%	156.7%	16.06	10.6%	99.9%	115.9%
2001	25.4%	77.8%	44.3%	22.8%	170.3%	18.02	9.9%	101.8%	113.3%
2002	26.1%	81.7%	47.5%	24.3%	179.6%	19.64	9.3%	98.5%	108.3%
2003	26.7%	84.7%	49.5%	26.1%	187.0%	21.42	9.2%	102.0%	116.1%
2004	27.7%	90.6%	53.2%	28.2%	199.7%	24.39	9.0%	103.5%	124.0%
2005	30.3%	94.0%	57.9%	28.6%	210.7%	27.46	9.4%	101.0%	128.4%
2006	32.0%	89.5%	57.6%	26.7%	205.9%	28.44	9.7%	99.9%	133.9%
2007	31.9%	80.9%	54.7%	24.0%	191.5%	27.68	10.0%	100.4%	136.7%
2008	29.4%	71.6%	50.4%	20.9%	172.3%	25.35	8.9%	93.0%	122.6%
2009	28.2%	68.2%	48.3%	20.7%	165.5%	23.91	9.4%	99.8%	130.4%
2010	26.4%	63.4%	45.8%	19.9%	155.4%	23.30	9.3%	102.3%	136.3%
2011	24.3%	59.6%	42.9%	19.5%	146.4%	22.75	9.2%	102.9%	136.1%
2012	23.0%	58.7%	41.8%	20.1%	143.7%	23.27	9.1%	104.3%	141.5%
2013	22.1%	62.5%	42.6%	22.4%	149.6%	25.10	9.3%	110.6%	149.3%
2014	21.2%	63.6%	43.6%	23.0%	151.5%	26.55	9.2%	109.3%	152.2%
2015	20.9%	65.6%	44.8%	23.5%	154.7%	28.22	9.0%	106.1%	149.2%
2016	21.2%	68.6%	46.4%	24.4%	160.6%	30.10	8.9%	106.3%	152.3%
2017	22.4%	70.2%	46.8%	24.9%	164.3%	32.11	9.1%	108.8%	158.4%
2018	23.8%	69.7%	47.0%	24.0%	164.5%	33.90	8.7%	103.5%	152.1%
2019	25.8%	68.1%	46.8%	23.0%	163.7%	35.08	8.9%	107.8%	161.8%

Source: Board of Governors of the Federal Reserve System. 'Distributional financial accounts of the United States,' 2020.

of the four social classes according to balance-sheet wealth (which is part of the problem).

The broader logic of financialization appears in the displacement of nonfinancial assets by financial claims. The current dollar totals of each of these data categories is displayed in Table 2.1. The value of nonfinancial assets held by US households does indeed increase from $8.92 to $35.08 trillion from 1989 to 2019. This is consistent with studies on the political economy of real estate and the importance of household consumption explored in the preceding chapter. However, the value of US household financial claims increases, nominally, in

	Total		Liabilities				Total		GDP
>1%	%GDP	$tri	<50%	51–11%	10–2%	>1%	%GDP	$tri	$trillion
72.3%	267.5%	15.09	16.5%	29.0%	9.0%	2.4%	56.8%	3.21	5.64
69.1%	263.0%	15.68	16.9%	28.9%	9.4%	2.7%	57.9%	3.45	5.96
76.3%	277.6%	17.10	17.3%	28.6%	10.6%	2.7%	59.2%	3.64	6.16
75.7%	276.8%	18.05	18.8%	26.1%	11.4%	2.5%	58.8%	3.83	6.52
81.7%	281.0%	19.27	19.5%	26.8%	10.5%	2.7%	59.5%	4.08	6.86
81.4%	274.5%	20.00	20.9%	27.1%	9.6%	2.8%	60.3%	4.40	7.29
93.0%	291.1%	22.24	22.3%	27.3%	9.2%	2.9%	61.7%	4.72	7.64
91.3%	297.5%	24.02	20.2%	29.4%	10.0%	3.2%	62.8%	5.07	8.07
97.2%	313.1%	26.85	19.5%	29.4%	10.9%	3.2%	63.0%	5.40	8.58
104.1%	331.1%	30.00	20.1%	29.4%	11.7%	3.2%	64.3%	5.83	9.06
109.0%	344.5%	33.17	20.6%	30.0%	12.6%	3.1%	66.3%	6.38	9.63
97.0%	323.3%	33.15	21.6%	30.4%	12.8%	3.1%	67.9%	6.96	10.25
91.1%	316.1%	33.45	21.4%	33.9%	12.3%	3.8%	71.4%	7.56	10.58
83.2%	299.3%	32.73	22.7%	36.5%	12.2%	4.4%	75.9%	8.30	10.94
94.4%	321.7%	36.86	24.2%	39.0%	13.5%	5.0%	81.7%	9.36	11.46
105.2%	341.8%	41.74	26.5%	39.2%	15.1%	4.9%	85.8%	10.48	12.21
108.9%	347.6%	45.32	28.8%	40.0%	15.8%	4.7%	89.2%	11.63	13.04
115.2%	358.8%	49.57	31.9%	39.6%	17.4%	4.4%	93.2%	12.88	13.81
116.7%	363.7%	52.57	33.3%	39.6%	18.2%	4.1%	95.2%	13.76	14.45
91.4%	315.9%	46.47	33.4%	38.2%	16.5%	4.5%	92.6%	13.63	14.71
100.8%	340.4%	49.18	33.9%	37.6%	17.0%	4.6%	93.1%	13.45	14.45
109.6%	357.5%	53.60	32.5%	34.9%	16.7%	4.3%	88.3%	13.24	14.99
106.5%	354.9%	55.15	30.9%	33.5%	15.9%	4.1%	84.2%	13.09	15.54
112.1%	367.1%	59.46	29.8%	31.6%	15.8%	3.6%	80.8%	13.09	16.20
124.4%	393.7%	66.08	27.2%	32.9%	15.1%	3.7%	78.9%	13.24	16.78
131.5%	402.3%	70.51	25.6%	32.9%	14.6%	3.8%	76.9%	13.48	17.53
130.3%	394.6%	71.97	24.8%	32.5%	13.7%	4.0%	75.0%	13.67	18.24
136.0%	403.5%	75.63	24.5%	33.0%	13.5%	4.2%	75.2%	14.09	18.75
146.5%	422.8%	82.62	25.7%	31.2%	14.0%	3.9%	74.8%	14.63	19.54
135.3%	399.6%	82.36	26.5%	29.2%	13.8%	3.7%	73.2%	15.08	20.61
152.2%	430.7%	92.31	26.9%	28.3%	14.1%	3.5%	72.8%	15.60	21.43

current dollar values, at a far greater pace – from $15.09 to $92.31 trillion (almost threefold the value of the increase reported for nonfinancial assets). And the liabilities of US households also increase from $3.21 to 15.6 trillion. This confirms both the far greater scale of financialization in the US, and the reality that household balance sheets do not balance along the same lines as banks, financial institutions, and the US financial sector generally.

What are the logics and limits to household financial portfolio management? How do they differ across social classes? This chapter explores the changing composition and strategic reorientation of US household portfolio strategies to

68 *Finance and American household inequality*

address these questions. The historical–institutional balance-sheet approach is to disaggregate the data, increase the number of observations back in time, and pay attention to the meanings of measures through conceptual analysis.

The first step is to place the data in context. The evolution of the three core aggregates of balance-sheet data (i.e. nonfinancial assets, financial claims, and liabilities), if considered as a percentage of US GDP, is even more impressive. The nonfinancial assets of US households increase from 158.1 percent of US GDP in 1989 to 210.7 percent of GDP in 2005. However, thereafter, the value of nonfinancial assets held by US household declines, returning 143.7 percent of GDP by 2012 (below the level reported for 1989), before returning to 164.5 percent in 2018, just slightly above the 1989 level of 158.1 percent. As discussed in previous chapters, the valuation of real estate in the US is seen to be a critical part of problems that contributed to the 2007–2008 financial crisis. However, the valuation of real estate pales in comparison to the valuation of financial claims and liabilities.

The value of US household *financial claims* as a percentage of US GDP increases from 267.5 percent in 1989 to *430.7 percent* in 2019 (with dips after the 2000 dot.com market crash and the 2007–2008 financial crisis). The total value of US household liabilities also increases, but from a far lower level: from 56.8 percent of US GDP in 1989 to peak at 95.2 percent of GDP in 2007, declining thereafter to 72.8 percent in 2019.

These trends indicate the far greater scale of financialization compared to the valuation of real estate and real assets. However, the aggregate trends in financial balance-sheet data conceal significant composition effects. The disaggregation by region, gender, race, and other indicators is beyond the scope of this chapter. However, decomposition of the data by social class reveals profound differences behind the aggregate data on US household balance sheets; specifically, the compounding of financial claims for the upper social classes and the compounding of liabilities (debt) for lower classes. This implies profoundly different strategies for the management of portfolios by US households. Presentation of the argument requires the elaboration of a series of comparisons.

The first set of comparisons turns on the unequal distribution of *nonfinancial assets*. The unequal holdings of nonfinancial assets may be seen in the first four columns of Table 2.1. Convex curves obtain for the trajectory of the value of all four social classes, with recoveries in the late 2010s. The bottom 50 percent increased the value of their nonfinancial asset holdings from 21.0 percent of GDP in 1989 to 32.0 percent in 2006, declining thereafter to 20.9 percent in 2015 and recovering to 25.8 percent in 2019. The nonfinancial assets of the next 40 percent (the 51st to the 11th top percentiles) increased in value from 74.6 to 94.0 percent of GDP from 1989 to 2005, then declined to 58.7 percent by 2012, then recovered to 70.2 percent of US GDP in 2017. The next 9 percent (the 10th to the 2nd top percentiles) increased the value of nonfinancial asset holdings from 45.1 to 57.9 percent of US GDP from 1989 to 2005, declining thereafter to 41.8 percent in 2012 before increasing, once again, in

Finance and American household inequality 69

the late 2010s to 46.8 percent in 2019. Finally, the richest 1 percent increased the value of nonfinancial assets from 17.5 percent of US GDP in 1989 to 28.6 percent in 2005, a value that declined to 19.5 percent by 2011 and then returned to 24.9 percent in 2017. The differences across social-class management of home finance are explored in due course. Comparison of the different compositions of nonfinancial assets and financial claims by social classes is required first.

The variance in *financial claims* is far greater. This informs the second set of comparisons. The value of financial claims held by the poorest 50 percent increased from 9.9 to 11.2 percent of US GDP from 1989 to 1999, then declined to 9.0 percent in 2004, increased once again to 10.0 percent in 2007, then declined to 8.7 percent in 2017. The value of financial claims held by the next 40 percent (the 51st to the 11th percentile) increased from *84.4 to 103.7* percent of US GDP 1989–1999, then declined twice to recover to 107.8 percent of GDP in 2019. The value of financial claims held by the top 9 percent (the 10th to the 2nd percentiles) increased in a similar trajectory from 100.9 percent of GDP in 1989 to peak at 136.7 percent in 2007 and, higher yet, at *161.8* percent of US GDP in 2019. Likewise, the top 1 percent increased the total value of financial claims from 72.3 percent in 1989 to 109.0 percent in 1999, a value that declined to 83.2 percent in 2002 before reaching 116.7 percent in 2007, to then decline once again to 91.4 percent in 2008, and increase thereafter to 152.2 percent in 2019.

Liabilities are distributed in the reverse. This can be seen in a third set of comparisons. The total value of liabilities held by the bottom 50 percent increased from 16.5 to 33.9 percent of US GDP from 1989 to 2009, declining thereafter to 26.9 percent by 2019. The next 40 percent (the 51st to the 11th percentiles) increased the value of liabilities from 29.0 to 40.0 percent 1989–2004. However, the value of liabilities incurred by the bottom 50 percent of Americans also declined thereafter to reach 28.3 percent in 2019, a value below that reported for 1989 at the beginning of the DFAs data. The value of the liabilities held by the next 9 percent (the 10th to the 2nd percentiles) increased from 9.0 to 18.2 percent of US GDP from 1989 to 2007, declining thereafter to 14.1 percent in 2019. Finally, the value of the liabilities held by the top 1 percent increased from 2.4 to 5.0 percent from 1989 to 2003, then declined to 3.5 percent of US GDP in 2019.

Further analysis of the nominal and proportional variance within and across social classes in the DFAs is beyond the scope of this chapter. However, the following observations are in order. First, the values registered on the data lines of the traditional 'T' shaped balance sheet of financial claims and liabilities (the 12 columns on the right side of Table 2.1, before the GDP totals) outpace, by far, the value of nonfinancial assets displayed in the first six columns. This is consistent with critical political economy accounts of financialization and endogenous money approaches (with the provisos that financial claims are neither assets nor money in the traditional sense). Second, the gains of the upper classes in the US far outpace those recorded for the lower classes. The

70 *Finance and American household inequality*

accumulation of nonfinancial assets and, especially, financial claims, increases substantially for the upper classes from 1989 to 2019.

In comparison, the accumulation of financial liabilities (debt) predominates in the lower-class percentile categories. Table 2.1 illustrates the basic trends that appear upon disaggregation of the balance-sheet data from the US. Further specification of the relations between the variance observed in financial balance sheets and the traditional macroeconomic aggregates of growth, labor, capital, savings, consumption, money, employment, prices, and wages follows below.

In sum, the DFAs permit the disaggregation of US household balance sheets by social class from 1989–2019. In this initial approximation to the data, tracing the value of nonfinancial assets, financial claims, and liabilities of the bottom 50 percent, next 40 percent, next 9 percent, and top 1 percent suggests a series of insights about financialization and inequality in the US. To further explore the DFAs data, the following section returns to the trends in the indices of financialization (financial claims over nonfinancial assets) and leverage (liabilities over total assets). However, instead of the aggregate trends for US households, these indicators are displayed for each of the US social classes as measured in the DFAs by wealth percentiles. This provides further information about the differences that obtain across American social classes in terms of financialization and the management of household portfolios.

Comparing ratios of financialization and leverage by US social class, 1989–2019

This section presents a second historical–institutional approach to the data on US household balance sheets by splitting the data on two indicators (ratios of financialization and leverage) from 1989 to 2019 according to the percentile groups as defined in the DFAs. The first measure of financialization is a simple ratio of financial claims over nonfinancial assets. The second measure of leverage is a simple ratio of liabilities over total assets. Figure 2.4 displays the ratio of financialization for each of the four social classes from 1989 to 2019 as defined in the DFAs by wealth percentiles. The largest variation obtains for the top 1 percent. From 1989 to 1998, the value of financial assets held by the top 1 percent of US households increases from between 4.0 to 6.0 times the value of nonfinancial assets on their balance sheets, before falling to 3.4 in 2002, then increasing to 5.5 in 2010 to remain at that level until 2018 and increasing to 6.6 during 2019. A similar, but flatter, trajectory obtains for the next 9 percent, with the ratio of household financial claims over nonfinancial assets increasing from 2.2 to 3.2 from 1989 to 1999, returning to 2.3 in 2002, then remaining at around 3.5 from 2013 to 2019.

The trend from 1989 to 2019 for this measure of financialization for the next 40 percent is similar, but at a lower level and flatter. The value of financial assets for the next 40 percent (the 51st to the 11th percentile) remain between 1 and 2 times the value of nonfinancial assets across the 30 years 1989–2019. The bottom 50 percentile sample decreases from 0.5 to 0.3 from 1989 to 2019. This

Finance and American household inequality 71

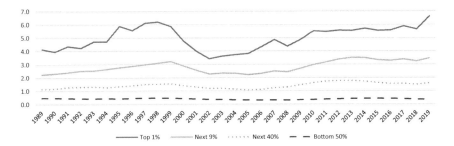

Figure 2.4 Financialization index by social class, 1989–2019.
Source: Board of Governors of the Federal Reserve System. 'Distributional financial accounts of the United States,' 2020.
Note: The index of financialization is a simple ratio of financial assets over nonfinancial assets.

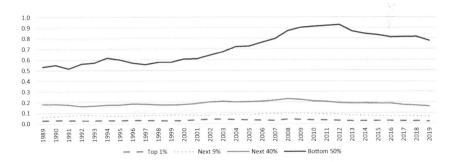

Figure 2.5 Leverage index by social class, 1989–2019.
Source: Board of Governors of the Federal Reserve System. 'Distributional financial accounts of the United States,' 2020.
Note: The index of leverage is a simple ratio of liabilities over total assets.

is tenfold below the values for the index of financialization for the top 1 percent, a quarter the levels for the next 9 percent, and less than one-third the levels reported for the next 40 percent. One of the central arguments of this book is that the balance sheets and financial portfolios of US social sectors do not balance, and that these empirical differences provide a profound opportunity to rethink central questions of political economy. One of the central arguments of this chapter is that this also applies to US social classes. Financialization for the DFAs sample of the top one percentile of US households, as measured in this index of financial claims over nonfinancial assets, remains tenfold the levels of the lowest 50 percent of households.

The opposite holds for leverage (see Figure 2.5). A second overview of the differences across social classes may be obtained by comparing the ratio of leverage (liabilities over total assets) for the four samples split by wealth

72 *Finance and American household inequality*

percentiles from 1989 to 2019. The data in Figure 2.5 indicate far greater variance in the leverage of US households classified in the bottom 50 percent. The value of liabilities over total assets held by the bottom 50 percent increases from around half (ratios near 0.5) from 1989 to 2001, before increasing to 0.9 in 2009, declining after 2012 to remain around 0.8. Figure 2.4 permits comparison of the ratio of financialization (financial claims over nonfinancial assets) for each social class from 1989 to 2019. The variance in the leverage of other social classes, compared to the bottom 50 percent, is (1) far lower and (2) the rank is in precisely the reverse order of (capitalized) wealth. The implications of these different levels of leverage for the management of household debt are explored below.

Taken together, comparison of the ratios of financialization and leverage by social class from 1989 to 2019 indicates the severity of composition effects and the need to disaggregate the data on household balance sheets. The unequal impact of financialization on US households also *disappears* upon the aggregation of the data. The macroeconomic effects of financial cycles and business cycles, and the profound differences in the strategic management of household portfolios during these cycles, are averaged out upon aggregation. In sum, the variance across US social classes in the ratios of financialization and leverage from 1989 to 2019 provides an initial indication of how the political economy of financialization differs by social class. The following section further disaggregates the balance-sheet data from the DFAs to explore the implications of these differences.

The balance sheets of US social classes and the financialization of inequality, 1989–2019

The historical–institutional method is to disaggregate the data further to compare the evolution of the balance sheets of the bottom 50 percent, next 40 percent, next 9 percent, and top 1 percent of households in the US from 1989 to 2019. The granular data on the balance sheets of each social class are reported in four separate tables (see Tables 2.2–2.5). The different weights of nonfinancial assets and financial claims, and the different composition of financial claims and liabilities, indicate the degree to which aggregation produces composition effects. From this perspective, it becomes clear that the causal logic of compounding financialization differs, fundamentally, for each social class. Initial observation of the skewed distribution of financial claims, liabilities, and net worth across social classes in the US informed the elaboration of the theory of compounding financialization in the preceding volume. This chapter decomposes these aggregates in the DFAs data to explore, more carefully, the processes of change for each social class from 1989 to 2019. Again, this may best be presented in a series of comparisons.

The first comparison is of the value of total assets declared on the balance sheets of each social class from 1989 to 2019. The bottom 50 percent of Americans increase the value of total assets (financial claims and nonfinancial assets) held

Table 2.2 The balance sheets of the bottom 50% income percentile of American households, 1989–2019

Assets	1989	1992	1995	1998	2001	2004	2007	2010	2013	2016	2019
Nonfinancial assets	68.0%	69.9%	70.7%	68.2%	71.9%	75.5%	76.2%	74.0%	70.3%	70.4%	74.4%
Real estate	46.7%	48.3%	49.4%	47.6%	51.2%	56.2%	57.8%	53.9%	49.3%	49.5%	54.7%
Consumer durables	21.3%	21.6%	21.3%	20.6%	20.7%	19.2%	18.4%	20.1%	21.0%	20.9%	19.7%
Financial claims	32.0%	30.1%	29.3%	31.8%	28.1%	24.5%	23.8%	26.0%	29.7%	29.6%	25.6%
Checkable deposits and currency	3.3%	3.4%	2.9%	1.9%	1.3%	1.0%	0.3%	0.9%	1.6%	1.6%	1.3%
Time deposits and S-term investments	6.1%	5.0%	3.3%	4.5%	4.9%	3.6%	3.6%	3.8%	4.7%	5.0%	3.9%
Money market fund shares	0.4%	0.2%	0.3%	0.4%	0.5%	0.4%	0.6%	0.4%	0.3%	0.3%	0.4%
Treasuries and municipal securities	0.8%	0.7%	1.0%	0.5%	0.3%	0.5%	0.5%	0.5%	0.5%	0.5%	0.4%
Corporate and foreign bonds	0.0%	0.0%	0.1%	0.1%	0.1%	0.1%	0.2%	0.3%	0.2%	0.1%	0.1%
Corporate equities and mutual fund shares	1.4%	2.3%	2.5%	3.7%	3.2%	2.0%	2.1%	1.8%	2.5%	2.6%	2.9%
Life insurance reserves	2.5%	2.4%	2.6%	2.7%	2.7%	2.1%	1.7%	2.1%	2.2%	2.3%	2.1%
Pension entitlements	12.4%	11.2%	12.0%	13.4%	10.8%	10.0%	9.3%	10.0%	11.8%	11.2%	9.7%
Equity in noncorporate business	2.6%	2.2%	2.2%	2.5%	1.6%	2.1%	2.6%	3.0%	2.1%	2.3%	1.6%
Other financial assets	2.4%	2.7%	2.5%	2.3%	2.5%	2.8%	2.8%	3.3%	3.7%	3.8%	3.2%
Total assets, percent	100.0%	100.0%	100.0%	100.0%	100.0%	100.0%	100.0%	100.0%	100.0%	100.0%	100.0%
Total assets, $billion	1,741.7	2,180.2	2,851.0	3,163.8	3,730.4	4,483.8	6,043.1	5,339.6	5,273.4	5,651.9	7,422.6

(*continued*)

Table 2.2 Cont.

Assets	1989	1992	1995	1998	2001	2004	2007	2010	2013	2016	2019
Liabilities (% total assets)											
Home mortgages	31.6%	35.4%	35.2%	32.4%	33.6%	46.2%	55.7%	61.8%	50.0%	42.9%	44.6%
Consumer credit	20.1%	19.5%	21.9%	24.1%	26.0%	25.4%	22.6%	27.1%	33.3%	34.7%	29.8%
Depository institution loans	0.0%	0.0%	0.2%	0.3%	0.0%	0.0%	0.2%	1.0%	1.7%	1.5%	1.7%
Other loans	1.4%	1.1%	2.3%	0.6%	1.1%	0.6%	1.1%	1.3%	1.6%	1.9%	1.5%
Life insurance premiums	0.1%	0.1%	0.1%	0.1%	0.1%	0.0%	0.0%	0.0%	0.0%	0.1%	0.0%
Total liabilities, percent total assets	53.3%	56.1%	59.8%	57.6%	60.8%	72.2%	79.7%	91.2%	86.7%	81.1%	77.6%
Total liabilities, $billion	928.6	1,222.9	1,705.4	1,821.5	2,268.5	3,238.8	4,815.8	4,872.1	4,570.97	4,585.3	5,763.4
Net worth	813.1	957.3	1,145.6	1,342.3	1,461.9	1,245.0	1,227.3	467.5	702.4	1,066.5	1,659.1

Source: Federal Reserve Board of Governors, Enhanced financial accounts, 'Distributional financial accounts of the United States,' 2020.

Table 2.3 The balance sheets of the next 40% (top 50–90%) income percentiles of American households, 1989–2019

Assets	1989	1992	1995	1998	2001	2004	2007	2010	2013	2016	2019
Nonfinancial assets	46.9%	43.5%	42.8%	39.6%	43.3%	46.7%	44.6%	38.2%	36.1%	39.2%	38.7%
Real estate	38.3%	34.5%	34.0%	31.6%	35.8%	39.7%	37.6%	30.6%	29.4%	32.6%	32.4%
Consumer durables	8.7%	9.1%	8.8%	8.0%	7.5%	6.9%	7.0%	7.6%	6.7%	6.6%	6.3%
Financial claims	53.1%	56.5%	57.2%	60.4%	56.7%	53.3%	55.4%	61.8%	63.9%	60.8%	61.3%
Checkable deposits and currency	1.7%	2.2%	1.9%	1.3%	0.9%	0.6%	0.2%	0.6%	1.1%	1.1%	1.0%
Time deposits and short-term Investments	10.8%	9.2%	7.9%	7.8%	7.4%	7.1%	8.1%	8.5%	8.7%	7.9%	7.5%
Money market fund shares	1.1%	0.9%	0.8%	1.3%	1.7%	1.5%	1.9%	1.4%	1.0%	1.1%	1.3%
Treasuries and municipal securities	1.5%	1.5%	1.5%	1.5%	0.8%	1.4%	1.3%	1.6%	1.4%	1.6%	2.0%
Corporate and foreign bonds	0.1%	0.4%	0.5%	0.5%	0.3%	0.5%	0.8%	1.3%	0.8%	0.4%	0.3%
Corporate equities and mutual fund shares	4.0%	5.5%	5.8%	9.0%	8.2%	6.5%	6.6%	6.2%	7.8%	7.6%	8.6%
Life insurance reserves	1.9%	2.1%	2.3%	2.5%	2.5%	1.8%	1.8%	2.1%	1.7%	1.8%	2.0%
Pension entitlements	23.9%	27.9%	30.4%	30.9%	28.6%	26.9%	27.9%	33.5%	35.0%	33.0%	32.6%

(continued)

Table 2.3 Cont.

Assets	1989	1992	1995	1998	2001	2004	2007	2010	2013	2016	2019
Equity in noncorporate business	6.4%	5.4%	4.8%	4.2%	4.7%	5.3%	4.8%	4.5%	4.3%	4.4%	4.0%
Other financial assets	1.9%	1.8%	1.7%	1.8%	1.9%	2.1%	2.2%	2.2%	2.3%	2.2%	2.2%
Total assets, percent	100.0%	100.0%	100.0%	100.0%	100.0%	100.0%	100.0%	100.0%	100.0%	100.0%	100.0%
Total assets, $billion	8,970.8	10,418.5	11,844.5	15,132.7	19,003.3	23,703.9	26,210.2	24,840.8	29,059.1	32,770.2	37,703.8
Liabilities (% total assets)											
Home mortgages	13.7%	12.8%	13.2%	13.4%	14.6%	16.3%	17.7%	16.7%	15.0%	14.4%	11.6%
Consumer credit	4.2%	3.0%	3.8%	3.4%	3.9%	3.6%	3.8%	3.8%	3.6%	4.0%	4.1%
Other Depository institution loans	0.0%	0.0%	0.1%	0.1%	0.0%	0.0%	0.0%	0.2%	0.1%	0.2%	0.2%
Other loans and advances	0.3%	0.3%	0.4%	0.6%	0.3%	0.3%	0.3%	0.4%	0.2%	0.2%	0.2%
Life insurance premiums	0.1%	0.1%	0.1%	0.1%	0.1%	0.0%	0.0%	0.0%	0.0%	0.0%	0.0%
Total liabilities, % total assets	18.3%	16.3%	17.6%	17.6%	18.9%	20.2%	21.9%	21.1%	19.0%	18.9%	16.1%
Total liabilities, $billion	1,641.7	1,698.2	2,084.6	2,663.4	3,591.6	4,788.2	5,740.0	5,241.4	5,521.2	6,193.6	6,070.3
Net worth, $billion	7,332.6	8,719.2	9,762.5	12,468.8	15,412.8	18,913.3	20,481.1	19,605.9	23,531.6	26,584.5	31,633.8

Source: Federal Reserve Board of Governors, Enhanced financial accounts, 'Distributional financial accounts of the United States,' 2020.

Table 2.4 The balance sheets of the next 9% (top 90–99%) income percentile of American households, 1989–2019

Assets	1989	1992	1995	1998	2001	2004	2007	2010	2013	2016	2019
Nonfinancial assets	30,9%	28,4%	26,6%	24,4%	28,1%	30,0%	28,6%	25,2%	22,2%	23,4%	22,4%
Real estate	25,8%	23,0%	21,5%	20,3%	24,3%	26,1%	25,2%	21,4%	19,1%	20,7%	20,3%
Consumer durables	5,1%	5,4%	5,0%	4,2%	3,8%	3,9%	3,3%	3,7%	3,1%	2,6%	2,1%
Financial claims	69,1%	71,6%	73,4%	75,6%	71,9%	70,0%	71,4%	74,8%	77,8%	76,6%	77,6%
Checkable deposits and currency	2,3%	2,0%	1,6%	0,8%	0,8%	0,6%	0,1%	0,5%	1,0%	0,8%	0,7%
Time deposits and short-term investments	11,5%	9,9%	8,1%	6,2%	6,1%	6,1%	7,6%	8,1%	7,5%	8,0%	7,5%
Money market fund shares	1,9%	1,8%	2,2%	2,7%	3,1%	2,4%	2,8%	2,5%	2,2%	1,9%	2,1%
Debt securities	5,4%	5,7%	5,1%	5,1%	2,9%	4,0%	3,8%	6,1%	4,3%	4,1%	4,8%
Treasuries and municipal securities	4,8%	5,0%	3,8%	4,0%	2,1%	3,2%	2,4%	3,4%	2,7%	3,2%	4,2%
Corporate and foreign bonds	0,6%	0,7%	1,3%	1,1%	0,8%	0,9%	1,5%	2,7%	1,6%	0,9%	0,6%
Corporate equities and mutual fund shares	10,1%	13,1%	15,5%	20,6%	18,2%	15,7%	17,5%	17,1%	19,4%	20,0%	22,1%
Life insurance reserves	1,4%	1,6%	1,3%	1,5%	1,4%	1,6%	1,2%	1,4%	1,3%	1,3%	1,2%
Pension entitlements	22,2%	24,7%	28,1%	27,2%	27,8%	27,1%	25,6%	29,0%	30,6%	29,7%	28,4%

(*continued*)

78 *Finance and American household inequality*

Table 2.4 Cont.

Assets	1989	1992	1995	1998	2001	2004	2007	2010	2013	2016	2019
Equity in noncorporate business	12.6%	10.9%	10.2%	9.8%	9.6%	10.1%	11.2%	8.5%	9.7%	9.1%	9.2%
Other assets	3.1%	2.9%	2.1%	3.0%	3.4%	3.8%	2.2%	2.5%	2.7%	2.9%	2.7%
Total assets, percent	100.0%	100.0%	100.0%	100.0%	100.0%	100.0%	100.0%	100.0%	100.0%	100.0%	100.0%
Total assets, $billion	8,236.4	9,184.7	10,249.3	13,798.9	16,675.1	21,642.0	27,655.4	27,294.0	32,200.9	37,243.0	44,713.1
Liabilities (% total assets)											
Home mortgages	4.8%	6.7%	5.7%	5.8%	6.0%	6.9%	8.0%	7.8%	6.4%	5.7%	5.6%
Consumer credit	0.7%	0.8%	0.8%	1.1%	0.9%	0.9%	0.7%	0.7%	0.7%	0.7%	0.8%
Other depository institution loans	0.0%	0.0%	0.0%	0.0%	0.0%	0.0%	0.0%	0.1%	0.1%	0.1%	0.1%
Other loans and advances	0.6%	0.6%	0.3%	0.7%	0.8%	0.7%	0.7%	0.6%	0.6%	0.3%	0.3%
Life insurance premiums	0.1%	0.1%	0.0%	0.0%	0.0%	0.0%	0.0%	0.0%	0.0%	0.0%	0.0%
Liabilities, percent total assets	6.1%	8.1%	6.9%	7.7%	7.8%	8.5%	9.5%	9.1%	7.8%	6.8%	6.8%
Liabilities, $billion	502.4	743.9	707.2	1,062.5	1,300.6	1,839.5	2,627.2	2,483.7	2,511.6	2,532.5	3,040.5
Net worth, $billion	7,730.9	8,441.1	9,544.5	12,742.4	15,375.8	19,793.2	25,031.0	24,796.9	29,674.2	34,716.8	41,691.3

Source: Federal Reserve Board of Governors, Enhanced financial accounts, 'Distributional financial accounts of the United States,' 2020.

Table 2.5 The balance sheets of the top 1% income percentile of American households, 1989–2019

Assets	1989	1992	1995	1998	2001	2004	2007	2010	2013	2016	2019
Nonfinancial assets	19.5%	19.1%	14.5%	13.9%	20.0%	21.1%	17.1%	15.4%	15.3%	15.2%	13.1%
Real estate	12.4%	14.5%	10.2%	10.3%	15.7%	17.7%	14.1%	12.6%	12.3%	12.4%	10.6%
Consumer durables	7.0%	4.6%	4.3%	3.6%	4.4%	3.4%	3.0%	2.8%	3.0%	2.8%	2.6%
Financial claims	80.5%	80.9%	85.5%	86.1%	80.0%	78.9%	82.9%	84.6%	84.7%	84.8%	86.9%
Checkable deposits and currency	0.7%	1.8%	1.3%	1.0%	0.6%	0.4%	0.1%	0.4%	1.0%	0.7%	0.7%
Time deposits and S-term investments	10.4%	5.0%	4.9%	4.0%	5.3%	7.0%	6.5%	8.8%	7.8%	10.1%	9.3%
Money market fund shares	2.3%	2.5%	2.7%	3.2%	5.5%	1.9%	2.9%	2.7%	2.0%	1.3%	1.6%
Debt securities	12.3%	13.5%	14.5%	10.5%	8.0%	9.7%	7.8%	12.8%	9.0%	6.5%	5.7%
Treasuries and Municipal bonds	9.9%	11.5%	10.2%	7.6%	5.9%	7.7%	5.9%	8.9%	6.2%	5.2%	4.8%
Corporate and foreign bonds	2.5%	2.0%	4.3%	2.9%	2.0%	2.0%	2.0%	3.9%	2.8%	1.4%	0.9%
Corporate equities and mutual fund shares	17.7%	23.4%	28.2%	36.1%	28.2%	27.3%	31.7%	30.4%	35.0%	35.9%	40.9%
Life insurance reserves	0.8%	0.5%	1.1%	0.5%	0.8%	1.4%	1.2%	1.4%	1.5%	1.3%	0.9%
Pension entitlements	8.2%	9.4%	8.1%	8.6%	6.4%	5.4%	7.1%	7.9%	6.6%	6.2%	6.0%
Equity in noncorporate business	26.7%	22.9%	22.5%	20.5%	22.1%	23.4%	21.7%	17.0%	19.2%	21.1%	20.8%

(*continued*)

Table 2.5 Cont.

Assets	1989	1992	1995	1998	2001	2004	2007	2010	2013	2016	2019
Other financial assets	2.5%	3.3%	4.0%	3.2%	5.6%	4.5%	7.3%	6.2%	4.7%	3.1%	1.8%
Total assets, percent	100.0%	100.0%	100.0%	100.0%	100.0%	100.0%	100.0%	100.0%	100.0%	100.0%	100.0%
Total assets, $billion	5,061.9	6,103.5	8,309.5	10,957.6	12,058.1	16,299.9	20,333.8	19,420.7	24,647.0	30,064.1	37,550.1
Liabilities (% total assets)											
Home mortgages	1.7%	1.9%	2.0%	1.8%	2.5%	2.7%	2.1%	2.1%	1.7%	1.6%	1.2%
Consumer credit	0.5%	0.2%	0.2%	0.1%	0.1%	0.2%	0.2%	0.4%	0.2%	0.3%	0.2%
Depository institution loans	0.0%	0.0%	0.1%	0.1%	0.0%	0.0%	0.1%	0.2%	0.1%	0.2%	0.1%
Other loans	0.4%	0.6%	0.5%	0.7%	0.7%	0.8%	0.5%	0.5%	0.6%	0.5%	0.4%
Life insurance	0.0%	0.0%	0.0%	0.0%	0.0%	0.0%	0.0%	0.0%	0.0%	0.0%	0.0%
Total liabilities, percent total assets	2.7%	2.7%	2.7%	2.6%	3.3%	3.7%	2.9%	3.3%	2.5%	2.6%	2.0%
Total liabilities, $billion	134.3	165.3	224.0	288.1	397.2	600.7	593.0	639.3	615.5	790.2	749.1
Net worth	4,927.6	5,938.2	8,085.4	10,669.4	11,660.9	15,699.1	19,740.8	18,781.3	24,031.4	29,273.8	36,800.9

Source: Federal Reserve Board of Governors, Enhanced financial accounts, 'Distributional financial accounts of the United States,' 2020.

Finance and American household inequality 81

from $1.7 to $7.4 trillion from 1989 to 2019 (see Table 2.2). However, the share of nonfinancial assets on the balance sheets of the bottom 50 percent remains quite high, increasing from 68.0 percent of total assets in 1989 to reach a peak of 76.2 percent in 2007, remaining thereafter at 74.4 percent in 2019 after slight declines in the late 2010s. The financial claims of the bottom 50 percent of Americans begin at 32.0 percent in 1989; and decline to 25.6 percent of total assets. Financialization therefore does not obtain in the data on the bottom 50 percent of US households. Instead of a turn to the holding of financial claims, real estate remains by far the most important component of the balance sheets of the bottom 50 percent; increasing from 46.7 percent of total assets in 1989, peaking at 57.8 percent in 2007 before declining to 49 percent in 2013 and, once again, in 2016, to end at 54.7 percent in 2019.

The preceding chapter explored the data from the US to reconsider debates about consumption in advanced capitalism. This chapter returns to this question with the DFAs data. In this respect, it is of note that the value of consumer durables on the balance sheets of the bottom 50 percent of Americans (measured in terms of total balance-sheet wealth, not income as in the aggregate data explored in the previous chapter) remains above the levels reported for other social classes, and declines, slightly, from 21.3 percent in 1989 to 18.4 percent to remain at 19.7 percent in 2019. Apparently, consumption among those worse off is greater, proportionally, because of necessity or, in mathematical terms, because of the far smaller denominator of total assets.

Further differences across social classes obtain. Disaggregating the financial claims of the bottom 50 percent suggests the dispersion across nine of the ten categories included in the DFAs data. The exception is pension entitlements that increase slightly from 12.4 to 13.4 percent from 1989 to 1998 before declining gradually to 9.7 percent of total assets in 2019.

In comparison, the values, and proportional shares, of liabilities for the bottom 50 percent of US households are far larger. The liabilities of the bottom 50 percent increase from $928.6 billion to $5.76 trillion from 1989 to 2019, an over sixfold increase. Subtracting the value of liabilities from the value of total assets implies an increase in the nominal (current dollar) net worth for this half of Americans and US residents; from $813.1 billion to $1.66 trillion over the thirty years 1989–2019. Financialization, from this perspective, implies the proportional accumulation of debt rather than the accumulation of nonfinancial assets or financial claims.

Decomposition of the data suggests further observations about the differences across US social classes. First, it is of note that the liabilities of the bottom 50 percent are concentrated in two categories: home mortgages and consumer credit. The value of home mortgages as a percentage of total assets increases from 31.6 to 61.8 percent from 1989 to 2019, declining thereafter to remain at 44.6 percent in 2019. Consumer credit increases from 20.1 percent of total assets to peak at 34.7 percent in 2018, declining in 2019 to 29.8 percent. The different weight of consumer durables and consumer credit on the balance sheets of the three upper classes are discussed below.[4]

82   *Finance and American household inequality*

To extend the comparison, the balance sheets of the next 40 percent of Americans (i.e. the top 50th to 90th percentiles of US households according to capitalized wealth from 1989 to 2019 in the DFAs), are displayed in Table 2.3. The total assets held by the top 40 percent increase from $8.9–37.7 trillion 1989–2019. However, compared to the data on the bottom 50 percent of US households in Table 2.2, the nonfinancial assets compose a far smaller part of the balance sheets of the next 40 percent of US households; and decrease from 46.9 to 38.7 percent of total assets from 1989 to 2019. For the next 40 percent sample, real estate remains the bulk of nonfinancial assets, albeit at a lower level than for the bottom 50 percent, and declining, from 38.3 to 32.4 percent 1989–2019. Meanwhile, consumer durables decline from 8.7 to 6.3 percent, also below the levels for the bottom 50 percent.

For the next 40 percent, financial claims increase from 53.1 to 61.3 percent during these two decades. Three types of financial claims predominate: pension entitlements, corporate equities and mutual fund shares, and time deposits and short-term investments. Pension entitlements increase from 23.9 to 32.6 percent of total assets; corporate equities and mutual fund shares increase from 1.1 to 8.6 percent of total assets; while time deposits and short-term investments decrease from 10.8–7.5 percent. This implies greater concentration and less dispersion compared to the bottom 50 percent, a trend that increases as one ascends the samples of social classes.

The liabilities of the next 40 percent increase from $1.64 to $6.07 trillion, values which remain below one-fifth of total assets held by these households during the 1989–2019 period. This implies an increase of net worth from $7.33 to $31.63 trillion, as emphasized in the previous volume. Although the liabilities of the next 40 percent are also concentrated in home mortgages and consumer credit, the proportions are far smaller compared to the bottom 50 percent. For the next 40 percent, home mortgages increase from 13.7 to 17.7 percent of total assets from 1989–2007, then decline to 11.6 percent by 2019. Consumer credit declines from 4.2–3.4 percent of total assets from 1989 to 1998, then increases to 4.1 percent in 2019. The far smaller weight of consumer credit on the portfolios of the next 40 percent of US households is marked.

The balance sheets of the next 9 percent (the top 90th to 99th percentile) of US households are displayed in Table 2.4. The value of total assets for the next 9 percent increase from $8.23 to *$44.71 trillion* (an aggregate also noted in the previous volume). The value of liabilities increases from $502.4 billion to $3.04 trillion. This represents 6.1 percent of the total assets held by the next 9 percent of US households in 1989; and 6.8 percent of total assets in 2019. Liabilities are also concentrated in the two categories of home mortgages and consumer credit. However, the weight of home mortgages is far lower than for the bottom 50 percent and next 40 percent, increasing from 4.8 to 8.0 percent from 1989 to 2007, then declining to 5.6 percent in 2019. Moreover, the share of consumer credit on the balance sheets of the next 9 percent remains low: 0.7 percent of total assets in 1989 and 0.8 percent in 2019. This implies that the weight of real estate on upper social classes is far lower, while the macroeconomic consequences of deleveraging since the financial crisis of 2007–2008 of the portfolio strategies of the upper classes is nonetheless greater.

The balance sheets of the top 1 percent of US households in the DFAs data suggest further differences across the portfolios of social classes. The total assets held by the top 1 percent increase from $5.06 to $37.55 trillion from 1989 to 2019. However, the share of nonfinancial assets remains almost one-half the level that obtains for the next 9 percent (counting from the top down). The nonfinancial assets of the top 1 percent rise and fall; from 19.5 percent in 1989 to peak at 21.1 percent in 2004, declining thereafter to 13.1 percent in 2019. The value of real estate retains far lower shares of the total assets for the top 1 percent of US households, declining from 12.4 percent in 1989 to 10.6 percent in 2019. At the beginning of the time series in 1989, consumer durables are recorded at higher levels for the sample of the top 1 percent in comparison to the next 9 percent, but decline thereafter, from 7.0 percent in 1989 to 2.6 percent in 2019.

The composition of financial claims for the top 1 percent also differs from other social classes. Corporate equities and mutual fund shares increase from 17.7 to *40.9 percent* of the financial claims reported by the top 1 percent from 1989–2019. Further equity in noncorporate business decreases from 26.7 to 17.0 percent from 1989 to 2010 (returning to over 20 percent in 2016 and 2019). The other categories of financial claims retain smaller shares and less variance.

The total value of liabilities incurred by the top 1 percent remain far lower than the other social classes, increasing from 2.7 to 3.7 percent of total assets held by this class from 1989 to 2004, but declining thereafter to 2.0 percent in 2019. The value of total liabilities increases from $134.3 to $749.1 billion during the 20 years 1989–2019. The net worth of the top 1 percent thereby increases from $4.92 to *$36.80 trillion* from 1989 to 2019.

In sum, decomposition of the balance-sheet data and portfolios of US households by social class permits a series of comparisons that help clarify the causal relations between financialization and inequality. The following section turns to the tendencies of wages and labor income shares to put the value of financial claims and liabilities in the DFAs data in context. However, comparison of the accumulation of financial claims by the upper classes and the accumulation of liabilities (debt) by the lower classes suggests that inequality is driven by financial factors far more than wage inequalities. This finding first appeared by tracing the shares of each social class in the total values of financial assets and liabilities, and the resultant net worth for each social class. Disaggregation of the data for each social class suggests the importance of compounding financial claims, but also the compounding of liabilities. This also brings into view new questions about how different social classes manage their balance-sheet portfolios. The different weight of real estate and real estate mortgages, the different levels of consumer durables and consumer credit, the greater reliance among lower-class households on traditional financial instruments, such as time deposits, and the effect of lower interest rates on the portfolios of each social

84 *Finance and American household inequality*

class all provide new perspectives on the different realities of financialization that obtain across social classes in the US.

The granular data in Tables 2.2 to 2.5 provide further evidence contrary to the claims of critical political economy about aggregate trends toward consumption in the US. This question was explored in Chapter 1 with data from the NIPAs from 1929 to 2019. Comparison of the balance sheets of US social classes from 1989 to 2019 suggests further questions about the composition, distribution, and place of consumption in the US political economy. Levels of consumption clearly differ across social classes, as do the respective weights of consumer durables and consumer credit on their respective balance sheets. However, another example of the particularities of US data arises here. Evidence of an increase of what is reported as consumer credit in the DFAs, especially for the bottom 50 percent of Americans, requires further disaggregation. This is because student loans are included in the category of consumer credit. Long-term investments in education may hardly be considered consumption. The fact that consumer credit is a residual category for all non-mortgage credit in the US data implies the overestimation of the former.

The tendencies of wages and labor income shares from 1929–2020 in the NIPAs

Given the importance of debates about the long-term tendencies of wages in political economy for the question of household inequality, this section returns to the NIPAs data from 1929–2018. The tendency of wages to decline in capitalist economies has remained a central focus of studies in critical political economy since Marx. The claim that financialization caused the labor share of national incomes to decline is a central argument in the critical political economy literature on advanced capitalist economies. Data from the NIPAs and secondary literature on labor shares of US income in the US support the broader ideas of critical political economy. However, the data from the US also suggest several anomalies and provisos.

Figure 2.6 displays the value of wages and salaries in the US as a percentage of total gross income in the US from 1929 to 2018 taken from the NIPAs. Several observations are in order. First, the labor share of US gross income does indeed increase from the 1930s to peak in 1969, and decline thereafter, especially after 1980. The decline of labor share from 58 percent to 52 percent of total US income in the US is considerable, and consistent with the literatures on financialization.

However, several provisos and anomalies appear that deserve consideration. First, the rise in wages and salaries associated with the New Deal occurs in the context of large losses incurred in property income because of the 1929 crash. This implies that increases in the labor share (the share of wages and salaries) is a result of the smaller denominator. The share of wages and salaries during the first years of the New Deal increases almost 2 percent, from 50.7 to 52.7 percent. This is consistent with political economy accounts. However, mobilization

Figure 2.6 The labor share of income: wages and salaries as percentage of US gross income, 1929–2018.
Source: NIPAs.

for WWII soon thereafter produces a far greater increase in the share of wages and salaries: of 5 percent, that is, from 51–56 percent of gross income in the US. Moreover, the second period of substantial increases in the share of wages and salaries occurs from 1965 to 1968 (from 55 to 58 percent). This occurs during the escalation of the war in Vietnam. A similar pattern obtains for the period of the Korean War, with wages and salaries increasing from 53 to 56 percent of gross income from 1950 to 1953. Three periods of increasing labor shares in the US are therefore associated with the realities of economic mobilization for war.

Moreover, the periods of declining labor shares also present anomalies for theories of financialization. Decreases in labor income shares are not exclusive to the period of high financialization after 1980 as emphasized in the critical political economy literature. Labor compensation does decline from 58 to 55 percent of gross income from 1980 to 1984. This may also be due to the distortions of high but declining inflation. However, the declines after 1992, 2001, and 2008 suggest the importance of business cycles and the lag of labor income during recoveries from recessions. Moreover, the three latter declines in the labor share of gross income are far greater than the decline recorded during the early 1980s. Given these four periods of decline and their correlation with business cycles, the relation between financialization and declining labor shares remains unclear, and less compelling.

Further anomalies arise in the data from the US on wages. Figure 2.7 displays the percentage annual change of real wages in the US from 1930 to 2019. After the periods of far greater volatility during the 1930s and 1940s, the data do indeed suggest a turning point in 1980. However, the tendency of wages is in the opposite direction than expected in theories of critical political economy and accounts of the structural consequences of financialization (both presuming the decline of real wages). The pace of annual increases in real wages declines from between 2 and 4 percent during the 1950s to around 2 percent during the 1960s, then falls into negative values in the early and late 1970s. This is most likely the result of the Great Inflation. The anomaly for theories

86 *Finance and American household inequality*

Figure 2.7 The percentage of annual change in real wages, 1930–2019.
Source: US BEA and St Louis Federal Reserve statistics.

Note: Percentage annual change in wage and salary accruals per full-time equivalent employee in domestic private industries, discounting consumer price inflation.

of financialization is that after 1980 the tendency is reversed. Real wages once again increase during the 1990s, 2000s, and 2010s, increases that hover around 1 percent. The declining pace of real wage increases from the late 1940s through the 1970s contrasts, clearly, with the increasing pace of changes since 1980. This may be due to inflation and deflation. However, in any case, the data from the US is not consistent with the claim that real wages have declined since 1980. Historical perspective suggests precisely the opposite.

To check this finding on the trajectory of real wages, the following section disaggregates the data on US personal income and its disposition in the NIPAs from 1929 to 2019.

US personal income and its disposition in the US NIPAs, 1929–2019

The NIPAs data on personal income and its disposition from 1929–2019 provide further information relevant to this anomaly about real wages in the US for critical political economy accounts of advanced capitalism. This also provides an opportunity to reexamine the evidence reported in the previous chapter on long-term changes in US household income, taxes, and transfers. Table 2.6 displays decade averages from the 1930s to the 2010s from the NIPAs on the four aggregate components used to calculate personal income. The four components are compensation of employees, proprietor's income, personal income on assets, and personal current transfer receipts from government social benefits. The decomposition of personal income into the underlying categories reveals further variance at odds with claims about declining labor shares. The decomposition of the NIPAs data on labor income indicates significant composition effects behind the single aggregate measure of total labor shares of gross income. The NIPAs permit the separation of wages and salaries paid by

Table 2.6 Decade average composition of US personal income and its disposition as percentage GDP, 1930s–2010s

	1930s	1940s	1950s	1960s	1970s	1980s	1990s	2000s	2010s
Gross domestic product, $billion	80.9	207.7	414.5	740.4	1,710.6	4,173.1	7,577.1	12,590.7	17,951.0
Personal income	81.6%	77.4%	77.3%	77.5%	80.0%	81.8%	82.7%	83.3%	85.9%
Compensation of employees	51.4%	53.6%	54.7%	55.7%	56.6%	55.8%	55.5%	55.1%	53.0%
Wages and salaries	49.7%	50.0%	50.2%	49.8%	48.7%	46.4%	45.4%	44.7%	43.0%
Private industries	41.9%	40.1%	41.5%	40.1%	38.7%	37.6%	37.2%	36.9%	35.8%
Government	7.9%	10.0%	8.7%	9.7%	10.0%	8.8%	8.2%	7.8%	7.1%
Supplements to wages and salaries	1.6%	3.6%	4.4%	5.9%	7.8%	9.4%	10.2%	10.4%	10.1%
Private pension and insurance	1.2%	2.2%	3.2%	3.9%	5.0%	6.0%	6.7%	7.1%	7.0%
Government social insurance	0.4%	1.4%	1.3%	2.0%	2.8%	3.4%	3.4%	3.3%	3.1%
Proprietors' income	11.8%	13.7%	10.8%	8.5%	7.1%	5.7%	6.5%	7.3%	7.9%
Farm	4.7%	5.4%	2.9%	1.6%	1.1%	0.5%	0.4%	0.3%	0.3%
Nonfarm	7.1%	8.3%	7.8%	6.9%	6.0%	5.2%	6.1%	7.0%	7.6%
Rental income of persons	4.5%	3.0%	3.0%	2.6%	1.2%	0.5%	1.4%	1.8%	3.4%
Personal income receipts on assets	12.0%	6.1%	7.0%	9.2%	11.7%	16.3%	15.1%	13.7%	13.3%
Personal interest income	7.4%	3.6%	4.6%	6.6%	9.6%	14.0%	11.7%	9.2%	8.0%
Personal dividend income	4.7%	2.5%	2.5%	2.5%	2.1%	2.4%	3.4%	4.5%	5.3%
Personal current transfer receipts	2.5%	3.0%	4.0%	5.3%	8.8%	9.9%	11.1%	12.1%	14.7%
Government social benefits	2.0%	2.8%	3.7%	5.0%	8.5%	9.5%	10.8%	11.9%	14.5%
Social security		0.1%	1.2%	2.4%	3.7%	4.2%	4.2%	4.1%	4.7%
Medicare				0.6%	0.9%	1.6%	2.2%	2.7%	3.5%
Medicaid				0.4%	0.7%	1.0%	1.8%	2.3%	2.8%
Unemployment insurance		0.5%	0.5%	0.4%	0.6%	0.4%	0.3%	0.4%	0.3%
Veterans' benefits	1.0%	1.3%	1.1%	0.7%	0.7%	0.4%	0.3%	0.3%	0.5%
Other	1.2%	0.8%	1.0%	1.1%	1.9%	1.9%	2.0%	2.2%	2.6%
Other net transfers from business	0.5%	0.2%	0.2%	0.3%	0.3%	0.4%	0.3%	0.3%	0.3%
Less: contr. to govt social insurance	0.6%	2.0%	2.2%	3.6%	5.3%	6.5%	6.9%	6.8%	6.5%
Less: Personal current taxes	1.6%	6.5%	8.0%	8.6%	9.5%	9.9%	10.3%	9.8%	9.9%
Equals: Disposable personal income	80.0%	70.8%	69.3%	68.9%	70.5%	71.8%	72.4%	73.5%	76.0%

(*continued*)

Table 2.6 Cont.

	1930s	1940s	1950s	1960s	1970s	1980s	1990s	2000s	2010s
Less: Personal outlays	76.7%	59.9%	61.9%	61.1%	62.1%	64.9%	67.3%	70.0%	70.4%
Personal consumption expenditures	75.3%	59.2%	60.8%	59.7%	60.5%	62.6%	64.7%	67.2%	67.9%
Personal interest payments	0.9%	0.4%	0.9%	1.3%	1.3%	1.9%	1.9%	1.8%	1.5%
Personal current transfer payments	0.5%	0.3%	0.2%	0.2%	0.2%	0.4%	0.7%	0.9%	1.0%
Equals: Personal savings	3.3%	11.0%	7.4%	7.8%	8.4%	6.9%	5.2%	3.5%	5.6%
Personal saving as % DPI	3.8%	15.9%	10.6%	11.2%	12.2%	9.9%	7.3%	4.8%	7.3%

Source: BEA NIPAs table 2.1. Personal Income and Its Disposition.

Finance and American household inequality   89

private industries from government wages and salaries, and report the value of supplements to wages and salaries from private pensions and insurance from government insurance. The value of farm income and nonfarm proprietors' income are also reported separately, which permits control for the long-term shift away from personal proprietary income from agriculture that, presumably, increases labor income values. Personal income receipts on assets are also disaggregated into interest income and dividend income. Personal current transfer receipts are separated into government social benefits, with lines reporting Social Security, Medicare, Medicaid, unemployment insurance, and veteran's benefits separately. Further aggregates are calculated by subtracting contributions to government insurance, current taxes, and personal outlays to measure personal consumption expenditures. Subtraction of personal interest payments and personal current transfer payments is used to calculate personal savings, reported both as a percentage of US GDP and a percentage of disposable personal income.

Personal income (wages and salaries and supplements) increases from 81.6 to 85.9 percent of US GDP from the 1930s through the 2010s. Proprietors' income decreases from 11.8 percent in the 1930s to 5.7 percent in the 1970s and 7.0 percent in the 2010s. However, this variance turns on the decline of farm income shares. In comparison, nonfarm income displays a convex curve from between 7 and 8 percent of GDP from the 1930s to the 1960s, declining during the 1970s to the 1980s, then returning to 7.6 percent of GDP in the 2010s. The value of personal rental income (not corporate rental income) as a percentage of GDP decreases from 4.5 percent in the 1930s to 0.5 percent in the 1980s, but increases thereafter to 3.4 percent of GDP in the 2010s.

Personal income receipts on assets increase from lows of 6.1 and 7.0 percent of GDP in the 1940s and 1950s to reach 16.3 percent of GDP in the 1980s, remaining at 13.3 percent in the 2010s. However, personal interest income outpaces personal dividend income (peaking at 14.0 percent of GDP in the 1980s). The value of personal dividend income increases, but from a low of 2.4 percent in the 1970s to reach 5.3 percent of GDP in the 2010s.

Greater variance obtains in the increase of personal current transfer receipts. Moreover, this increase is composed largely of government social benefits that increase from 2.0 percent of GDP during the 1930s (the decade of their inauguration), to reach 14.5 percent of GDP in the 2010s. Other net transfers from business remain between 0.2 and 0.5 percent during the nine decades from the 1930s to the 2010s. The increases in contributions to government social insurance (from 0.6 to 6.5 percent GDP) are consistent with the findings above on the cumulative importance of social policy programs and transfers in the US since their creation in the 1930s. The increase of personal current taxes from 1.6 percent in the 1930s to remain near 10 percent of GDP through the 2010s also confirms the data on taxation explored in the previous section of this chapter.

The NIPAs calculate disposable personal income by subtracting contributions to government social insurance programs and personal taxes. Disposable personal income declined from 80.0 percent of GDP in the 1930s to 70.8 percent in the

90　*Finance and American household inequality*

1940s, then increased slightly through the following decades to reach 76.0 percent of GDP in the 2010s. The NIPAs accounts then subtract personal outlays (composed of personal consumption expenditures, personal income payments, and personal current transfer payments) to arrive at the calculation of personal savings. Personal savings are reported as a percentage of US GDP and a percentage of disposable personal income in the last two lines of Table 2.6. The trajectory of personal savings increases substantially from the 1930s to the 1940s (from 3.3 to 11.0 percent of GDP and 3.8–15.9 percent of disposable personal income). This involves both the effect of new government social programs and the wartime economy of the 1940s. Thereafter, personal savings declines to 7.4 percent of GDP in the 1950s, then increases to 8.4 percent in the 1970s, then declines to 3.5 in the 2000s. However, like many of the aggregates explored in this book, this trend changes in the 2010s. During the 2010s, personal savings increase from 3.5 to 5.6 percent of GDP and from 4.8 to 7.3 as a percentage of disposable personal income.

In sum, the NIPAs data on personal income and its disposition suggest that the key macroeconomic aggregates vary considerably according to the concepts and categories used to compile personal, household, and domestic accounts. Chapter 1 explored the US data on savings, labor income, wages, and other indicators at the center of debates about financialization in advanced capitalist economies. This section disaggregated the NIPAs data on personal income and its disposition to control for underlying trends in taxation, government social policy programs, and consumption. Personal savings, taken as an indicator in isolation, does indeed suggest a significant decline since the 1980s. However, the increase of savings implied in government social benefit programs, and the large variance observed for the 1930s, 1940s, and, especially, the 2010s suggest anomalies for claims about unilateral trends in the US (based on cross-national comparisons of aggregates during shorter time spans). The historical–institutional approach is to increase the number of observations back in time, disaggregate the data, and pay attention to the original meanings of measures.

Personal consumption in the US NIPAs, 1929–2019

Further data from the NIPAs on personal consumption expenditures by major type of product help control for the variance in the disposition of personal income over time, explored above. Further composition effects arise because of the transition away from the consumption of manufactured goods to the consumption of services. Table 2.7 displays the composition of personal spending by types of product in billions of dollars and percentage of US GDP. The total value of personal spending declines, proportionally, from the 1930s to the 1940s because of the doubling of the nominal GDP during the mobilization for World War II. Thereafter, from the 1940s to the 2010s, the share of personal spending in US GDP increases gradually from 62.5 to 67.9 percent of GDP. An increase of 5.4 percent in the share of personal spending as a percentage of US GDP over eight decades is hardly evidence of a rise in consumption.

Table 2.7 US personal spending on goods and services, 1930s–2010s

Personal spending	1930s	1940s	1950s	1960s	1970s	1980s	1990s	2000s	2010s
Goods	55.0%	59.0%	56.5%	51.5%	47.7%	42.0%	36.9%	34.8%	32.0%
Durable goods	9.9%	11.4%	14.6%	14.6%	14.6%	13.7%	12.9%	12.4%	10.5%
Motor vehicles and parts	3.1%	3.1%	5.9%	6.1%	5.9%	5.8%	5.2%	4.5%	3.7%
Home furnishings	4.3%	5.0%	5.3%	4.6%	4.2%	3.5%	3.0%	2.9%	2.4%
Recreational goods and vehicles	1.3%	1.5%	2.0%	2.4%	2.9%	2.8%	3.0%	3.4%	2.8%
Other durable goods	1.3%	1.7%	1.4%	1.4%	1.6%	1.6%	1.6%	1.6%	1.6%
Nondurable goods	45.1%	47.5%	41.9%	37.0%	33.1%	28.3%	24.0%	22.3%	21.5%
Food and beverage take away	22.2%	23.7%	20.4%	16.8%	14.6%	11.4%	9.0%	7.8%	7.4%
Clothing and footwear	10.4%	11.6%	8.7%	7.5%	6.5%	5.5%	4.7%	3.5%	3.0%
Gasoline and other energy goods	5.2%	4.2%	4.8%	4.3%	4.5%	4.0%	2.7%	3.1%	2.9%
Other nondurable goods	7.3%	8.0%	8.0%	8.4%	7.5%	7.3%	7.6%	8.0%	8.2%
Services	45.0%	41.0%	43.5%	48.5%	52.3%	58.0%	63.1%	65.2%	68.0%
Housing and utilities	17.5%	12.7%	15.6%	17.2%	17.1%	18.4%	18.3%	18.2%	18.3%
Health care	3.2%	3.1%	4.1%	6.0%	8.6%	11.4%	14.2%	15.1%	16.7%
Transportation services	2.8%	3.0%	2.8%	2.8%	3.2%	3.3%	3.5%	3.3%	3.2%
Recreation services	2.2%	2.2%	1.9%	2.1%	2.3%	2.7%	3.6%	3.8%	4.0%
Food services and accommodations	5.4%	8.1%	6.6%	6.1%	6.7%	6.7%	6.4%	6.1%	6.7%
Financial services and insurance	3.6%	2.7%	3.5%	4.3%	5.0%	6.0%	7.1%	7.5%	7.7%
Other services	8.7%	7.8%	7.7%	8.3%	7.8%	7.6%	8.0%	8.6%	8.3%
Nonprofit spending	1.7%	1.4%	1.4%	1.6%	1.6%	1.8%	2.1%	2.6%	3.1%
Personal spending	100.0%	100.0%	100.0%	100.0%	100.0%	100.0%	100.0%	100.0%	100.0%
Personal spending, $billion	59.3	122.9	259.2	454.0	1,035.4	2,611.1	4,902.3	8,463.8	12,187.8
Personal spending, %GDP	73.3%	59.2%	62.5%	61.3%	60.5%	62.6%	64.7%	67.2%	67.9%

Source: BEA NIPAs table 2.3.5. Personal Consumption Expenditures by Major Type of Product.

92 *Finance and American household inequality*

Moreover, the aggregate trend of personal spending conceals a decline in personal spending on goods, from 59.0 to 32.0 percent from the 1940s to the 2010s, especially nondurable goods from 45.1 to 21.5 percent. This is further evidence of both the skewed baselines in the data from before 1950 and counter to the claim that financialization caused an increase in consumption in the US political economy.

The data on the increase in consumption of services is more compelling. Personal spending on services increases from 45.0 to 68.0 percent of GDP from the 1940s to the 2010s. Personal spending on finance does indeed increase from 2.7 to 7.7 percent of GDP during these eight decades. However, health care increased from 3.2 to 16.7 percent of GDP during this period, and other service sectors retain far larger shares of personal spending than finance, especially housing and utilities (18.3 percent).

It is also of note that the value of nonprofit spending (traditionally reported as part of the household sector in the NIPAs, IMAs, and Federal Reserve Z1 Reports data), are reported separately in Table 2.7. According to this measure of personal spending (not the operational receipts of nonprofits), nonprofit spending increased from 1.4 percent of US GDP in the 1950s to 3.1 percent in the 2010s.

In sum, the composition of personal spending in the US NIPAs data from the 1930s to the 2010s suggests that claims about increased consumption due to financialization in the US require caution. The transition from industrial manufacturing to the provision of services involved large variance that overshadows the evidence of a turn to consumption and/or the rise of finance. The financial sector does increase its share of US GDP from the 1930s to the 2010s. However, the financial sector increases at a far slower pace than health care and, indeed, remains a distant third in the rank of service sectors in terms of growth. Finally, once again, the financial sector remains small part of US GDP if measured in terms of the traditional measures of income and production in the NIPAs. This avoids loading on the dependent variables of financial claims and liabilities. The following section takes a closer look at the NIPAs data to explore further these counterintuitive patterns of continuity and change in the US economy.

A closer look at personal income, consumption, private investment, and government, 1929–2020

The decade averages explored from the NIPAs data may be traced by year from 1929 to 2019 to further examine these findings on savings, consumption, and finance. This section examines personal income receipts on assets, the pace of annual change in personal consumption, private investment, and government as a share of US GDP from 1929 to 2019. The data confirm the anomalies for theories of financialization reported in Chapter 1 and explored above. Figure 2.8 displays the total current dollar value of personal income receipts received from personal assets from 1929 to 2019. Once again, a sharp decline in personal income receipts was caused by the Great Depression, one that continued

Finance and American household inequality 93

Figure 2.8 Personal income receipts as percentage personal income, 1929–2019.
Source: BEA NIPAs, Table 2.1 Personal income and its disposition.

through the end of World War II (unlike the indicators of industrial production, wages, and salaries). The uptick in 1980 expected by theories of financialization also appears in the data. However, the sharp increase during the years of high interest rates adopted by Federal Reserve Chair Paul Volker appears to plateau in 1982, and decline thereafter, with the exception of an increase during the 2007–2008 financial crisis. The fact that personal income receipts on assets plateau so soon (three years after the policy change) suggests the repositioning of markets and investors. Thereafter, personal income generated from assets declines. This runs counter to the idea that financialization, as measured in terms of personal income on assets, continues unabated during the three decades since the 1980s in the US.

A second broader view of personal consumption in the US may be obtained from comparing the percentage annual change of personal consumption from 1934 to 2019 alongside the two other components of the economy at this level of aggregation: private investment and government consumption and investment (see Figure 2.9). As indicated in the best fitting line through the values for personal consumption, the tendency in the percentage annual change declines from 4.5 to 4.0 percent from 1934–2019. It is also of note that the dark line of personal consumption remains far more stable compared to the paces of change in government spending and private domestic investment. From this perspective, personal consumption remains a more stable part of economic growth in the US, exhibiting a one-half of 1 percent decline in the pace of change during the eight decades from the 1930s to the 2010s.

In comparison, private investment remains far more volatile, even after discounting the extreme variance experienced during the 1930s and 1940s. Private investment rises and falls sharply during business cycles, with peaks in 1966, 1973, 1981, 1988, from 1997 to 2000, and in 2015. Unfortunately, the data on US government investment and spending are not reported separately. However, as reported in the NIPAs, the government sector's contribution to the annual change in US GDP displays less variation, but with peaks in the late 1960s, the late 1980s, the early 2000s, and at the end of the period in 2019.

94 *Finance and American household inequality*

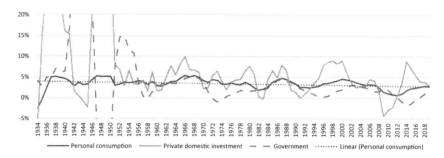

Figure 2.9 The percentage of annual change in US personal consumption, private investment, and government, 1929–2018.
Source: BEA NIPAs, Table 1.1.1.
Note: Percentage change from preceding period in real gross domestic product, seasonally adjusted at annual rates.

Although not displayed here, the data on personal consumption, private investment, and government as percentage shares of US GDP indicate the structural importance of the former and far less variance for all three sectors. After the large variance experienced from the 1930s to the 1950s, personal consumption remains near 60 percent of US GDP, increasing slightly after 1980 to reach 68 percent in 2018 (reported as decade averages above). Private investment decreases gradually, from between 22 and 24 percent in the 1960s to remain near 20 percent until declining in the latter 2010s and declining to 18 percent in 2019. Government spending remains just below the level of private investment from the 1950s to the 1990s, then remains close to private investment at 20 percent (except for the years of financial crisis and recovery from 2008 to 2012).

This chapter has explored the traditional data reported in the US NIPAs. The further indicators such as gross value-added, as compiled for the IMAs data and comparative financial balance-sheet data, require caution. New data categories require caution because they mix together what is, in the NIPAs data, kept apart: on the one hand, the traditional nonfinancial aggregates according to the theory, method, and logic of national income accounts and, on the other hand, the new measures of financial claims and liabilities that compose financial balance sheets. The latter are based, not on macroeconomics but, instead, financial theory, concepts, and measurements. Comparison of the changing shares of households, nonprofits, and the federal and subnational government sector in the US NIPAs from 1929 to 2019 suggest counterintuitive trends because they avert loading on the dependent variables of finance.

In sum, the NIPAs data from 1929 to 2019 suggest a variety of anomalies and provisos for claims about structural change in the US political economy. In the nonfinancial data of the NIPAs, the shares of households and traditional income sources such as wages, salaries, and interest income remain far more stable than

Finance and American household inequality 95

claims about how financialization has changed the US economy. Personal consumption, savings, social policy funds and transfers, wages, and the respective shares of households, private business, and government in the US economy as measured in the traditional aggregates of the NIPAs, suggest a variety of observations about continuity and change. Few support generalizations about financialization or the syndromes of advanced capitalism as forwarded by critical political economy research. Having traced the traditional macroeconomic indicators, consideration of the financial balance-sheet data on US households in the IMAs from the 1960s to the 2010s is in order.

US household balance sheets in the IMAs, 1960s to 2010s

This section turns to the data on US household balance sheets in the IMAs from the 1960s to the 2010s. Several patterns of continuity and change suggest provisos and anomalies for studies of the US and advanced economies. To explore the basic trends, on aggregate, in US household balance sheets, the data from the IMAs is split into two tables. The first table (Table 2.8) displays the aggregate items of nonfinancial assets, financial claims, and liabilities. The second table (Table 2.9) displays the disaggregated items that compose these categories. Regarding the aggregate categories, the first observation is the marked continuity of proportional levels amid the geometric increase in current dollar values. Over the six decades from the 1960s to the 2010s, nonfinancial assets

Table 2.8 US household aggregated balance sheets, decade average percentage total assets, 1960s–2010s

	1960s	1970s	1980s	1990s	2000s	2010s
Nonfinancial assets	30.6%	35.0%	38.4%	34.0%	36.7%	29.8%
Financial claims	69.4%	65.0%	61.6%	66.0%	63.3%	70.2%
Equity and investment fund shares	34.2%	27.1%	23.3%	27.4%	27.5%	31.0%
Insurance and pension schemes	18.0%	20.0%	19.9%	23.4%	22.6%	24.4%
Currency and deposits	11.7%	13.5%	13.1%	8.6%	7.5%	8.9%
Debt securities	4.1%	3.5%	4.4%	5.5%	4.4%	4.8%
Liabilities (percent total assets)	10.9%	11.8%	13.0%	14.1%	16.5%	14.1%
Loans	10.6%	11.5%	12.4%	13.4%	15.9%	13.5%
Other liabilities	0.3%	0.3%	0.6%	0.7%	0.6%	0.6%
Total assets, percent	100.0%	100.0%	100.0%	100.0%	100.0%	100.0%
Total assets, $trillion	3.1	6.7	17.6	35.6	69.0	104.8
Total assets, CPI discounted $trillion	3.1	3.9	5.1	7.4	11.1	13.9

Source: BEA IMAs, table S.3.a. Households and Nonprofit Institutions Serving Households.

Note: Consumer price index (CPI) calculated at mid-decade, i.e. 1965–1975 etc.

96 *Finance and American household inequality*

Table 2.9 US household disaggregated balance sheets, decade average percentage total assets, 1960s–2010s

	1960s	1970s	1980s	1990s	2000s	2010s
Nonfinancial assets	30.6%	35.0%	38.4%	34.0%	36.7%	29.8%
Real estate	22.8%	26.2%	30.2%	26.6%	30.6%	24.5%
Consumer durable goods	7.6%	8.4%	7.9%	7.0%	5.7%	4.8%
Equipment and Intellectual property	0.2%	0.4%	0.4%	0.4%	0.4%	0.6%
Financial claims	69.4%	65.0%	61.6%	66.0%	63.3%	70.2%
Currency and deposits	11.7%	13.5%	13.1%	8.6%	7.5%	8.9%
Currency and transferable deposits	2.9%	2.4%	2.1%	1.6%	0.6%	1.0%
Time and savings deposits	8.8%	11.1%	11.0%	7.0%	6.8%	7.8%
Debt securities	4.1%	3.5%	4.4%	5.5%	4.4%	4.8%
Treasury securities	2.5%	1.5%	1.5%	2.0%	0.5%	1.1%
Municipal securities	1.2%	1.0%	2.0%	1.5%	1.8%	1.8%
Corporate and foreign bonds	0.4%	0.9%	0.6%	1.3%	1.4%	1.4%
Agency- and GSE-backed securities	0.1%	0.2%	0.2%	0.7%	0.6%	0.4%
Equity and investment fund shares	34.2%	27.1%	23.3%	27.4%	27.5%	31.0%
Corporate equities	17.5%	9.2%	6.3%	11.8%	10.6%	13.1%
Equity in noncorporate business	15.7%	17.2%	14.5%	10.0%	10.1%	9.7%
Mutual fund shares	1.0%	0.6%	1.3%	3.8%	4.6%	6.6%
Money market fund shares	0.0%	0.1%	1.2%	1.7%	2.3%	1.6%
Insurance and pension schemes	18.0%	20.0%	19.9%	23.4%	22.6%	24.4%
Pension entitlements	14.1%	16.9%	17.5%	21.0%	20.0%	21.9%
Insurance reserves	7.5%	5.9%	4.5%	4.7%	4.5%	4.1%
Liabilities	10.9%	11.8%	13.0%	14.1%	16.5%	14.1%
Loans	10.6%	11.5%	12.4%	13.4%	15.9%	13.5%
Short term	3.7%	4.1%	3.9%	3.8%	3.9%	3.9%
Long term (mortgages)	7.0%	7.4%	8.5%	9.6%	12.0%	9.6%
Insurance and pensions	0.1%	0.1%	0.1%	0.0%	0.0%	0.0%
Total assets, percent	100.0%	100.0%	100.0%	100.0%	100.0%	100.0%
Total assets, current $trillion	3.1	6.7	17.6	35.6	69.0	104.8
Total assets, CPI discounted $trillion	3.1	3.9	5.1	7.4	11.1	13.9

Source: BEA IMAs, table S.3.a Households and Nonprofit Institutions Serving Households.

Note: Consumer price index (CPI) calculated at mid-decade, i.e. 1965–1975 etc.

Finance and American household inequality   97

begin and end near 30 percent of total household asset holdings, with financial claims at near 70 percent. In comparison, liabilities increase from 10.9 to 16.5 percent of household assets, but decline to 14.1 percent in the 2010s. Quarterly data are explored below. The total current dollar values are discounted by the Consumer Price Index to provide a rough estimate of the real accumulation of assets by households over time.

The composition of financial claims also suggests anomalies for theories of financial change in the US toward money managers and disintermediation. The top category of household financial claims is shares in equity and investment funds. However, the shares of equity and investment fund decrease from 34.2 to 23.3 percent of total household financial claims from the 1960s to the 1980s, before returning to 31.0 during the 2010s. This is hardly the transition to financial intermediaries suggested by contemporary banking theory and financial intermediation theory. The second largest category of US household financial claims is composed of the reserves of insurance and pension schemes. The gradual trajectory of increasing shares from 18.0 to 23.4 percent, and the recovery from the slight decline incurred during the 2000s implied by the 24.4 percent recorded for the 2010s, suggest the gradual accumulation of assets consistent with the long-term financial accumulations and management typical of insurance companies and pension funds in the US.

In sum, the major categories of aggregate US household balance sheets display remarkable continuity, with the structure of balance sheets over six decades changing little, and certainly not in the direction supposed by theories of financialization or, indeed, a fundamental shift of US households toward real estate holdings. These findings are checked through the disaggregation of the data as follows – first intra-category, then in terms of the profound differences across US social classes.

Before proceeding, however, a note about the minor categories and liability structure is in order. The value of US household liabilities as a percentage of total assets does increase from 10.9 to 16.5 percent over the five decades from the 1960s to the 2000s. However, the aggregate leverage (liabilities as a percentage of total assets) declines during the 2010s to 14.1 percent. This also differs profoundly across social classes as will be seen in due course.

Disaggregation of the data on US household balance sheets, and display of the decade averages from the 1960s to the 2010s, provide further insights into the unexpected patterns of continuity and change. First, the stability of nonfinancial assets as a proportion of US household balance sheets results from dual peaks in the shares of real estate, the steady decline of consumer durable goods, and the marginal but increasing share of equipment and intellectual property. The valuation of real estate increases from 22.8 to 30.2 percent of household portfolios from the 1960s to the 1990s, but declines twice thereafter, once to 26.6 percent in the 1990s and again to 24.5 percent during the 2010s. The declining shares of consumer durable goods also counters research in critical political economy and studies of the US and other advanced economies about the relations between financialization (even if real estate valuation

98 *Finance and American household inequality*

is considered as part of financialization), and increases in consumption. The share of consumer durable goods in US household portfolios declines from a peak of 8.4 percent in the 1970s to 4.8 percent in the 2010s.

In sum, evidence of deleveraging and reduced consumption during the 2010s suggests fundamental changes in the American political economy. Disaggregation of the data by social class follows.

Disaggregation of the major types of financial claims[5] held by US households by decade average from the 1960s–2010s presents further provisos for theories of financialization. First, corporate equities are the largest single type of equity and investment shares held by households. This is consistent with the importance of debates about the shareholder revolution (Knafo and Dutta, 2019) and, indeed, the focus of much of financial economics on corporate finance. However, from the 1960s through the 1990s, the value of *equity in noncorporate businesses* held by households remained above the value of stocks purchased by household from incorporated businesses. The importance of investments made by households in unincorporated businesses, and the gradual increase of mutual fund shares and money market fund shares, suggest a more complex picture than a unilateral trend toward capital market-centered banking that is implied in theories of financialization and studies of corporate finance.

The weight of government bonds (Treasury and Municipal) in the second largest category of US household financial claims (debt securities) presents another proviso for theories of financialization that focus primarily on corporate finance. Although the share of total assets held by US households remains small, two trends in the composition of debt securities held by US households are of note. First, the two largest categories of debt securities held by US households are US government Treasury securities and municipal government securities. Moreover, the direct purchase of corporate and foreign bonds, although quite small in comparison to the household purchase of equity and investment funds, increases during the latter decades.

Household financial portfolios in the Z1 financial accounts of the United States

Another historical–institutional view of the financial portfolios of US households may be obtained from the Board of Governors of the Federal Reserve Z1 Reports, or Financial accounts of the United States. Figure 2.10 displays the five largest categories of financial claims held by US households from 1951 to 2020 as a percentage of total US financial claims. The rank order in 1951 is the following: first, household equity holdings in unincorporated business (39 percent total); second, corporate equities (20 percent of total); third, the net holdings of households in insurance policies and pension schemes (21 percent of total); fourth, time and savings deposits (9 percent of total); and, finally, mutual funds and money market funds (near zero percent, but included to capture later variance).

Finance and American household inequality 99

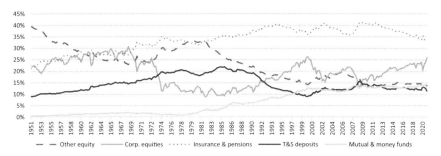

Figure 2.10 Principal US household financial claims; percentage total household financial claims, 1951–2020.
Note: Other equity = equity in unincorporated businesses and other entities. Insurance and pensions = net holdings. T&S deposits = Time and savings deposits. Mutual & money funds = Mutual funds and money market funds.
Source: Board of Governors of the Federal Reserve System, Financial accounts of the United States Z1 Reports.

The following observations about these principal types of US household financial holdings over time focus on their relevance for debates about financialization, bank change, and the political economy of advanced capitalism. First, the displacement of the single largest category of US household financial claims in 1951 (equity in unincorporated business enterprises), from over twice the level of the second and third ranked types (insurance and pensions, and corporate equity) downward to the third largest type of financial holding, is the largest variance. This is consistent with theories of financialization, especially the emphasis on the shareholder revolution, long-standing debates about the separation of ownership from management (Bearle and Means, 1932), and the rise of stockholding corporations in the US. These themes are explored in the following chapter. However, the data on US household balance sheets also indicate the existence of limits to the displacement of the traditional household practice of holding noncorporate equity. Specifically, the decline of 'other equity' is *reversed* after the 2000 dot.com crisis. Moreover, the share of noncorporate equity holdings stabilizes at around 15 percent of total household financial claims through 2020. The reversal of the trend from 1951 to 1999, and the stabilization thereafter, are anomalies for claims about the inexorable advance of financialization toward the shareholding model of corporations and corporate governance; an expectation shared by research in corporate finance and economic approaches – mainstream, heterodox, and critical alike.

The trajectory of the second largest category of US household financial claims at the outset of the Z1 Reports data in 1951 suggests further anomalies for theories of financialization and economic approaches. The value of corporate equities, as a percentage of total US household financial claims, does indeed increase from 20 percent in 1952–1953 to reach 30 percent in 1965.

100 Finance and American household inequality

However, this is far earlier than the 1980 turning point emphasized in theories of financialization and critical political economy. Moreover, the share of corporate equities declines thereafter to 11 percent by 1974; then fluctuates around 10 percent through 1990. After 1990, the share of corporate equities on US household financial balance sheets does increase, once again, to 26 percent until the 2000 stock market crash. Thereafter, the share of corporate equities falls twice after stock market reversals; once to 15 percent by 2003 and, once again, to 13 percent in 2009. Thereafter, corporate equities increase their share of US household financial claims to 26 percent in 2020, recovering from the collapse in the NYSE caused by the COVID-19 pandemic.

The share of corporate equities in US household financial portfolios thereby ends, in 2020, at levels similar to the levels in the early 1950s, as reported at the outset of the Z1 data. The volatility is substantial, indicating the effect on household balance sheets of the rise and fall of the NYSE and the associated business cycles in the US economy. However, the historical–institutional evidence from the balance sheets of US households suggests that the forces of financialization are far longer term than the focus of research on a turning point around 1980. And the shift toward the holding of corporate equities by US households reached limits, both in the 2000 dot.com crash and the 2007–2008 financial crisis.

The third largest category of US household financial claims in 1951 is the net holdings of insurance policies and pension fund schemes. The net value of household insurance and pensions combines the different types of insurance and the variety of pension funds into a single indicator. This may conceal variance. However, for broader comparative purposes, a single aggregate measure permits an overview of the sector alongside the other principal types of financial claims of US household portfolios.

The trajectory of the net insurance and pension claims of US households displays a far more stable parabolic curve, which increases from 21 percent of total household financial claims in 1951 to peak at 41 percent in 2009. Periodic declines appear to covary with the recovery of the economy stock markets (producing increases in the share of corporate equities), especially after 1994. However, the parabolic curve of net insurance and pension claims is far less volatile than the value of equity in business enterprises, incorporated and unincorporated. Given the simpler, more conservative, and longer-term investments of insurance companies and pension funds in the US, the rise of net value of the financial claims of insurance policies and pension schemes on US household balance sheets provides another anomaly for claims about a universal trend toward short termism caused by financialization in advanced economies. Instead, the trajectory appears to reflect more gradual processes typically the result of generational trends and long-term accumulation of household savings invested in insurance and pensions.

The fourth largest category of US household financial claims is composed of time deposits and savings deposits. This traditional category increases from 9 to 22 percent of total household financial portfolios from 1951 to 1985,

Finance and American household inequality   101

before declining to 9 percent in 2000. This is consistent with theories of disintermediation in contemporary banking theory and financial intermediation ('re-intermediation' in this study). This trend is also consistent, partially, with theories of financialization and studies of market-centered banking in the US in the sense that it indicates a shift away from traditional deposit-taking and loan-making activities at banks, and toward capital market funding of banks and, in this case, financial investments on the part of households.

However, the data after 2000 differ. This implies that the preceding trend may well be due to the long-term, gradual increase of inflation during the 1960s and 1970s (the Great Inflation). This can be assumed to have produced the long-term increase of time deposits and savings from 1951 to 1985. Thereafter, upon the control of inflation, and declining interest rates, the reverse tendency ensued. And like the many other measures explored in this section, the proportional decline of time deposits and savings deposits on US household financial portfolios reverses after the 2000 dot.com crash. The percentage share of time deposits and savings deposits increases from 9 to 15 percent of total US household financial claims from 1999 to 2009; and remains between 11 to 15 percent of the total from 2009 to 2020. The stabilization of time deposits and savings deposits at this level (alongside similar, and similarly stable, shares of mutual- and money market funds and equity in unincorporated business enterprises), indicates marked continuity in the third-, fourth-, and fifth-largest types of financial holdings on the part of US households since the financial crisis of 2007–2008. The inversion of the two major holdings (net values on insurance policies and pension funds, and corporate equities) indicates the systematic valuation of the latter during the bull markets in the 2010s, valuations only briefly interrupted during the 2020 COVID-19 pandemic.

The fifth major type of financial claim in US household financial portfolios, as measured in the Federal Reserve Z1 Reports from 1951 to 2020, is the combined value of mutual funds and money market funds. These holdings breach 1 percent of household financial holdings in 1958, and remain at 1 percent through the 1970s. In a pattern consistent with theories of financialization, as well as contemporary banking theory, financial intermediation theory, and endogenous money theory, the (combined) value of mutual funds and money market funds increases from 1 percent in 1979 to reach 12.5 percent of total US financial holdings in 2000. However, once again, the data after 2000 differ. The value of these holdings does indeed reach 14 percent in 2008. However, thereafter, the value of mutual funds and money market funds held by US households remains between 13 and 14 percent of the total through 2020. This is another indicator of the different patterns of financialization in the US during the 2010s, patterns that contrast with the rise of financial market holdings at US households for the previous periods. The strategic portfolio decisions of US households since the 2000 dot.com crash, and the financial crisis of 2007–2008, indicate the stabilization of trends rather than change in the direction implied by financialization, contemporary banking theory, financial intermediation theory, and post-Keynesian endogenous money approaches.

102 *Finance and American household inequality*

In sum, the evidence from US household financial holdings, according to the categories of the Board of Governors of the Federal Reserve Financial Accounts of the United States Z1 Reports from 1951 to 2020, suggests the longer-term process of compounding financialization, one that begins long before the turning point of 1980, as emphasized in critical political economy research (and shared by other economic approaches). The parabolic ascendent curve of the net value of private insurance policies and pension funds; the volatile trajectory of corporate equities that, nonetheless, end in 2020 at the same level reported at the beginning of the Z1 Report data (1951); the declining share of household equity in unincorporated business that recovers after 2000 and stabilizes after 2008; and the reverse trajectory of mutual funds and money market funds (a gradual increase after 1980 that reverts after 2000 and stabilizes after 2008), combine to suggest a more complex picture of financialization and its limits. Unfortunately, more granular data on the underlying composition of these trends are not available in the Z1 Reports. The following sections, therefore, turn to additional sources before concluding.

An addendum on household debt, 1980–2020

Unfortunately, the Federal Reserve Financial accounts of the United States (Z1 Report) do not report data on US household financial claims by social class. The profound differences across US social classes found in the DFAs data (published in March 2019) are concealed by the aggregation of a single measure for the composition of US household financial portfolios in the Federal Reserve Z1 reports. However, before turning to further data on the differences across social classes in the management of household debt available from the FDIC Consumer Finance Surveys from 1989 to 2016, consideration of another indicator of household debt is in order. The same proviso about composition effects holds. However, the cost of US household debt service payments from 1980 to 2020 suggests both a significant degree of *deleveraging* by US households during the 2010s, and the counterintuitive finding of *lower* levels of household leverage in 2020 than in 1980.

Figure 2.11 displays the aggregate value of US household debt service payments as a percentage of disposable personal income, each quarter, from 1980 to 2020. The increased indebtedness of US households from around 10.5 percent of disposable personal income in 1983 to 12.1 in 1988, and again from 10.4 to 13.2 percent from 1994 to 2008, are consistent with theories of financialization in critical political economy.

However, three periods of decline are also notable and suggest significant deleveraging. The first period of deleveraging that reduced US household debt service payments coincides with the 1987 crash on US capital markets through the first quarter of 1994. This brought the cost of debt payments back to the preceding level of 10.5 percent of disposable personal income that obtained from the first quarter of 1980 through the first quarter of 1984. The second period of deleveraging is far more substantial, endures far longer, and dates from the first

Finance and American household inequality 103

Figure 2.11 US household debt service payments, percentage disposable personal income, 1980–2020.
Source: St Louis Federal Reserve statistics.

quarter of 2008 through the third quarter of 2012. This level also remains quite stable, under 10 percent, until 2020. This second period of deleveraging in the sample from 1980 to 2020 occurred from 2008 to 2012, precisely during the latter stage of financial crisis and the recession and recovery that followed. From 2008 to 2012, the cost of US household debt service payments as a percentage of disposable personal income dropped from 13.1 in the first quarter of 2008 to 9.8 percent by the third quarter of 2012. The mechanisms of this reduction, the importance of business cycles, and the differences in the ability of social classes to reduce debt service payments require further analysis. However, the data since the financial crisis of 2007–2008 clearly differ from the preceding periods. Finally, the steep drop in the value of household debt service payments during the first quarter of 2020 is also counterintuitive. However, it is consistent with the pattern after the 2007–2008 financial crisis and, to a lesser extent, after the 1987 financial crisis.

In sum, the data on household debt in the US suggests several anomalies for theories of financialization. The aggregate data on household debt suggest profound differences between the increasing burden of debt experienced from the 1980s through the 2000s and the substantial deleveraging of households during the early 2010s, a deleveraging that was sustained throughout the decade. Further data from the triennial FDIC Consumer Finance Surveys from 1989 to 2016 suggest profound differences across social classes behind these aggregate trends.

Unequal household financial management: Perspectives from FDIC Consumer Finance Surveys, 1989–2016

One of the central arguments of this chapter is that the aggregation of data on household financial portfolios conceals large composition effects due to profound differences across social classes. This section turns to two indicators that capture these differences in the FDIC Consumer Finance Surveys from 1989

104 *Finance and American household inequality*

Table 2.10 Percentage of families with debts 60 days or more past due, 1989–2016

	1989	1992	1995	1998	2001	2004	2007	2010	2013	2016
1st Quintile	17.9	10.9	10.0	13.2	13.3	16.5	15.1	21.1	16.4	14.0
2nd Quintile	12.2	9.3	10.8	12.7	11.6	13.5	11.3	15.2	14.0	11.0
3rd Quintile	4.9	6.9	8.7	9.5	8.0	10.1	8.3	10.4	10.0	9.3
4th Quintile	5.9	4.4	6.3	5.8	3.9	7.2	4.2	8.8	7.3	4.4
80–90%	1.0	1.8	2.8	3.7	2.5	2.3	1.9	5.3	4.2	2.6
90–100%	2.3	0.9	0.9	1.7	1.3	0.3	0.1	2.1	1.0	0.8

Source: Federal Deposit Insurance Company (FDIC), Consumer Finance Surveys, 1989–2016.

to 2016. The first indicator is the ratio of debt payments to family income. The second indicator is the number of debtor families with debt payment ratios greater than 40 percent of family income. Comparison of class differences is facilitated by the separation of the FDIC survey data into four quintiles (from the poorest to the richest), and splitting the 5th quintile into the two top ten percentiles of American families (by income). Table 2.10 displays the percentage of families in each income class with debts 60 days or more past due from 1989 to 2016. In 1989, the variance spans from 17.9 for the first quintile (the poorest 20 percent of families in the US) to 1.0 and 2.3 for the top two 10 percent quintiles. For the first quintile, the number of families with debts 60 days or more past-due decreases from 17.9 to 10.0 percent from 1989 to 1995. However, thereafter, the percentage of families with debts past-due increases to reach 21.1 in 2010 (declining thereafter to 14.0 percent in 2016. This does suggest that part of the variance of deleverage on the aggregate level reported above involves the reduction of debt for poorer households in the US. Further data on the proportional shares of debt stocks and other factors are beyond the scope of this chapter. However, the evidence suggests profound differences across social classes. The percentage of families with debts 60 days or more past due in the other quintiles, and the two top deciles, suggests both substantially lower leverage and a far greater capacity to deleverage.

The second comparison possible in the FDIC Consumer Finance Survey data is that of the number of families with debt payments greater than 40 percent of total household income. Table 2.11 displays the stark differences that obtain in this ratio for the first quintile of US families (considered from the bottom up) compared to wealthier families. For the lowest quintile of US families, those with debt payments over 40 percent of income increase from 25.9 to 29.7 percent from 1989 to 2001. However, thereafter, this figure declines to 21.9 percent by 2016. This is further evidence that deleveraging obtains for those worst off, albeit at a slower pace from far greater levels of debt and leverage. Like the above data, similar trends from far lower levels obtain for the other quintiles. The percentage of families with debt payments over 40 percent of income falls markedly as one ascends the quintiles according to total income in the FDIC Consumer Finance Survey data. Such that, for the top 10 percent

Table 2.11 Percentage of families with debt payment ratio greater than 40 percent income, 1989–2016

	1989	1992	1995	1998	2001	2004	2007	2010	2013	2016
1st Quintile	25.9	27.0	27.1	29.5	29.7	27.3	26.7	26.2	23.4	21.9
2nd Quintile	14.7	15.4	19.1	19.5	15.9	18.5	19.7	18.6	18.1	13.4
3rd Quintile	11.1	11.7	8.9	15.9	12.8	13.9	14.5	15.3	11.2	8.5
4th Quintile	5.4	7.8	7.8	9.6	6.1	7.3	12.8	11.1	5.9	4.3
80–90%	2.3	3.6	4.9	3.4	3.7	2.7	8.1	5.3	4.1	4.2
90–100%	2.2	2.4	2.9	3.0	2.0	1.6	3.8	2.9	1.6	1.5

Source: Federal Deposit Insurance Company (FDIC), Consumer Finance Surveys, 1989–2016.

of families in the US according to income, only 2.2 percent lived with debt payments above 40 percent of income; one-tenth of the level reported for the bottom (1st) quintile. And although this number increased to 3.8 percent in 2007, deleveraging for the top 10 percent of US families reduced the percentage of families with debt payment ratios over 40 percent of income from 3.8 to 1.5 percent. These differences are consistent with the data on household deleveraging reported above, and indicate the importance of both low interest rates during the 2010s and the importance of decomposing financial aggregates by social class. The different levels and trends reported in this section indicate the need to consider the different logic and limits of financial portfolio management by social class.

In sum, data from the FDIC Consumer Finance Surveys from 1989 to 2016 provide information about the political economy of late debt payments and the degree of debt burdens across social classes in the US. This provides further evidence of how financial aggregates may conceal fundamental differences and inequalities.

Before concluding, a final look at social-class differences is in order. This time in terms of home equity as an indicator of household financial management. The valuation and devaluation of real estate is central to debates about the political economy of financialization and change in advanced economies. A rich variety of new, highly specialized data sources, academic research, and studies of real estate in government agencies and international entities have become available since the financial crisis of 2007–2008. The political-economic complexities of real estate, and real estate finance, are beyond the scope of this chapter. However, the DFAs make it possible to compare the different realities of real estate in the portfolios of US social classes from 1989 to 2019.

This chapter began by comparing the weight of real estate holdings in the balance sheets of the bottom 50 percent, next 40 percent, next 9 percent, and top 1 percentiles of American citizens and residents according to the DFAs data. The DFAs provide further insight here through comparison of the value of home equity in the balance-sheet portfolios of US social classes. Figure 2.12 displays the value of home equity for each of the wealth percentiles.

106 *Finance and American household inequality*

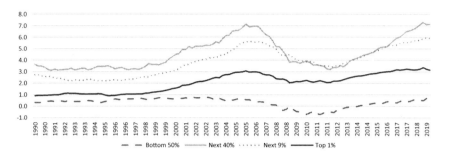

Figure 2.12 Home equity by social class, 1990–2019, $ trillion.
Source: Board of Governors of the Federal Reserve System. 'Distributional financial accounts of the United States,' 2020.

Several observations are in order. First, the bottom 50 percent is the only class than dipped below zero. The total value of home equity owned by the bottom 50 percent of US households remained below one trillion dollars from 1989 to 2019. From 2008 to 2013, the value of home equity for the bottom 50 percent of US households remained negative. In comparison, the total value of home equity held by the top 1 percent, next 9 percent, and next 40 percent remained stable at one, two, and three trillion dollars respectively from 1989 to 1998. From 1999 to 2005, the total value of home equity held by the top 1 percent increased from 1.25 to 3.07 trillion dollars, while the next 9 percent increased home equity holdings from 2.6 to 5.6 trillion, and the next 40 percent from 3.31 to 7.16 trillion. Translation of these valuations into macroeconomic effects and the ups and downs of business cycles is beyond the scope of this chapter. The point here is to demonstrate the importance of disaggregation. The decomposition of home equity by social class in the DFAs provides insights into the profoundly different context for the strategic management of household portfolios. The immense valuation of real estate, and home equity, for the top three social classes, and the negative valuation of home equity held by the bottom 50 percent of US households suggest the continued importance of a core category of classic modern political economy: social class.

In sum, data from the DFAs and FDIC Consumer Finance Surveys provide insight into the fundamentally different strategies and realities of household portfolio management. A critical dimension in the political economy of advanced economies is the place of real estate in broader macroeconomics. Home acquisition and mortgage finance has been at the center of debates about social inclusion and the excessive cycles of valuation that increasingly drive economies, but also produce boom and bust cycles. This section has used the DFAs to disaggregate the value of home equity value by social class. The far greater equity value of the upper classes contrasts with the far lower values of the bottom 50 percent of American citizens and residents. Indeed, negative home equity levels obtains for this half of the DFAs sample from 2008 to 2014.

Further analysis of these trends and the cost and benefits of lower interest rates during these cycles is beyond the scope of this chapter.

Conclusion

This chapter explored the data on US household balance-sheet portfolios and related trends in personal income, taxes, government social policies, and the share of wages, consumption, savings, and other traditional indicators of household economics. Both the traditional sectoral and national income accounts data from the NIPAs, and further data from official US government statistics on income, taxes, and social policy transfers supplement the historical–institutional analysis of the US Department of Commerce Bureau of Economic Analysis (BEA) IMAs data that provide in-depth coverage of the composition of US household balance sheets from 1960 to 2019. Of special value is the data from the Distributional financial accounts of the United States that were launched in March 2019. The DFAs provide the opportunity to disaggregate the US household sector by social class, and trace patterns of continuity and change in the nonfinancial assets, financial claims, and liabilities for the bottom 50 percent, next 40 percent, next 9 percent, and top 1 percent of American citizens and residents according to the total value of wealth and the composite measures used to calculate wealth. This permits the estimation of how nonfinancial and financial factors have increased inequality in the US. The distribution of gains and losses from financial claims and liabilities are found to be far more important than nonfinancial factors. And the differences across social classes are found to be far more important than aggregate household trends.

Traditional measures used since 1929 in the US NIPAs belie profound changes in both the fundamental indicators of macroeconomics, such as wages, salaries, taxes, government social policy transfers, and the real estate and durable goods that compose household balance sheets. Profound change does occur in terms of the decline of industrial manufacturing of goods and the rise of the service sector. However, neither financialization, nor, unexpectedly, profound declines in wages, salaries, or government social policy transfers appear in the traditional economic aggregates of the NIPAs. This is partially a function of the longer time span of the NIPAs data from 1929 to 2019. However, this also suggests that the variance emphasized by studies of financialization and comparative analysis of advanced capitalist economies may turn on the use of financialized indicators rather than the traditional income and production aggregates as embodied in the NIPAs.

The historical–institutional balance-sheet approach was used in this chapter to focus on the proportional decline of households as reported at the outset of this study. This variance appeared by comparing the percentage shares of US social sectors of the total value of financial claims from 1960 to 2019. This chapter used a variety of additional sources to place this variance in context and to disaggregate the data by social class and type of asset, financial claim, liability, and the traditional indicators of the NIPAs.

108   *Finance and American household inequality*

The framework for the analysis of these diverse sources and indicators remained the classic modern categories of political economy. Further analysis of the complex relations across the wide variety of indicators in traditional sectoral and national income and production accounts, and the financial accounts as reported by the US Federal Reserve and BEA Integrated macroeconomic accounts, is beyond the scope of this chapter. However, the basic categories of classic modern political economy and the traditional aggregates of the NIPAs have provided a variety of insights about the political economy of households in the US. And comparison of the traditional data in the NIPAs and the financial balance-sheet data in the IMAs suggest that the core arguments of this book on compounding financialization and the political economy of banking and finance in the US are valid. So, too, are the claims about the need for historical–institutional analysis.

Increasing the number of observations back in time, paying attention to the traditional meanings and measure of the NIPAs to put the financial balance-sheet data into context, and disaggregating the variance to check for composition effects and underlying causes have revealed, in this chapter, a variety of insights into continuity and change in the place of households, labor, and the traditional sources of income and wealth in the US. However, the DFAs also indicate the profound differences across social class and the consequences of the financialization of income and wealth. Stretching the concepts of income and the double-counting of changes in the values of financial claims and liabilities are far more important than underlying structural changes in consumption, savings, wages, salaries, taxes, social policy transfers, and other complexities of US economic activities. However, to pursue the causal logic of compounding financialization, it is necessary to turn to an other social sector in US national accounts, the nonfinancial business sector.

Notes

1 The traditional term of households is defined as individuals living under the same roof. No bias toward traditional families or against new identities or living arrangements are implied.

2 The question of low inflation is central to the broader discussion of financialization in the previous volume, especially Chapters 1 and 2, while government policies of low interest rates are discussed in Chapter 3.

3 From 1979 to 2014 the Gini coefficient of Brazil fell from 6.0 to 5.3. This implies that wealth inequality in the US and Brazil were largely the same (5.3 vs 5.2) in 2014, notwithstanding the fact that the *per capita* income of the US remained four times that of Brazil, depending on foreign exchange value and other considerations.

4 Caution is also required with this aggregate of consumer credit because, among other types of credit, student loans are included. This is because of the practice of classifying credit as either long-term mortgages or other types of (supposedly) short-term credits.

5 Like the preceding volume, this book uses the term 'financial claims' instead of financial assets to avoid confusing the attributes of these items with the attributes of

nonfinancial assets. This is taken from Financial Stability Board reports and helps readers avoid the misconceptions in economic approaches that are the object of critique in this study.

References

Atkinson, Anthony. (2015). *Inequality*. Cambridge, MA: Harvard University Press.

Atkinson, Anthony and François Bourguignon. (eds). (2015). *Handbook of income distribution*. Amsterdam: New Holland (2 vols).

Atkinson, Anthony., Thomas Piketty, and Emmanuel Saez. (2011). 'Top incomes in the long run of history.' *Journal of Economic Literature*, 49(1): 3–71.

Auclert, Adrien. (2019). 'Monetary policy and the redistribution channel.' *American Economic Review*, 109(6): 2333–67.

Barnes, Karen. (2020). *Low income families and the new welfare state*. Ann Arbor, MI: University of Michigan Press.

Barnes, Jonathan and Anthony Kenny. (eds). (2014). *Aristotle's Ethics: Writings from the complete works*. Princeton, NJ: Princeton University Press.

Bartscher, Alina K., Moritz Kuhn, Moritz Schularick, and Ulrike I. Steins. (2020). 'Modigliani meets Minsky: Inequality, debt, and financial fragility in America, 1950–2016.' Institute for New Economic Thinking, Working Paper No. 124.

Batty, Michael., Jesse Bricker, Joseph Briggs, Elizabeth Holmquist, Susan McIntosh, Kevin Moore, Eric Nielsen, Sarah Reber, Molly Shatto, Kamila Sommer, Tom Sweeney, and Alice Henriques Volz. (2019). 'Introducing the distributional financial accounts of the United States.' Washington, DC: Board of Governors of the Federal Reserve System: Finance and Economics Discussion Series 2019–17.

Benhabib, Jess., Alberto Bisin, and Mi Luo. (2017). 'Earnings inequality and other determinants of wealth inequality.' *American Economic Review*, 107(5): 593–97.

Berle, Adolf A. and Gardiner Means. (1932). *The modern corporation and private property*. New York: Transaction.

Bowles, Samuel and Herbert Gintis. (2002). 'The inheritance of inequality.' *Journal of Economic Perspectives*, 16(3): 3–30.

Bureau of Commerce. (1934). 'National income 1929–1932.' Washington, DC: Government Printing Office.

Champernowne, David G. (1953). 'A model of income distribution.' *Economic Journal*, 114: 318–51.

Collier, David., Fernando D. Hidalgo, and Andra O. Maciuceanu. (2006). 'Essentially contested concepts: Debates and applications.' *Political Ideologies*, 11(3): 211–46.

Congressional Budget Office. (2019). 'Projected changes in the distribution of household income. Data underlying figures.' Washington, DC.

Foley, Duncan K., Thomas R. Michl, and Daniele Tavani. (2019). *Growth and distribution*. Cambridge, MA: Harvard University Press.

Gallie, Walter B. (1956). 'Essentially contested concepts.' *Proceedings of the Aristotelian Society*, 56: 167–98.

Gordon, Robert and Ian Dew-Becker. (2008). 'Controversies about the rise of American inequality: A survey.' Chicago, IL. NBER Working Paper No. 13982.

Gornemann, Nils., Keith Kuester, and Makoto Nakajima. (2016). 'Doves for the rich, hawks for the poor? Distributional consequences of monetary policy.' Washington, DC: Board of Governors of the Federal Reserve System: International Finance Discussion Papers No. 1167.

110 *Finance and American household inequality*

Gouge, William. (1833). *A short history of paper money and banking.* New York: T. W. Ustick.

Greve, Bent. (ed). (2018). *The Routledge handbook of the welfare state.* London: Routledge.

Klein, Steven. (2020). *The work of politics: Making a democratic welfare state.* Cambridge: Cambridge University Press.

Knafo, Samuel and Sahil J. Dutta. (2016). 'Patient capital in the age of financialized managerialism.' *Socio-Economic Review,* 14(4): 771–88.

Kuznets, Simon. (1955). 'Economic growth and income inequality.' *The American Economic Review,* 45(1): 1–28.

Luetticke, Ralph. (2015). *Transmission of monetary policy with heterogeneity in household portfolios.* Bonn: University of Bonn.

Mettenheim, Kurt. (2021). *Political economy, banking, and financialization: A historical-institutional balance-sheet study of the United States.* London: Routledge.

Nell, Edward. (2019). *Henry George and how growth in real estate contributes to inequality and financial instability.* New York: Palgrave Macmillan.

Piketty, Thomas. (2014). *Capital in the twenty-first century.* Cambridge, MA: Harvard University Press.

Piketty, Thomas., Emmanuel Saez, and Gabriel Zucman. (2018). 'Distributional national accounts: Methods and estimates for the United States.' *The Quarterly Journal of Economics,* 133(2): 553–609.

Saez, Emmanuel and Gabriel Zucman. (2016). 'Wealth inequality in the Unites States since 1913: Evidence from capitalized income tax data.' *The Quarterly Journal of Economics,* 131(2): 519–78.

Stiglitz, Joseph E. (2015). 'New theoretical perspectives on the distribution of wealth and inequality among individuals.' NBER Working Paper Nos. 21189–92. Part I, The wealth residual (21189); Part II, Equilibrium wealth distributions (21190); Part III, Life cycle savings vs inherited savings (21191); Part IV, Land and credit (21192).

Stiglitz, Joseph E. (1969). 'Distribution of income and wealth among individuals.' *Econometrica,* 37(3): 382–97.

3 The financialization of American nonfinancial business

Olivier Butzbach

Introduction

The literature on financialization lays much emphasis on the increasing reliance of nonfinancial firms on financial revenue as symptom of the transformation of the Chandlerian, Fordist business corporation into vehicles for value extraction to the benefit of rentier investors. This view seems to be confirmed by a significant number of empirical studies. However, it has also been criticized for overlooking problems of measurement and misidentification. This chapter revisits these issues by drawing on a variety of aggregate data sources and broadening the focus to consider both the income structure and balance-sheet structure of nonfinancial business enterprises in the US. The US business sector does indeed exhibit strong signs of income and asset financialization. However, both trends may reflect the long-term increase in the overall indebtedness of the US corporate sector. A historical–institutional approach to these trends in the US sheds new light on the financialization/rentieralization narrative. The evidence also suggests these channels of financialization are concentrated in the largest and most internationalized US corporations. The data from the US also evidence significant differences between the trajectories of financialization that obtain for unincorporated and incorporated business enterprises.

Financialization is a multi-sided phenomenon, reflecting the rise of the financial sector, the increasing importance of financial sector profits for the economy as a whole, and the rise of financial claims, revenue, and debt for nonfinancial sectors; households, government, nonfinancial firms; and between domestic economies and the rest of the world (Epstein, 2015; Krippner, 2011; Orhangazi, 2008; Crotty, 2005). This phenomenon is usually historically situated after the 1970s, representing a significant break between a 'pre-financialized' era and a 'post-financialized' era (see, for instance, Krippner, 2011, and Orhangazi, 2008). Within the many debates about financialization, the transformation of nonfinancial corporations (NFCs) is particularly important because it purportedly reveals the growing reliance of NFCs on finance and financial markets for their income and profits. It is widely argued, thereby, that the 'Fordist' or 'Chandlerian' NFC of the pre-financialization era was mostly shielded from financial market pressures and driven to achieve mostly nonfinancial results.

DOI: 10.4324/9781003223320-4

112 *Finance and American business*

This is the view held within the part of the financialization literature that focuses on the governance of firms and associates financialization with the emergence and impact of the 'shareholder primacy' revolution or 'shareholder value' paradigm on the governance and business strategies of NFCs. According to this perspective, the emergence and dominance of shareholder primacy has led to a shift in NFC strategy from 'retaining and reinvesting' cash flows to 'downsize-and-distribute' payouts to shareholders (Lazonick and O'Sullivan, 2000).

Such a shift in strategy is widely believed to have contributed to socially damaging outcomes from firm-level phenomena, such as increased short-termism (Davis, 2018; Epstein, 2015; Stout, 2012; Crotty, 2005); hoarding (Clarke, 2013); and the enrichment of the rentier class at the expense of the firm's stakeholders through higher payouts and, especially, buybacks of shares (Lazonick, 2014, 2015). Paradoxically, moreover, the pursuit of shareholder value has not benefited shareholders: resulting neither in significant improvements in profitability (Fligstein and Shin, 2007), nor in increased shareholder returns (Stout, 2012). These findings are partially in line with claims made in the heterodox economics literature concerning the macroeconomic effects of financialization. A staple of such claims is that financialization may explain the so-called 'profits-without-investment' puzzle that is seen to characterize the US, and other advanced economies, since the 1980s (Hein, 2012; Stockhammer, 2004; and see Sotiropoulos and Hillig, 2020 for a review).

This 'profits-without-investment' puzzle has a potentially significant bearing on the explanations of the shifts in inter-sectoral dynamics, as reflected in the structural shifts in macro-sectoral balance sheets that are a central concern of this study. Drawing on a Neo-Kaleckian model, Hein observed that profits can survive low investment only through either one (or a combination) of the following trends: higher consumption, rising exports, or increasing government surpluses (Hein et al., 2015; Hein, 2012). However, in the context of low or stagnant wages (a key mechanism leading to a return to NFC profitability in the 1980s), and against the backdrop of the decline in the labor income share of national incomes, this is possible only through increased indebtedness. According to this perspective, financialization in the US (prior to the 2007–2008 financial crisis), took the form of a debt-driven consumption boom (Hein, 2012; Hein and Van Treeck, 2010; van Treeck, 2009). Moreover, this particular growth regime may be self-sustaining. The decreased purchasing power from 'real' income leads households to rely more and more on price increases on the market for financial liabilities. On the other hand, this consumption boom cannot sustain effective demand at a high level. Depressed long-term demand therefore reduces the quasi-rents that NFCs could previously expect to earn from capital (real) investments, thus encouraging NFCs to rely on financial investments (Dögüs, 2018).[1]

More broadly, most heterodox approaches emphasize the endogenous causes of financialization, incorporating the 'shareholder primacy' narrative within more structuralist frameworks. For Marxist approaches and neo-Marxian schools (such as the French Regulation School), the collapse of the Fordist

Finance and American business 113

accumulation regime and its gradual replacement with a finance-dominated regime were caused by a continuous decline in the profitability of NFCs, which resulted, in turn, from a combination of endogenous causes (exhaustion of the Fordist regime) and external shocks such as the oil price shocks of the 1970s (Aglietta, 1976, 2019). For post-Keynesians, on the other hand, financialization reflects the restoration of the power of the 'rentier' class, who reacted against a long period of negative real interest rates (Hein et al., 2015; Smithin, 1996) by reasserting their claims on economic policy. Within the post-Keynesian framework, furthermore, a distinction may be made between two approaches. First, the Neo-Kaleckian approaches of Hein and colleagues see the financialization of NFCs as associated with a 'rentierialization' of capitalism. From this perspective, the increasing payments of NFCs to the rentier class (i.e. financial investors) are the main cause of the slowdown in capital accumulation (Hein, 2012; Hein and Van Treeck, 2010). Second, Minskian approaches, on the contrary, emphasize the 'overcapitalized' nature of NFCs and support the idea of weak capital accumulation being caused primarily by depressed demand (Dögüs, 2018).

The heterodox economic accounts of financialization are partially compatible with narratives that take politics more seriously, such as the influential thesis of Krippner, who argued that the shift to financialization was the inadvertent outcome of US government policies geared toward 'avoid[ing] a series of social, economic and political dilemmas' that they faced in the late 1960s and 1970s (Krippner, 2011). However, this book, and its preceding volume, argue that the specific trajectory of financialization in the US cannot be reduced to general 'laws of motion' of capitalism. In fact, Krippner's account illustrates, precisely, the specificity of the dilemmas of the late 1960s and 1970s in the US. Moreover, recent studies have shown how the account of a shareholder-driven, stock market-based transformation of the NFCs in the 1980s may be overstated. Indeed, as Knafo and Dutta have pointed out, the financialization of NFCs may owe much more than originally thought to the managerial strategies put in place in US conglomerates in the 1960s – what they call 'financialized managerialism' (Knafo and Dutta, 2016, 2020). Such techniques and strategies were adopted by outsiders to the established corporate elite, successfully challenging incumbent executives by using the leverage provided by financial markets. This historical explanation is consistent with Baines and Hager's analysis of corporate leverage as power (Baines and Hager, 2020), which also explains the different debt trajectories of large and small firms, as will be seen below. Perhaps more importantly, Knafo and Dutta's narrative provides an insight relevant for understanding the organizational changes undergone by large US conglomerates in subsequent decades. In particular, the *de jure* disintegration of US corporations in the 1980s and 1990s (Schwartz, 2020) may be viewed as the continuation of managerial strategies to draw on financial techniques and instruments to ensure the persistence of dominant positions in a changed macroeconomic environment.

The validity of such narratives, however, can be fully ascertained only with the hindsight of a detailed empirical investigation of the financialization of US NFCs over the past few decades. This chapter combines the approaches of

114   *Finance and American business*

historical–institutionalism and balance-sheet analysis to argue that a broader view of financialization (than the one offered in the heterodox literature on financialization) is required to capture important aspects of the transformation of the US business sector in the past 40 years. This implies consideration of different measures of financialization; looking first at income and profits, then sectoral balance sheets to consider nonfinancial assets, financial claims, and liabilities. Finally, a closer look at the differences and similarities between the trajectories of incorporated and unincorporated business firms will be used to shed light on the financialization of NFCs in the US and explore the importance of alternative paradigms.

Nonfinancial corporations and the rise of financial income

A good starting point for a discussion of the financialization of NFCs is the analysis of income and profits. A widespread view in the financialization literature is that, over time, NFCs have increasingly relied on financial sources of income and profits. Various measures have been proposed to capture this phenomenon. Orhangazi uses interest and dividend income as a percentage of gross value-added (Orhangazi, 2008); Krippner uses the ratio of portfolio income to corporate cash flows, with portfolio income construed as total earnings from interest, dividends, and capital gains on investments, and corporate cash flow corresponding to profits plus depreciation allowances (Krippner, 2011: 34). For Krippner, net measures of financial income, such as the one used by Duménil and Lévy in their 2004 book, can be misleading when assessing the extent of financialization. Krippner notes: 'if the objective is to provide a measure of financialization, netting out assets and liabilities is a problematic procedure' (Krippner, 2011: 174). Both Orhangazi and Krippner calculate financial income ratios with data from the Bureau of Economic Analysis (BEA) National income and product accounts (NIPAs) and, in Krippner's case, from the Internal Revenue Service (IRS) Statistics of Income.

Both Orhangazi and Krippner find a significant increase in the value of their respective measures of financial income, starting in the early 1970s. It is of note that most of the rise in portfolio income experienced by US corporations since the 1970s consisted in interest income (less so in dividends and capital gains). In other words, as Krippner points out, 'the increase in portfolio income was more a product of interest income swelling firm coffers as higher interest rates became embedded in the economy than it was a result of the soaring stock market of the 1980s and 1990s' (Krippner, 2011: 37). This argument is in line with the observation made by Orhangazi (2008) and several widely cited works within the first wave of financialization studies (see, for instance, Stockhammer, 2004). Yet other scholars, like Fiebiger (2016), find the high correlation between US NFC interest income, on the one hand, and monetary policy interest rates, on the other, further evidence of the conjunctural nature and volatility of financialization. Indeed, by replicating Krippner's measure of NFC portfolio income as a percentage of cash flow, Fiebiger finds a sharp decline in the value of this indicator starting in the early 1990s – corresponding to a decrease in interest rates set by US monetary policy (Fiebiger, 2016).

Table 3.1 displays, from 1950 to 2017 in decade averages, the value of the indicator used by Orhangazi (2008); that is, financial income divided by gross value-added. The latter, one may argue, may be more appropriate than cash flow measures used by Krippner (2011) and Fiebiger (2016) given that the latter are more susceptible to accounting and financial decisions. Table 3.1 indicates that, indeed, the 'financialization of income' of NFCs proceeded apace during the period in consideration, that is, between the 1970s and mid-2000s. Indeed, the significantly higher weight of financial income on value-added continued until the 2007–2008 financial crisis, after which it started to drop.

Figure 3.1 provides further information on the persistent high level of financial income over time, displaying nonfinancial corporate financial income and financial payout ratios from 1958 to 2019. While there is indeed some correlation between financial income to value-added and the real interest rate, this correlation is not perfect. Noticeably, as can be seen in Figure 3.1, monetary policy easing and low inflation, first in the mid-1980s to the mid-1990s, then

Table 3.1 Decade average value of the financial income ratio for US nonfinancial corporations

	1958–1968	1969–1979	1980–1990	1991–2001	2002–2007	2008–2017
Financial income ratio	2.07%	3.50%	6.03%	5.56%	5.78%	3.35%

Source: Internal Revenue Service (IRS) Sources of Income.

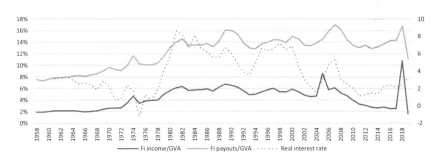

Figure 3.1 US nonfinancial corporate financial income and financial payout ratios, 1958–2019.
Note: The financial income ratio is calculated, following Orhangazi (2008), as interest+dividend/gross value-added; the financial payout ratio is calculated as interest paid+dividend paid/gross value-added. Financial income and financial payout ration = left scale. Real interest rates = right scale.

Sources: Internal Revenue Service (IRS) (for income data); International Monetary Fund International Financial Statistics and World Bank (for real interest rates).

116 *Finance and American business*

in the early 2000s, have not led to a significant decrease in the importance of financial income (and especially interest income) over that period, contrary to what Fiebiger argues (Fiebiger, 2016).

The income statements of US NFCs highlight another important aspect of financialization, that is, the increasing weight of financial payouts of NFCs to investors and shareholders. This is where the rentierialization of corporations becomes more obvious. This aspect has already been pointed out in the financialization literature (see, for instance, Orhangazi, 2008), and is a key argument raised by scholars emphasizing shareholder value maximization as the logic underpinning financialization (Lazonick, 2014, 2015; Lazonick and O'Sullivan, 2000). Figure 3.1 displays a first rough measure of a 'financial payout ratio' similar to the one used by Orhangazi (2008). Several observations can be made about the data showed in that figure. First, the two ratios (financial income and financial payout) show similar patterns, that is, an increase in their significance (with respect to value-added) in the 1970s (the early 1970s for the financial payout ratio) until the 1980s and their persistent high levels (compared to the post-WWII era) throughout the 1990s until the 2007–2008 crisis.

Second, the financial payout ratio has been consistently higher than the financial income ratio for the whole period. This lends support to the view of NFCs as an important site of value extraction for rentier investors, which is a staple of financialization (Lazonick, 2015; Crotty, 2005; Duménil and Lévy, 2004). Indeed, the financial payout ratio has consistently been higher than 12.8 percent of gross value-added between 1980 and 2018 – a remarkable stability dented by two accelerations (in the late 1980s and 2004–2006). Moreover, while the increase in real interest rates may explain part of the rise in interest paid during the late 1970s to mid-1980s, it is the increase in dividends paid, from the mid-1980s, that fed the increase in financial payouts. This can be seen in greater detail in Figure 3.2: dividend payouts have increased from 4.01 percent of gross value-added in 1987 (the same level as in the mid-1970s), to a peak of 11.6 percent in 2018 (but note a similarly high average level of 7.8 percent during the 2010s). This, again, seems to run counter to Fiebiger's objections.

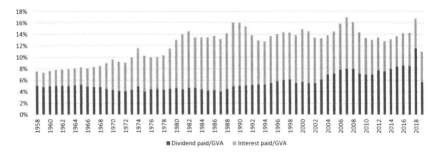

Figure 3.2 Breakdown of financial payout ratios, 1958–2019.
Source: Internal Revenue Service (IRS) Sources of Income.

Finance and American business 117

The financial payout ratio used here, it should be emphasized, does not incorporate the value of share buybacks, which have been common practice among the large US public corporations over the last two decades (Aramonte, 2020; Zeng and Luk, 2020; Davis, 2016, 2018; Lazonick, 2014). According to one estimate, share buybacks have exceeded dividends since 2007 (Zeng and Luk, 2020). Another author estimates that, between 2010 and 2019, US corporations have distributed $4 trillion in dividends and $6 trillion in buybacks – while they issued equity for about $6 trillion (Aramonte, 2020). Incorporating into the financial payout ratio, calculated above, a very rough estimate of buybacks (at an average value of 3/2 of dividends of the period 1997–2017), we obtain an approximate value comprised between 25 percent and 33 percent of gross value-added.

Perhaps a more accurate measure of the rentieralization of NFCs can be obtained by measuring financial payouts as a percentage of profits. This can be proxied as net operating surplus, displayed in Figure 3.3 from 1947 to 2019. The value extraction implied by financialization is even more blatant, as one can see that the part of profits destined to financial stakeholders (creditors and shareholders) more than doubled between the 1960s and 1980s, with peak years where together, interest and dividend payments represented more than 100 percent of net operating surplus.

However, comparing gross financial flows with profits might be misleading, as Krippner has shown. Moreover, the nature of financial income as it is accounted for can also lead to overestimation of financialization. In particular, Krippner acknowledges that outsourcing and subsidiary ownership may question the validity of her findings – whereby financialization 'may in reality be an artifact of the reorganization of firms, such that financial activities that once took place inside nonfinancial firms now take place outside of them' (Krippner, 2011: 42). She answers these concerns by arguing, first, that outsourcing affects financialization in two opposite ways: it decreases NFCs' portfolio income by depriving corporations from interest income captured by financial

Figure 3.3 Financial payouts as percentage of net operating surplus, 1947–2019.

Note: Financial payouts are calculated as the sum of interest and dividends paid.

Source: Federal Reserve Flow of Funds Accounts.

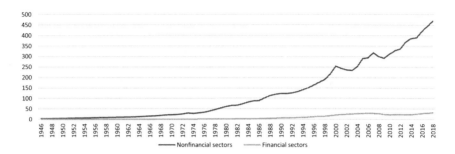

Figure 3.4 Nonfinancial and financial trade receivable assets, 1946–2019, $billion.
Source: Federal Reserve Z1 Accounts.

corporations, while it increases the ratio of financial sector profits. Of course, when focusing on nonfinancial corporations only, as in this chapter, the negative impact of outsourcing on financialization should stand out. Is that the case? Krippner mentions trade receivables, which, she argues, have been, since the 1970s, increasingly outsourced to financial firms. Does the data support such a claim? Figure 3.4 reports current US dollar values of trade receivable assets held by US nonfinancial and financial firms since 1946. As one can see, the values of nonfinancial corporations' holdings of trade receivables has significantly increased over the period – much more than trade receivables assets held by the financial sector. While not in line with Krippner's argument,[2] this reinforces the central thesis of the book, that is, that financialization has represented a fundamental transformation in the financial position of the main sectors of the US economy – not simply a redistribution of financial claims across sectors.

In her 2011 book, Krippner also addresses the issue of subsidiary formation, an important feature of the transformation of US corporations over the past 50 years (see Boies and Prechel, 2002). Krippner argues that such a type of corporate reorganization might threaten the validity of her analysis; the creation of subsidiaries 'artificially' inflates dividend income, by contrast with higher dividend income resulting from the 'growing orientation of nonfinancial firms to financial markets' (Krippner, 2011: 43). Yet such dividend income inflation might very well vindicate a logic of financialization as well, whereby top management seeks to increase capital extraction from the firm's business divisions. In other words, financialization can encompass corporate strategies that go beyond direct operational involvement in financial markets. Here, Krippner's approach can be combined with Knafo and Dutta's historical account of 'financialized managerialism' (Knafo and Dutta, 2016, 2020); and especially with Schwartz's recent study of the 'franchise model of the corporation,' which substituted the conglomerate model of the 1960s and early 1970s (Schwartz, 2020). In this model, large corporations rely on de facto control of legally autonomous subsidiaries and intellectual property rights to extract monopolistic rents (Schwartz, 2020).

Finance and American business 119

Another issue addressed by Krippner concerns the potential confusion of financialization with the consequences of the globalization of US corporation production processes, whereby 'production increasingly occurs offshore but financial functions continue to be located in the domestic economy' (Krippner, 2011: 45). Krippner minimizes this risk by showing, first, that the foreign portfolio income of US corporations has remained, between 1978 and 1999, quite small with respect to domestic portfolio income. Second, the offshore activities of US corporations are even more financialized than domestic ones.

Recent studies have reiterated this challenge. Fiebiger argues that what US corporations have been subjected to in the past 30 years is not financialization (defined as shareholder pressure for downsize-and-distribute policies), but, instead, globalization, pursued by senior managers seeking to shift 'operations to the international sphere to expand foreign market share and to export back to advanced-economy markets while minimising labour costs and taxation' (Fiebiger, 2016: 354–5). In particular, Fiebiger criticizes the use of corporate dividends as proxies for financialization, showing that they represent, instead, a measure of the growing strategy of 'external accumulation' preferred by US NFCs. Indeed, both Fiebiger (2016) and Rabinovich (2019) show that, since the late 1990s, US NFCs have shifted an increasingly significant part of their operations and assets overseas, for a variety of motives that are only, in part, financial. Notably, the ratio of US NFC overseas affiliate assets to parent company assets has risen substantially; from about 0.3 in 1990 to 1.05 in 2012 (Fiebiger, 2016). Fiebiger further argues that this rise in the assets of foreign affiliates has arisen, in large part, from the outsourcing of operations.

More importantly, according to Rabinovich, NFC financial income as a proportion of total income has not dramatically increased, as is claimed by proponents of the financial rentieralization hypothesis (Rabinovich, 2019). In fact, both Fiebiger and Rabinovich aim at rebuking this hypothesis by demonstrating the low degree to which the profits of US NFCs originated in financial investments. However, both acknowledge some degree of increase in NFC financial assets as a proportion of total assets (Rabinovich, 2019; Fiebiger, 2016). In addition, the significant financial losses found by Rabinovich for a sample of large US NFCs during the 2010s do not disprove, but rather confirm, the growing (if ill-conceived or managed) financialization of those corporations. Overall, therefore, the data showed here confirms the widely held view that NFCs' financial revenues and income have significantly increased as a proportion of total income, since the late 1970s. This financialization of NFCs' income, moreover, reflects more than a conjuncture more favorable to financial income: real interest rates did increase very significantly with the monetarist turn of the Federal Reserve's policy under Chairman Paul Volcker after 1979, but they remained at a high level for only a handful of years – while 'income financialization' is a much longer-lasting phenomenon. This, therefore, must reflect more fundamental changes in NFCs' strategies and in their balance sheets.

In addition, and more fundamentally, this book suggests that basing claims about financialization on income streams exposes the observation to potential

120 *Finance and American business*

conceptual stretching and mis-aggregation – and the netting of financial claims and liabilities. This is why the analysis must disentangle claims from liabilities, which is done in the next two sub-sections.

Nonfinancial corporations and the rise of financial assets

One of the drivers of financialization, according to the studies linking financialization to rentierealization, is the lure of higher returns from financial investment as opposed to productive investment (Lin and Tomaskovic-Devey, 2013; Krippner, 2011; Orhangazi, 2008; Stockhammer, 2004). This is reflected in changes in the structure of NFC balance sheets, with a rise in financial assets in proportion to total assets. Many different studies have reported evidence to document such increases (Davis, 2016, 2018; Krippner, 2011; Orhangazi, 2008; Crotty, 2005). Drawing on Compustat firm-level data, Davis shows a remarkable increase in 'median financial asset holdings' from 27 percent of sales in 1971 to 41.8 percent of sales in 2014 (Davis, 2018). Those findings are in line with earlier studies on US corporate cash holdings (Bates et al., 2009). Aggregate, Flow of funds data confirm these findings (see also Orhangazi, 2008, who uses the same data). The preceding volume to this book found that the most rapid increase in value of the financialization index (the ratio of financial over nonfinancial assets), among US social sectors was experienced by the nonfinancial business sector (corporate especially, but also unincorporated business), together with the federal government. In addition, as one can see from Figure 3.5, the ratio of NFCs' financial assets to total assets has increased from about 22 percent in 1951 to 47.99 percent in 2002, and remained between 44.5 percent and 50 percent over the subsequent 16 years.

A primary item that, in the literature, regularly embodies the increase in financial assets held by NFCs is cash. In mainstream corporate finance studies, the cash holdings of nonfinancial corporations are determined by firm-level factors, such as cash flow risk and the availability of growth opportunities. Cash holdings thus result from managerial decisions about optimal cash levels, driven

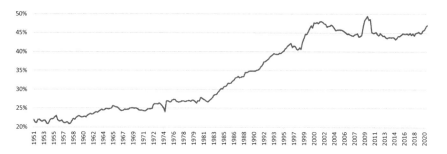

Figure 3.5 The financial assets of nonfinancial corporations, percentage total US assets, 1951–2020.
Source: Federal Reserve Flow of Funds Accounts, FRED database.

by a trade-off between the costs and benefits attached to cash (Opler et al., 1999). The strong influence of agency theory on mainstream corporate finance means that the costs of cash are, indeed, costs to shareholders more than to the firm itself (Jensen, 1986). However, the empirical results generated by such literature are not conclusive as to whether agency costs do drive cash holdings (Opler et al., 1999); indeed, there is little evidence to argue so (Bates et al., 2009). Yet, the cash holdings of US NFCs have markedly increased since the 1970s, as widely observed (for example, Davis, 2016, 2018; Bates et al., 2009). Bates et al. (2009) for instance, find a doubling of cash holdings among US industrial firms between 1980 and 2006; Davis (2018) finds a threefold increase in cash holdings relative to sales, between 1971 (with 4.8 percent) and 2014 (14.6 percent). Davis finds these results to be in line with the financial rentierialization of NFC hypothesis since, as she notes, the measure for cash she uses in her analysis of firm-level (Compustat) data includes short-term interest-bearing assets – such as short-term investment, commercial paper, marketable securities, money market funds, repurchase agreements, and term deposits (Davis, 2018: 5).[3] In contrast with the low causal purchase of agency cost theory, Davis finds, indeed, that cash holdings are positively and strongly correlated with a growing 'shareholder orientation' within firms' management (proxied by stock repurchase frequency; see Davis, 2018).[4]

Beyond cash holdings, the interpretation of the increase in financial assets depends on the type and source of data used. As Krippner points out in her 2011 book, her data on corporate income sources does not enable her to assess 'whether increases in portfolio income over the period reflect the increased acquisition of financial assets or higher returns on an existing portfolio of assets' (Krippner, 2011: 37). Krippner then argues that the available data does not allow us to convincingly answer this question. The data she presents (extracted from the Federal Reserve Flow of Funds database) does show a marked increase, starting in the early 1980s, of the net acquisition of financial assets (relative to other assets). However, the broad category of 'financial assets' used by the Fed incorporates unspecified items, such as 'other assets' that includes items ambiguously linked to financialization, like goodwill. Financialization 'skeptics' such as Fiebiger and Rabinovich, emphasize this point. Through a simple breakdown of financial assets as construed by the Federal Reserve in its 'Flow of funds' data, both authors show the very rapid growth, since the 1970s, of 'unidentified miscellaneous financial assets' (Rabinovich, 2019; Fiebiger, 2016).

As a matter of fact, the growth in such assets represents the most important component, by far, of the growth in financial assets broadly defined (a phenomenon also emphasized by Orhangazi, 2008 and Crotty, 2005). There is, by definition, little certainty as to what these assets are. Fiebiger cites some sources who mention goodwill and intangible assets, such as copyrights, patents, trademarks; in a footnote, he notes that in 2012, US NFCs reported to the IRS a total value of intangibles that represented 72 percent of the category of 'unidentified miscellaneous financial assets' in the Fed Flow of funds (Fiebiger, 2016: 367). As mentioned by Rabinovich, a more recent publication by the Federal Reserve

122   *Finance and American business*

provides a more specific definition of such assets, including goodwill together with deferred charges, intangibles and inter-corporate holdings of corporate equity (Rabinovich, 2019; see also Orhanghazi, 2019).

Goodwill is important because it constitutes a large chunk of intangible assets on US NFC balance sheets.[5] However, the financial or nonfinancial status of goodwill is uncertain. Goodwill corresponds to the difference between the book value of an acquired firm and the amount paid by the acquirer,[6] which is supposed to embody the routines, culture, procedures that make up the acquired firm's value. It is measured through annual impairment tests, in accordance with International Accounting Standards (IAS), specifically IAS 36. According to authors such as Rabinovich (2019), goodwill must be distinguished from financial assets strictly defined. But can it?

Goodwill, after all, reflects the market value (rather than some kind of accounting value) given to a business firm's idiosyncratic intangibles. Indeed, impairment is construed by reference to the price effectively paid by the acquirer, and the overall amounts of goodwill (and goodwill impairment) mirror, obviously, the overall value of mergers and acquisitions (M&As). Thus, changes in the significance of goodwill over time may be seen as reflecting the trends of M&As rather than any change in nonfinancial assets. For instance, a recent report by the specialized goodwill firm Duff & Phelps shows that goodwill was estimated at an overall $386 billion in 2018, up from 2017, with a 125 percent increase in goodwill impairment during that year; remarkably, goodwill impairment is very concentrated, with the top five cases of impairment corresponding to large M&A transactions that represent 57 percent of the overall increase (Duff and Phelps, 2020).

Furthermore, accounting for goodwill and goodwill impairment also changes over time. The increase in goodwill impairment that may be reconstructed from the 'miscellaneous' asset classes in Flow of Funds data might reflect such changes. Indeed, according to Ding et al. (2008), current goodwill accounting practices, which they call 'actuarial,' tend to recognize goodwill as full-fledged assets with no automatic amortization or write-offs (Ding et al., 2008).

In addition, as Rabinovich's data show, a growing share of NFC cash holdings has been destined, since the 1980s, to acquisitions (Rabinovich, 2019). This is consistent with the view that increasing goodwill reflects growing activism on the market for corporate control, expressing one type of financialization. Indeed, the hostile takeover wave of the 1980s, which established the importance of the market for corporate control in NFC business strategies, also ushered in an era dominated by the 'portfolio view' of the NFC (Crotty, 2005), a development seen as a key component of financialization. Finally, goodwill can be directly related, as Thorstein Veblen has pointed out (Veblen, 1908), to monopolistic rents that are perfectly in line with the rentieralization of the US corporation. As Schwartz argues, 'most mergers enhance or protect some kind of monopoly position that financial market actors then capitalize in equity markets' (Schwartz, 2020: 5). According to Crouzet and Eberly, rising industrial concentration and the increased importance of intangibles are both largely responsible for weak physical capital investment by US NFCs (Crouzet and Eberly, 2019).

The intensification of activities on the market for corporate control is perfectly compatible with rising monopolistic rents and might well constitute a further characteristic of financialization in the US. Indeed, there is evidence that US industries over the past two decades have become more concentrated (Grullon et al., 2019; Davis and Orhangazi, 2021), and that US firms' market power has increased (De Loecker et al., 2020). In conclusion, the increased significance of goodwill in 'miscellaneous' assets is more than consistent with increasingly financialized NFCs.

Beyond the issue of miscellaneous assets, however, some authors have cast doubt on the financialized nature of the increase in conventional financial assets, pitting, again, a globalization hypothesis against the financialization hypothesis (Rabinovich, 2019; Fiebiger, 2016). As Rabinovich points out, a large chunk of the increase in US NFC conventional financial assets consisted in the rise of US direct investment abroad. Rabinovich observes that 'it's dubious to directly consider FDI as a financial asset,' given that foreign direct investment implies a lasting interest in the investee – an argument reinforced by the fact that most US foreign affiliates are majority-owned (Rabinovich, 2019; Fiebiger, 2016). As a matter of fact, FDI has increased its share in the total financial assets of NFCs. According to the Federal Reserve Z1 accounts, foreign investment represented 7.5 percent of total financial assets in 1946; 12 percent in 1956; 18 percent in 1966; and 22.2 percent in 1976. After stagnating during the 1980s, US NFCs' FDI resumed their growth in the 1990s, reaching a plateau of 20–27 percent between 2004 and 2018 (except for 2008, when the global financial crisis depressed FDI across countries). However, between the 1970s and the 1990s, US NFCs also significantly increased their holdings of other types of financial assets, such as commercial paper, repos, and money market fund shares. Rabinovich presents evidence of the near complete disappearance of debt securities, which in 1945 represented 25 percent of NFCs' financial assets (minus miscellaneous assets) but declined to a few percentage points in 2015. Conversely, money market fund shares increased significantly, from zero in the 1970s to about 10 percent in 2015 (Rabinovich, 2019).

To conclude, the data show that financialization and globalization have walked hand in hand over the past 40 years. It is likely that part of what appears, in national accounts, as an increase in financial assets actually reflects ongoing processes of internationalization, at least among large US business firms. However, it is equally true that, over the same period, US NFCs have significantly increased their holdings of cash and a variety of liquid financial assets. This 'asset financialization' explains in part the 'income financialization' discussed above: rising NFC investment in financial assets has provided the basis for increasing generation of financial revenue.

A central argument of this book, however, is that a focus on income and asset financialization ignores the important dynamics characterizing the other side of corporate balance sheets, to which we now turn.

Nonfinancial corporations and the rise of debt

Much less attention, in the financialization literature, has been paid to the high indebtedness of nonfinancial corporations than to the rise of financial income or financial assets. Yet this is a critical aspect of financialization. As a matter of fact, increasing indebtedness can be seen as a 'way out' of the profit-investment puzzle mentioned above (Crotty, 2005; Duménil and Lévy, 2004). As Fiebiger points out, higher financial payouts to rentier investors may originate in increased borrowed funds, thus not weighing on productive investment (Fiebiger, 2016: 357). Debt, in addition, shows another set of critical economic relationships between business firms, on the one hand, and other social sectors.

Is debt or leverage really a good indicator of financialization? Increased or decreased leverage, *at the aggregate level*, may simply be the outcome of individual capital structure decisions taken by business enterprises. Swapping debt for equity and vice versa would signal shifts in financial strategy driven by changing conditions on the debt and equity markets. Such shifts may actually provide significant benefits to business firms. Thus, in his rebuttal of income financialization arguments, Fiebiger argues that the concern expressed about stock repurchase – one of the key arguments against financialization formulated by critical scholars such as Lazonick (2015) – is really misplaced: 'Swapping equity for debt may be conducive to accumulation if the strategy reduces claims on net income' (Fiebiger, 2016: 355).

A likely reason for the relatively lower attention paid to debt by the financialization literature may consist in the oft-repeated observation that US business firms have, between the early 1980s and the late 1990s, de-leveraged (see, for instance, D'Mello et al., 2018; Grennan et al., 2017). Indeed, as Figure 3.6 shows, whereas between 1954 and 1989 nonfinancial business debt never grew below 4 percent a year, 1990 and 1991 saw negative growth rates for the first time in 45 years. However, in the first quarter of 1993 nonfinancial business debt resumed growing at a fast pace again – before decreasing again ten

Figure 3.6 Nonfinancial business debt annualized quarterly percentage growth rate, 1952–2020.

Source: Federal Reserve Z1 Accounts.

Finance and American business 125

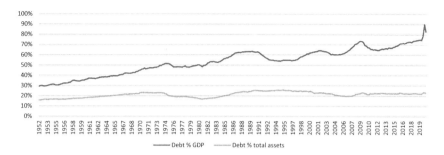

Figure 3.7 US nonfinancial business debt as percentage of GDP and total assets.
Source: Federal Reserve Z1 Accounts.

years later (specifically during the second half of 2003). Debt growth resumed apace again and, yet again, turned negative in 2009 – in the wake of the 2007–2008 financial crisis, the most severe financial crisis experienced by the US since 1929. De-leveraging was registered during 2020 during the COVID-19 pandemic.

Overall, therefore, nonfinancial business firms have experienced, in the past 65 years, four circumscribed episodes of de-leveraging – all concentrated in the second half of that 65-year period, and two of which (the last two) can be ascribed to severe external shocks. This seriously puts in question the de-leveraging narrative. More importantly, debt is cumulative. A broad measure of leverage as debt to GDP shows an almost constant increase of leverage in the nonfinancial business sector since the beginning of the period of observation (see Figure 3.7).

Figure 3.7 also shows a measure of nonfinancial corporate debt to total assets. This is a typical measure used in the capital structure literature – although, perhaps, not extremely useful in terms of capital structure analysis because, as Welch pointed out (Welch, 2011), its converse, (1−TD/TA) is comprised both of equity and nonfinancial liabilities. However, for our present purposes it can give us a rough estimate of the relative importance of total debt for US NFCs. Although less spectacular than the overall rise of debt as percentage of GDP, we do observe a significant increase of that measure over time – from around 16 percent in the beginning of the period to about 23.6 percent at the end.

Here again, like in the case of cash holdings, analyzed above, firm-level characteristics used in mainstream corporate finance cannot account for such a cumulative rise. As Graham, Leary, and Roberts put it in a recent study of US corporate leverage during the twentieth century, 'none of the average or aggregate [usual firm-level] characteristics change over the century in a way that would support greater debt capacity or higher optimal leverage' (Graham et al., 2015: 659); yet, leverage has undoubtedly increased over the years.

Changes in the composition of nonfinancial corporate debt in time are also significant. As Figure 3.8 shows, more than half of overall nonfinancial corporate

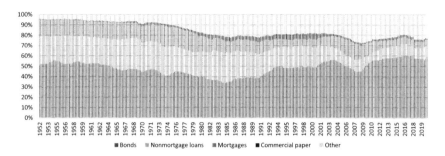

Figure 3.8 Composition of US nonfinancial corporation financial debt, 1952–2020.
Source: Federal Reserve Z1 Accounts.

debt consists of corporate bonds. However, this proportion has changed over time, experiencing a decline between the 1950s and the mid-1980s, only to bounce back since to reach a historical peak in 2016 at 60 percent of overall corporate debt. Equally remarkable is the decline of loans over the years, from about 45 percent at the beginning of the period to about 18 percent in 2020. Instead, 'other debt' has grown in importance.

A remarkable fact about US business firms' growing indebtedness is the timing of such a phenomenon: as shown in Figures 3.6 and 3.7, the lasting increase in corporate debt started in the early 1960s – roughly two decades before the rise of the 'shareholder primacy' paradigm usually seen as the main driver of NFCs' financialization. This is a crucial piece of information because it may change our view of the causal factors of financialization: in line with the 'compounding financialization' conceptualized in this book, long-term patterns of US corporate debt point to a liability-driven financialization of the US NFC, whereby the increasing weight of financial (debt) liabilities of NFCs may have led the latter to symmetrically increase their financial income-earning assets over time. This view is not at odds with the main arguments behind the 'rentierialization' thesis; it is just that the push to transform US corporations into rent-extraction machines did not originate in the increasing power of the shareholder and stock markets. Rather, the rentierialization of the US NFC may plunge its roots in the increasing financial interdependence of the latter with the financial sector – and, in particular, the banking and shadow banking system.

Nonfinancial corporations versus unincorporated business firms

Another central argument of this book is that financialization in the US varies for types of nonfinancial business enterprises. In studies relying on firm-level data, size is the usual parameter that allows the observer to differentiate individual trajectories of financialization (see, for instance, Davis, 2018). Indeed, increasing empirical evidence shows how financialization in the US corporate sector is driven by the largest, internationalized US firms (Soener, 2020). Thus Davis (2018) shows that share buybacks have been almost exclusively concentrated in large firms; Pinkowitz et al. (2013) show how high, abnormal cash holdings are concentrated in firms that are large and highly profitable; and Gu (2017) shows that US multinational corporations hold much more cash than domestic firms. On the liabilities side of the balance sheet, furthermore, Baines and Hager (2020) show that large and small US firms have experienced radically different trajectories, with regard to corporate debt, in the past decades: while large firms have combined rising leverage with debt service burden, smaller firms have been de-leveraging.

However, in addition to size, another useful distinction can be made: that between incorporated and unincorporated nonfinancial business enterprises. In the US, this distinction is quite relevant, as can be seen in Figures 3.9 and 3.10. Both figures draw on data from the BEA Integrated macroeconomic

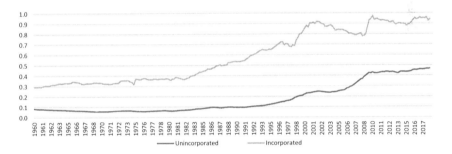

Figure 3.9 Financialization index for corporate and noncorporate business, 1960–2018.
Source: Department of Commerce Bureau of Economic Analysis, Integrated Macroeconomic Accounts.

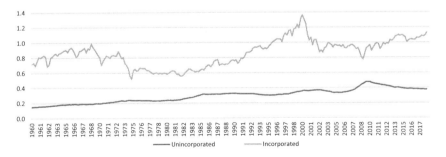

Figure 3.10 Leverage ratio for US corporate and noncorporate business, 1960–2018.
Source: Department of Commerce Bureau of Economic Analysis, Integrated Macroeconomic Accounts.
Note: Leverage ratio = liabilities / total assets.

accounts (IMAs) from 1960 to 2019 to show the financialization and leverage indexes, for incorporated and unincorporated business firms. The differences are striking. While both unincorporated and incorporated business sectors have undergone a significant increase in financialization, corporations overall appear to be much more financialized than unincorporated business firms. Similarly, while both sectors have experienced a higher exposure to debt (our leverage ratio), unincorporated business firms are significantly less levered, at the end of the period under study, than incorporated ones.

Figures 3.11 and 3.12 further break down our data into the quarterly current US dollar values of financial assets, nonfinancial assets, liabilities and net worth for, respectively, unincorporated nonfinancial businesses (Figure 3.11) and incorporated nonfinancial businesses (Figure 3.12).

Again, the differences are striking: Both sectors start the period of observation (1960) with (a) a higher level of nonfinancial assets than financial assets

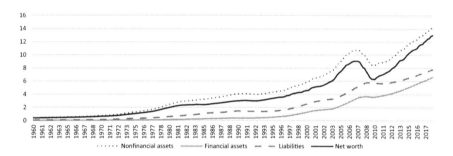

Figure 3.11 Balance-sheet totals for noncorporate business enterprises, 1960–2018, $trillion.

Source: Department of Commerce Bureau of Economic Analysis, Integrated Macroeconomic Accounts.

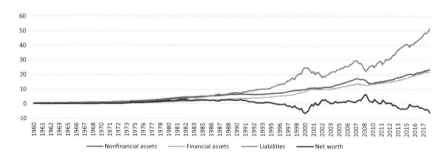

Figure 3.12 Balance-sheet totals for US corporate business enterprises, 1960–2018, $trillion.

Source: Department of Commerce Bureau of Economic Analysis, Integrated Macroeconomic Accounts.

Finance and American business 129

and (b) lower debt than nonfinancial assets. In 1960, both sectors reported a positive net worth. In subsequent years, both financial and nonfinancial assets have increased, together with liabilities. But while liabilities and financial assets of unincorporated business firms have grown at a similar pace (with liabilities being constantly below financial assets), enabling unincorporated firms to continue to report positive values of net worth, this has not been the case for incorporated businesses. As shown in Figure 3.12, US nonfinancial corporations (incorporated business enterprises), saw their liabilities (driven by financial debt, as seen in the previous section) increase exponentially during the 1990s, leading to negative net worth. Moreover, the liabilities of incorporated business enterprises exhibit a consistently higher degree of volatility over time. The variance of incorporated business liabilities is *33 times* higher than the variance of unincorporated business liabilities.

Distinguishing the trajectories of incorporated and unincorporated businesses is important for several reasons. First, as many authors have pointed out, the model of the US public corporation has been in decline for many years (see, for instance, Kahle and Stulz, 2017). Some observers have attributed this decline to financialization: The pressures of shareholder value maximization being such that the whole *raison d'être* of the corporate form (i.e. locking in capital for long-term investment) started to crumble (see Blair, 2003). Furthermore, the corporate form in general (not necessarily just the public corporation) seems to be less popular among business firms: Corporations accounted for 20.8 percent of all business returns to the IRS in 1980, against 17.5 percent in 2015. Second, whereas the aggregate data for the business sector does show common trends, it is important to identify the factors that may enhance or impede such trends – factors that can then be more conclusively observed with firm-level data, in studies such as the one by Rabinovich (2019).

Third, if these differences may lend credence to the latter, still, the fact that unincorporated business firms display common trends to incorporated ones does lend further support to the financialization thesis. Indeed, unincorporated business firms are less likely than incorporated ones to internationalize or outsource. This, however, represents a serious challenge for US capitalism, as the corporate form has been, historically, the main conduit for sustainable capital accumulation.

Conclusion

US business firms have undergone a radical transformation in the last quarter of the twentieth century – a well-documented shift from the 'Chandlerian-Fordist' firm, driven to retain profits, reinvest, and redistribute value to a broad range of stakeholders, to a leaner, more finance-oriented firm seeking to cut down and cost and distribute value to financial investors (Epstein, 2015; Lazonick, 2015; Orhangazi, 2008; Crotty, 2005; Lazonick and O'Sullivan, 2000). The data presented in this chapter confirms, to a large extent, the view of a largely financialized nonfinancial corporation. However, it does so by re-framing the

130 *Finance and American business*

financialization of NFCs within the broader context of inter-sectoral dynamics, whereby (1) NFCs have undergone a process of rentierialization starting in the late 1970s, a process reflecting the strategic shift represented by increased investment in financial assets and increased dependence on financial revenue for generating profits; and that (2) while such process can be partly attributed to the pressures of the shareholder value paradigm, it also relates to the increasing indebtedness of nonfinancial corporations, which did not result from conscious firm-level capital structure decisions, but the growing interconnectedness of the nonfinancial sector with the financial sector.

This is an important finding, as it helps recast the financialization of the US NFC within longer-term patterns of transformation of US capitalism, as suggested by Knafo and Dutta (2016, 2020). In this perspective, financialization is no longer seen as a transformation imposed upon the nonfinancial corporation from the outside – by rentier investors buoyed by booming financial markets. Rather, in line with Keynes' arguments, followed by Minsky and others, finance and 'real' production are not only 'co-determinants of the growth process' (Kregel, 2017): they have also been combined within managerially driven transformations of the corporation for quite some time.

In addition, the view of a liability-driven financialization of US NFCs compounds the notion that inter-sectoral dynamics are key to understand financialization in broad terms. The confusion of household savings with banks' and financial institutions' assets has already been explored at length in previous chapters; what this chapter shows is that the build-up of banks' and financial institutions' balance sheets were then instrumental in transforming the US corporation into rent-extraction vehicles. Thus, contrary to narratives that focus exclusively on the relationship between shareholder primacy and the financialization of US NFCs, we argue that there is a strong link between the financialization of households' balance sheets and the epochal transformation of the US business firm in the late twentieth century.

Notes

1 The main empirical findings that underlay heterodox economists' accounts of financialization are contested. The turnaround in corporate profits since the 1980s is generally not disputed (see Barkai and Benzell, 2018, for a recent longitudinal study). However, as Chapter 1 shows, it can be argued that investment in the US, *as a whole*, has not declined significantly since the 1980s. This is also the argument made by non-post-Keynesian heterodox economists such as Kliman and Williams (2015). However, there is solid evidence that, at the *firm-level*, physical capital accumulation has, indeed, decreased since the 1970s. This obtains relative to firm profitability (Gutiérrez and Philippon, 2016, 2017), as measured either as net operating surplus or as Tobin's Q. Moreover, this lower investment or investment gap seems to be structural in the US – as opposed to European economies, where it seems to be cyclical (Döttling et al., 2017). Divergent findings may be due to the types of data used, or measurement techniques. It may also reflect significant facts about the financialization of NFCs, such as the concentration of the 'profits-without-investments' puzzle within a small group of large corporations. This point will be further explored below.

Finance and American business   131

2 Our findings are also not strictly in line with Rabinovich (2019). Rabinovich argues that a meaningful assessment should take into consideration the value of receivables as percentage of total assets – whereby one can observe a decline in that ratio since the late 1960s. We are not contesting this result. Instead, we attempt to understand the specific implications for Krippner's explanation of financialization.

3 However, Rabinovich writes that 'the fact that NFCs are holding a higher proportion of cash and short-term investments does not seem to be related to a significant increase in the flow of financial income or an increased financial profitability. Therefore, the increase in cash and short-term investment is due to other motives' (Rabinovich, 2019: 15). One could argue that it is equally likely that low financial incomes and/or profitability might simply reflect the low returns associated with cash holding and short-term investment. In other words, the increase in the latter does not necessarily imply nonfinancial strategies.

4 In addition, focusing on the cash flow structure of US NFCs, Rabinovich notes that both the use and source of cash flows have changed over time. Notably, he points to the dramatic fall in the 'capital expenditure' use of cash flows, consistent with a drop in the value of fixed assets on US NFCs' balance sheets since the late 1960s – and with the hypothesis of financialization broadly defined (Rabinovich, 2019).

5 According to Rabinovich, who draws here on firm-level data from the Compustat database, goodwill represents between 50 percent and 60 percent of all intangibles (Rabinovich, 2019).

6 More precisely, goodwill is defined in international financial reporting standards as 'an asset representing the future economic benefits arising from other assets acquired in a business combination that are not individually identified and separately recognised' (IFRS, 2021).

References

Aglietta, Michel. (ed). (2019). *Capitalisme. Le temps des ruptures*. Paris: Odile Jacob.

Aglietta, Michel. (1976). *Régulation et crises du capitalisme*. Paris: Odile Jacob.

Aramonte, Sirio. (2020). 'Mind the buyback, beware of the leverage.' *BIS Quarterly Review*, December issue.

Baines, Joseph and Sandy Brian Hager. (2020). 'The great debt divergence and its implications for the Covid-19 crisis: Mapping corporate leverage as power.' *New Political Economy*. Available at: https://doi.org/10.1080/13563467.2020.1865900.

Barkai, Simcha and Seth G. Benzell. (2018). '70 years of US corporate profits.' Stigler Center for the Study of the Economy and the State, University of Chicago Booth School of Business, New Working Paper No. 22.

Bates, Thomas W., Kathleen M. Kahle, and René M. Stulz. (2009). 'Why do US firms hold so much more cash than they used to?' *The Journal of Finance*, 64(5): 1985–2021.

Blair, Margaret M. (2003). 'Locking in capital: What corporate law achieved for business organizers in the nineteenth century.' *University of California Law Review*, 51: 387.

Boies, John and Harland Prechel. (2002). 'Capital dependence, business political behavior, and change to the multilayered subsidiary form.' *Social Problems*, 49(3): 301–326.

Clarke, Thomas. (2013). 'Deconstructing the mythology of shareholder value: A comment on Lynn Stout's "The shareholder value myth."' *Accounting, Economics and Law: A Convivium*, 3(1): 15–42.

Crotty, James. (2005). 'The neoliberal paradox: The impact of destructive product market competition and "modern" financial markets on nonfinancial corporation

132 *Finance and American business*

performance in the neoliberal era,' in Gerald A. Epstein (ed) *Financialization and the world economy*. Cheltenham: Edward Elgar, pp. 77–110.

Crouzet, Nicolas and Janice Eberly. (2019) 'Understanding weak capital investment: The role of market concentration and intangibles.' NBER Working Paper No. 25869.

Davis, Leila. (2018). 'Financialization, shareholder orientation and the cash holdings of US corporations.' *Review of Political Economy*, 30(1): 1–27.

Davis, Leila. (2016). 'Identifying the "financialization" of the nonfinancial corporation in the US economy: A decomposition of firm-level balance sheets.' *Journal of Post Keynesian Economics*, 29(1): 115–141.

Davis, Leila and Özgür Orhangazi. (2021). 'Competition and monopoly in the US economy: What do the industrial concentration data show?' *Competition & Change*, 25(1): 3–30.

De Loecker, Jan., Jan Eeckhout, and Gabriel Unger. (2020). 'The rise of market power and the macroeconomic implications.' *The Quarterly Journal of Economics*, 135(2): 561–644.

Ding, Yuan., Jacques Richard, and Hervé Stolowy. (2008). 'Towards an understanding of the phases of goodwill accounting in four western capitalist countries: From stakeholder model to shareholder model.' *Accounting, Organizations and Society*, 33(7–8): 718–55.

D'Mello, Ranjan., Mark Gruskin, and Manoj Kulchania. (2018). 'Shareholders valuation of long-term debt and decline in firms' leverage ratio.' *Journal of Corporate Finance*, 48(C): 352–74.

Dögüs, Ilhan. (2018). 'A Minskyan critique of the financial constraint approach to financialization.' *Review of Keynesian Economics*, 6(2): 202–20.

Döttling, Robin., Germán Gutiérrez, and Thomas Philippon. (2017). 'Is there an investment gap in advanced economies? If so, why?' Unpublished Working Paper.

Duff & Phelps. (2020). '2019 US goodwill impairment study.' Available at: www.duffandphelps.com/GWIStudies.

Duménil, Gérard and Dominique Lévy. (2004). *Capital resurgent: Roots of the neoliberal revolution*. Cambridge, MA: Harvard University Press.

Epstein, Gerald A. (2015). 'Financialization: There is something happening here.' University of Massachusetts Amherst, Political Economy Research Institute, Working Paper No. 394.

Fiebiger, Brett. (2016). 'Rethinking the financialisation of non-financial corporations: A reappraisal of US empirical data.' *Review of Political Economy*, 28(3): 354–79.

Fligstein, Neil and Taekjin Shin. (2007). 'Shareholder value and the transformation of the US economy, 1984–2000.' *Sociological Forum*, 22(4): 399–424.

Graham, John R., Mark T. Leary, and Michael R. Roberts. (2015). 'A century of capital structure: The leveraging of corporate America.' *Journal of Financial Economics*, 118(3): 658–83.

Grennan, Jillian, Roni Michaely, and Christopher J. Vincent. (2017). 'The deleveraging of US firms and institutional investors' role.' Unpublished Working Paper, available at SSRN 1941902.

Grullon, Gustavo, Yelena Larkin, and Roni Michaely. (2019). 'Are US industries becoming more concentrated?' *Review of Finance*, 23(4): 697–743.

Gu, Tiantian. (2017). 'US multinationals and cash holdings.' *Journal of Financial Economics*, 125(2): 344–68.

Gutiérrez, Germán and Thomas Philippon. (2017). 'Declining Competition and Investment in the US.' NBER Working Paper No. 23583.

Gutiérrez, Germán and Thomas Philippon. (2016). 'Investment-less Growth: An Empirical Investigation.' NBER Working Paper No. 22897.

Hein, Eckhard. (2012). *The Macroeconomics of finance-dominated capitalism – and its crisis.* Cheltenham: Edward Elgar.

Hein, Eckhard and Till Van Treeck. (2010). 'Financialisation and rising shareholder power in Kaleckian/post-Kaleckian models of distribution and growth.' *Review of Political Economy,* 22(2): 205–33.

Hein, Eckhard, Nina Dodig, and Natalia Budyldina. (2015). 'The transition towards finance-dominated capitalism: French Regulationist School, Social Structures of Accumulation, and post-Keynesian approaches compared,' in Eckhard Hein, Daniel Detzer, and Nina Dodig (eds) *The demise of finance-dominated capitalism. Explaining the financial and economic crises.* Cheltenham: Edward Elgar, pp. 7–53.

IFRS (International Financial Reporting Standards). (2021). 'Issued standards.' Available at: www.ifrs.org/issued-standards/list-of-standards/.

Jensen, Michael C. (1986). 'Agency costs of free cash flow, corporate finance, and takeovers.' *The American Economic Review,* 76(2): 323–29.

Kahle, Kathleen M. and René M. Stulz. (2017) 'Is the US public corporation in trouble?' *Journal of Economic Perspectives,* 31(3): 67–88.

Kliman, Andrew and Shannon D. Williams. (2015). 'Why "financialisation" hasn't depressed US productive investment.' *Cambridge Journal of Economics,* 39(1): 67–92.

Knafo, Samuel and Sahil Jai Dutta. (2020). 'The myth of the shareholder revolution and the financialization of the firm.' *Review of International Political Economy,* 27(3): 476–99.

Knafo, Samuel and Sahil Jai Dutta. (2016). 'Patient capital in the age of financialized managerialism.' *Socio-Economic Review,* 14(4): 771–88.

Kregel, Jan. (2017). '"Isms" and "zations": On fictitious liquidity and endogenous financialization.' *Economia e Sociedade,* 26(SPE): 879–93.

Krippner, Greta R. (2011). *Capitalizing on crisis. The political origins of the rise of finance.* Cambridge, MA: Harvard University Press.

Lazonick, William. (2015). 'When managerial capitalism embraced shareholder-value ideology.' *International Journal of Political Economy,* 44(2): 90–99.

Lazonick, William. (2014). 'Profits without prosperity: Stock buybacks manipulate the market and leave most Americans worse off.' *Harvard Business Review,* September, 46–55.

Lazonick, William and Mary O'Sullivan. (2000). 'Maximizing shareholder value: a new ideology for corporate governance.' *Economy and Society,* 29(1): 13–35.

Lin, Ken-Hou and Donald Tomaskovic-Devey. (2013). 'Financialization and US income inequality, 1970–2008.' *American Journal of Sociology,* 118(5): 1284–329.

Opler, Tim, Lee Pinkowitz, René Stulz, and Rohan Williamson. (1999). 'The determinants and implications of corporate cash holdings.' *Journal of Financial Economics,* 52(1): 3–46.

Orhangazi, Özgür. (2019). 'The role of intangible assets in explaining the investment–profit puzzle.' *Cambridge Journal of Economics,* 43(5): 1251–86.

Orhangazi, Özgür. (2008). *Financialization and the US economy.* Cheltenham: Edward Elgar.

Pinkowitz, Lee, Rene M. Stulz, and Rohan Williamson. (2013). 'Is there a US high cash holdings puzzle after the financial crisis?' Ohio State University Fisher College of Business, Working Paper No. 2013–07.

Rabinovich, Joel. (2019). 'The financialization of the non-financial corporation: A critique to the financial turn of accumulation hypothesis.' *Metroeconomica,* 70(4): 738–75.

134 *Finance and American business*

Schwartz, Herman M. (2020). 'Intellectual property, technorents and the labour share of production.' *Competition & Change* (online). DOI: 10.1177/1024529420968221.

Smithin, John. (1996). *Macroeconomic policy and the future of Capitalism. The revenge of the rentiers and the threat to prosperity.* Cheltenham: Edward Elgar.

Soener, Matthew. (2020). 'Did the "real" economy turn financial? Mapping the contours of financialisation in the non-financial corporate sector.' *New Political Economy* (online). DOI: 10.1080/13563467.2020.1858775.

Sotiropoulos, Dimitris P. and Ariane Hillig. (2020). 'Financialization in heterodox economics,' in Philip Mader, Daniel Mertens, and Natascha van der Swan (eds) *The Routledge international handbook of financialization.* London: Routledge, pp. 125–35.

Stockhammer, Engelbert. (2004). 'Financialization and the slowdown of accumulation.' *Cambridge Journal of Economics*, 28(5): 719–41.

Stout, Lynn. (2012). *The shareholder value myth: How putting shareholders first harms investors, corporations, and the public.* San Francisco, CA: Berrett-Koehler.

van Treeck, Till. (2009). 'The political economy debate on "financialization": A macroeconomic perspective.' *Review of International Political Economy*, 16(5): 907–44.

Veblen, Thorstein. (1908). 'On the nature of capital: Investment, intangible assets, and the pecuniary magnate.' *The Quarterly Journal of Economics*, 23(1): 104–36.

Welch, Ivo. (2011). 'Two common problems in capital structure research: The financial-debt-to-asset ratio and issuing activity versus leverage changes.' *International Review of Finance*, 11(1): 1–17.

Zeng, Liyu and Priscilla Luk. (2020). 'Examining share repurchasing and the S&P buyback indices in the US market.' S&P Dow Jones Indices Research. Available at: www.spglobal.com.

Conclusion

On July 24, 2020, Elon Musk, the chief executive officer of Tesla Inc., tweeted 'We will coup anywhere we want. Get used to it.' On January 6, 2021, President Trump openly encouraged an assault on the US Congress to interrupt confirmation of the election of the Democratic party ticket of Joe Biden and Kamala Harris. Weeks later, the measures of voter exclusion approved by the Georgia State Legislature engendered censure, first by the executives of multinational corporations headquartered in the state, then, on April 14, 2021, by hundreds of chief executive officers of American corporations as featured in *The New York Times*. The new political cleavages of corporate America are beyond the scope of this book. However, these events add to the anomalies and provisos about political economy and financialization encountered in this study. The level of authoritarian threat, the shifting allegiance of corporate elites from the Republican to the Democratic administration, the massive emergency measures of 2020 and 2021 designed to counter the COVID-19 pandemic, and the bold legislation passed for economic recovery, social inclusion, and the greening of the US economy during the first months of the Biden–Harris administration reinforce the central intuition of this study: the need to reassess core ideas about politics, banking, and financialization.

This book, and its companion volume, are the results of decades of research on banking and finance. However, writing began in earnest in 2017 amid the rise of authoritarian populism that had extrapolated from the confines of distant peripheries to threaten, instead, the very paradigms of liberal representative government at the financial centers of the world economy (Berberoglu, 2018; Brown et al., 2018). The end of the easy phase of capitalism seemed at hand. After decades of transitions from military and authoritarian rule around the world, the rise of political reaction seemed overwhelming. However, during the completion of this book (amid the national elections of 2020 and unprecedented drama of transition through early 2021), the political coordinates became somewhat less frightening, at least in the US. Only time will tell. Forecasting is not a part of this study.

However, in retrospect, several observations may now be made at the end of this second volume, many of which were far from clear at the outset. To begin with, this second volume proved necessary because adequate consideration of the

DOI: 10.4324/9781003223320-5

136 *Conclusion*

primary materials and secondary literatures on the US overflowed the confines of a reasonable single volume. More space was required to present the details of evidence and arguments; to recover the theories and methods of classic modern political economy; to adapt the techniques of historical–institutionalism to balance-sheet analysis; to clarify the basics of social sector financial portfolios; and to do justice to the data from the US. This required working through dozens of primary sources and the foreboding complexities of diverse academic debates relevant to the questions raised by financialization studies. In this sense, the first chapter of this book was somewhat of a detour, one that became necessary to verify the validity of the macroeconomic claims of comparative and critical political economy about financialization. Unexpectedly, this imposing task was facilitated by returning to the meanings and measures of the 1934 US constitution of national accounts (Bureau of Commerce, 1934). This good fortune – which is not so unusual in historical–institutional analysis – helped retrace the relevant trends in the US National income and product accounts (NIPAs) from 1929 to 2019.

Remarkably, none of the deleterious consequences associated with financialization appeared in the NIPAs data (nor the Integrated macroeconomic accounts (IMAs) data from 1960 to 2019), with two exceptions: substantial increases in income inequality and unused industrial capacity. This belies central claims in the international literature on financialization and suggests the continued importance of classical Keynesian approaches to demand management, social inclusion, and countercyclical economic policies. The original 'non-financialized' meanings and measures of US national income accounts were elaborated in 1934 by Simon Kuznets. These measures provided 'new' perspectives, and decades of evidence, that ran contrary to many commonly held views in economic approaches. In retrospect, this was perhaps the most unexpected finding of this study. The traditional categories of classic modern political economy that still inform the NIPAs data from the US made it possible to elaborate a critique of the conceptual stretching, double-counting, and mis-aggregation that flaw macroeconomic approaches of all stripes, Keynesian, monetarist, heterodox, critical, and neoclassical.

Chapter 2 argued that the very same errors and ideologies of post-1945 economics, which had cast a veil over financial capital, had also caused, and concealed, the financialization of household inequality. The decomposition of the balance-sheet data on US households by social class from 1989 to 2019 revealed further consequences of compounding financialization. This was possible thanks to the publication, in March 2019, of the Distributional financial accounts (DFAs) of the United States. The decomposition, by social class, of the financial claims, nonfinancial assets, and liabilities on American household balance sheets over the three decades (1989–2019) confirmed (1) the basic elements of the theory compounding financialization; (2) the performative fallacies of conceptual stretching; (3) the flaws of mis-aggregation and double-counting, and; (4) the confusion between the basic categories of sectoral and national income and production accounts and the very different basic categories of financial and nonfinancial balance-sheet portfolios. The very same errors and ideologies of post-1945 economics that contributed to the displacement of US households as the predominant holders of US financial assets were also found to be behind the endogenous capitalization of household inequality.

The third chapter explored the evidence, historical and recent, in the NIPAs data, the financial balance-sheet data, and further income data to better understand the consequences of financialization for nonfinancial business enterprises in the US. The literature on financialization has revealed many different forces, and measurement problems, behind changes in the structure and management of American business over the last decades. Increasing the number of observations back in time and paying attention to the original meanings of measures (and the differences between the aggregates of sectoral and national income and production accounts, and the aggregates of financial accounts and balance sheets), provided new perspectives on current debates about precisely how financialization hollowed out nonfinancial corporations. The data from the US also suggests the importance of controlling for alternative paradigms, especially the degree to which *unincorporated* business enterprises were able to avert the downsides of financialization.

By tracing the causal logics and consequences of compounding financialization across the balance-sheet portfolios of all five US social sectors, this volume completed the scope of analysis originally envisioned for this study. The previous volume focused on two of the five social sectors (the financial sector and the government sector as defined in balance-sheet studies). However, explaining the rise and fall of finance and the transformation of monetary authority in the US soon outgrew the confines of a single book. It was necessary to delve into the complexities of bank change and explore the shift (that became apparent only after the 2007–2008 financial crisis), from the endogenous production of private money claims to the public accommodation and support of the exorbitant and murky claims of a select number of large bank holding companies.

This second volume has considered the equally imposing complexities of how financialization transformed American households and nonfinancial businesses. It was also necessary to extend the analysis beyond the evidence from the financial portfolio data on US social sectors (despite the remarkable data of the IMAs from 1960 to 2019 and the DFAs from 1989 to 2019). Tracing the historical–institutional evidence in the NIPAs from 1929 to 2019 made it possible to control for both broader macroeconomic changes and the domestic consequences of changing relations between the US and the rest of the world. The anomalies and provisos encountered throughout the chapters of this book provide a series of challenges for influential ideas across the standard approaches in economics and political economy. This does not disqualify the many contributions, and explanations, drawn herein from mainstream, heterodox, and critical traditions to explain specific aspects of financialization.

The defeat of a sitting US president in the 2020 elections is further indication of political change in the opposite direction emphasized in studies of financialization, advanced capitalism, and comparative political economy. The

138   *Conclusion*

step back from the brink of the nightmares of political reaction implied by the 2020 election in the US reinforces another intuition behind this study: That the concepts and categories of American exceptionalism (Ramrattan and Szenberg, 2019), provide alternative perspectives on basic questions of politics and political economy. For a particular reason that is not obvious: The differences between the concepts and theories that have been elaborated to understand American *political* institutions and the concepts and theories that inform studies of political institutions abroad.

This point may be explained with an apparently mundane observation about political science. The differences between the US and other countries are manifold. However, in terms of core ideas about politics and political economy, the central paradigms about the US emerged, after 1950, in opposition to (and as critiques of) the Eurocentrism and liberal reformism that had, theretofore, also biased studies of American political development. The claim here is that these very same biases (of Eurocentrism and liberal reformism), continue to skew research in the subdisciplines of comparative politics and comparative political economy.

This is not just an obscure detail from the annals of political science. The massive financial support from the US government for area studies and, by extension, comparative politics was forthcoming for the purpose of understanding politics, and political risk, in the vast number of newly independent nations produced by the waves of decolonization after 1945. It is a project that responded to the necessities that arose from the radical expansion of American power abroad after 1945. However, the point here is not about US foreign policy. The point here is that this produced an enduring divide between two subdisciplines of political science. The basic concepts, theories, and paradigms of comparative politics remained largely European, despite the massive increase in the number of newly independent nation-states that began to receive the empirical and conceptual attention necessary to understand their postcolonial experiences and trajectories. The consequences of this division of labor, and these biases, have been long-lasting. Today, in the third decade of the twenty-first century, Eurocentrism and liberal reformism continue to bias the predominant frameworks, assumptions, and paradigms of comparative political economic analysis.

These dimensions of neocolonialism are beyond the scope of this Conclusion. The point here is more positive and more specific: That the paradigms of American political science provide a profoundly different view of political economy. Comparative analysis obviously has a far longer pedigree in the social sciences. The contributions of political theory (classical, modern, contemporary, critical, and positive), have indeed provided bulwarks against the biases of Eurocentrism and liberal reformism. Indeed, rereading the classics is an essential part of the historical–institutional method. However, the point here is that this study of the political economy of financialization was *facilitated* by the explicit rejection of the Eurocentrism and liberal reformism that tend, still, to skew research in the subdiscipline of comparative politics (in the US and

Conclusion 139

abroad), including studies in the comparative political economy of advanced capitalist economies and, by extension, the growing international literature on financialization. This study therefore took a different approach. An approach based on the non-European paradigms, theories, and concepts about American politics and political institutions. Alexis de Tocqueville, James Bryce, and Max Weber were among the many foreign observers who, long ago, recognized the fundamentally different trajectory of democratization in the US (passive democratization as Weber called it, for the classics were not ideologues, despite their work often being claimed by ideologues).

Stated in these terms, the argument is not surprising. As mentioned, since the founding work of Antonio Gramsci, the advance of capitalism has been seen as a process of *Americanization* abroad (Aglietta, 2015). From this perspective, it is counterintuitive (especially for those not versed in the intricacies of political science), that research in comparative politics and comparative political economy, with all due respect, has largely failed to incorporate the advances in the understanding of American political institutions over the last decades. This is ironic, in part, because American political science is composed, overwhelmingly, by studies of US politics. Consequently, as is true of the public sphere and political culture in the US generally, European ideas (and indeed cosmopolitanism itself), are suspect in American political science to a far greater degree than supposed by observers from abroad.

This broader context is necessary to clarify the less than usual approach of this book. Indeed, the alternative paradigms of American political science and political economy proved essential to pursue the goals defined at the outset of this study: to reconsider the causal logics and counterforces of financialization. Decades have passed since the founding works that changed the study of American politics. However, Eurocentrism and liberal reformism nonetheless continue to bias research in comparative political analysis and comparative political economy. This study does not seek to substitute one neocolonialism or exceptionalism for another. The goal is far more limited: To elaborate an in-depth case study while controlling for the exceptional elements and particular global status of the country in question.

These observations may seem out of place in a conclusion. They raise more questions than answers. However, they are required to explain how, and why, this study of financialization differs so markedly from other studies of financialization (and how, and why, it found such different evidence). The cross-national empirical comparisons in the preceding volume stand on their own. Unfortunately, this second volume was restricted to the analysis of the data and secondary literature on the US. The sources to elaborate comparisons of US household inequality, the nonfinancial business sector, and macroeconomic trends were found to be lacking, or biased by the financialization of categories, or beyond the scope of this study.

This study of financialization in the US was nonetheless able to tap the quite different traditions of pragmatism, pluralism, the separation of powers, federalism, and populism, and the non-European ideas about American political

140 Conclusion

development and democratization. Among the essential landmarks, in this respect, are: the concept of critical elections (Key, 1955); the realist approach to the expansion of the scope of conflict (Schattschneider, 1960); the recognition of the executive-centered political realignment of party machines and voters (Burnham, 1970); the separationist design of American political institutions (Jones, 2005); and the functionality of divided government (Mayhew, 2005).

These theories of American politics were built on the traditions of federalism, pluralism, and the separation of powers. These theories recognized that American political institutions reflected the voracious capitalist occupation of the New World, a process fundamentally different than the transition from feudalism to capitalism in Europe. This difference is not confined to the mainstreams of social science. Critical theorists and classic and contemporary Marxist political economy from the US also provided concepts and theories for this study.

However, the argument here is that political economy in the US also experienced its own Kuhnian scientific revolution (Kuhn, 1962). One that is exemplified by Charles Lindblom's 'The science of muddling through,' (Lindblom, 1959). In the US, the traditions of separationism, federalism, populism, pluralism, pragmatism, and democratic principles of government are all behind the popular expression of 'muddling through.' Taken together, they provide an alternative theory of democratic policymaking, especially economic policymaking. From this perspective, the decentering of the subject is not an import of postmodernism from Europe. Lindblom's science of muddling through was home grown. It was part of broader, transdisciplinary, post-behavioral movements across the social sciences in the US. This is part of what are described in this book as the traditions of classic modern critical and pluralist political economy. These traditions provide time-tested alternative approaches to economics, public policy, and democratization in the US and abroad.

The vast literatures on the types and phases and political phenomena of public policy are beyond the scope of this Conclusion. However, the implications of these differences for understanding the logic and limits to financialization merit a final word. Four implications stand out. First, the differences discussed above between the study of American politics and the politics of other countries matter for two reasons. One reason is that Eurocentrism and liberal reformism continue to bias research in comparative political economy. This critique was alluded to throughout this study, perhaps too obliquely. However, the second reason is more positive and, it is hoped, was presented with more clarity: That the theories and concepts of politics and political economy from the US provide alternative paradigms to the predominant approaches to financialization.

A second set of differences arises between social policies in the US and Welfare States abroad. These differences matter, in part because of their different political and historical origins (Skocpol, 1992). This is recognized in comparative studies of social policy. However, the evidence explored in Chapter 2 suggested serious anomalies and provisos about the degree of dismantlement of social policies wrought by neoliberals and neoconservatives in the US since

Conclusion   141

1980. The evidence from the 2010s (and the early evidence from studies of the dramatic challenges presented by the COVID-19 pandemic since 2020), belie generalizations about social exclusion and impoverishment in the US. The data on taxes, government transfers, and the US macroeconomy explored in Chapter 2 suggest important trends in the other direction.

For example, the US does not have universal public health insurance. However, the data on health insurance coverage since the financial crisis of 2007–2008 nonetheless indicates compelling change. Millions of people in the US remain without health insurance (31.6 million in 2019 according to the US Department of Health and Human Services). This is shocking if compared to the full coverage of many European public health insurance programs.

However, the trends in the data from the US since 2013 are also compelling. The number of uninsured in the US falls from *15.5 percent* of the population in 2010 (46.4 million) to 9.2 percent in 2019 (31.6 million). In comparative (and moral and ethical) perspective, this still represents a profound disappointment. However, the trend is not one of unilateral exclusion or expulsion. To the contrary, it implies the extension of health insurance to 14.8 million individuals during the 2010s (ignoring differences that surely obtain across social classes, in the quality of coverage provided by public and private insurance, the details of Obamacare provisions, and the effects of switching from private to public coverage and vice versa).

The third set of implications that arises from the alternative approaches to politics and political economy in the US turn on the importance of decentralization. In a broader sense, all disputes about politics may be seen to turn on a single axis, with centralization and decentralization at opposite ends. Regime theory, in political science, turns on the opposing logics of totalitarian centralization and the decentralization implied by liberal democracy (Friedrich and Brzezinski, 1956). Lenin described the same dual dynamic in the theory of dual power (Lenin, 1917).

However, this also applies to the more restricted typologies and comparisons of democracy and representative government. The combination of federalism and the separation of powers in the US has long been seen to have produced far more decentralized political institutions than the unitary states and parliamentary systems of Europe. From this perspective, the concept of presidentialism is another misleading residual concept in comparative political analysis (Mettenheim, 1997). Studies of American politics therefore emphasize, not the presidency but, instead, the separation of powers and how this contrasts with the concentration of powers in the legislative branch of government in European parliamentary systems.

Alexis de Tocqueville became perhaps the single most important author to inform the self-understanding of any country, precisely because of his focus on local governments and voluntary associations in the US in the 1830s. Hanna Arendt also argued that the decentralization of New England Townships embodied a lost treasure of the revolutionary tradition, precisely because it differed so radically from the tendency to centralize revolutionary power

142 *Conclusion*

(Arendt, 1963). Samuel Huntington lamented that the US retained what he called a Tudor system of government, a peculiar legacy of Puritan thought that opposed government and the centralization of political power of any kind (Huntington, 1968). The virtues of local government and civil society have also become American ideologies. However, this study has attempted to employ the scientific paradigms advanced by American political science since the 1950s, while averting these ideologies.

From this perspective, the critiques elaborated by studies of financialization may be considered far more mainstream than generally supposed. The central phenomena of financialization – such as the extreme concentration of banking and financial industries, the centralization of monetary authority, and the capitalization of inequality – all run counter to the core ideas of American exceptionalism. By ignoring these affinities, critical and heterodox economic approaches to financialization contribute, unnecessarily, to their own estrangement.

A fourth set of implications that arises from the different concepts and theories about American politics turn on the importance of debates about power in critical theory and Marxist traditions. The long history of debates about power and politics in American sociology and political science is also beyond the scope of this Conclusion (Lukes, 2005). However, the same point applies. The economic determinism of political economy, and the excessively broad strokes of sociological approaches, also fail to explain the most important political phenomena behind financialization. The issues of theory and method at stake here were treated in the preceding volume and require more careful attention than is possible here.

However, the same tendency of unnecessary estrangement from the mainstreams of social science appears to obtain. The contributions from political sociology, critical theory, and recent studies of financialization are especially promising as means to explore the implication of the anomalies and provisos encountered in this study. Moreover, recent approaches to critical theory and the micropolitics of financialization are, also, far more mainstream than supposed.

Two observations are in order here. The first is about origins: The origins of academic ideas about the autonomy of politics and the division of labor that emerged during the 1960s across the sister disciplines of social science (economics, sociology, and political science). The founders of political sociology, as a subdiscipline of political science, were a generation of researchers who collaborated in the Research Committee on Political Sociology of the International Sociological Association.

The work of this generation can be summarized as *political development theory*: From Karl Deutsch's concept of the political gap (Deutsch, 1962), through Samuel Huntington's *Political Order in Changing Societies* (1968), and exemplified by the volumes published from 1965 to 1979 in the Princeton University Press series entitled 'Political Development Studies.' This generation of political sociologists forged the central ideas about the autonomy of politics and the causal relations between politics, economic forces, and society that still inform the discipline of comparative politics (Remmer, 1997).

Conclusion 143

A second observation about the potential for convergence between financialization studies and mainstream social science requires brief consideration of yet another topic that may appear, once again, to take this Conclusion astray: The unraveling of the ideologies of modernization theory and the reconsideration of the place of democracy in Max Weber, who remains perhaps the single most important founder of modern sociology and its division of labor with the sister social sciences of economics and political science.

A final word on Max Weber and the principle of democracy as a fourth type of legitimate domination

False impressions of distance between critical theory and mainstream social science also continue because the new perspectives of Max Weber studies, and the organization of Max Weber's complete works, have yet to overturn the ideologies of modernization theory. The obsolescence of modernization theory has been noted. However, mention of the new perspectives provided by studies of Max Weber's political sociology may illustrate the problem here. The division of labor between economics, sociology, and political science envisioned by Weber remains valid. The preceding volume alluded to the implications of this traditional division of labor. Two further points are relevant here. One is to recognize an essential part of Weber's *The Methodology of the Social Sciences* (1949): That the key to social science is the suspension of one's personal ethical and moral views, *temporarily*, in favor of empirical and conceptual research and the consideration of alternative explanations. This maxim has informed the empirical analysis of the historical–institutional and balance-sheet evidence from the US.

The second comment is alluded to in the subtitle of this subsection. It bears repeating that one of the most pernicious ideologies of American sociology was the widespread acceptance of an idea that was erroneously credited to Weber. This originated in Talcott Parsons' misleading interpretation of three types of authority. The ideology of modernization envisioned paths from traditional, through charismatic, to legal-rational forms of authority. This interpretation has been decisively contested. It is antagonistic to the core ideas of Weber's work and an unfortunate result from the posthumous organization of his writings for the publication of *Economy and Society*. However, the point here, once again, is more limited and more positive.

Scholarship on Max Weber since the 1980s helps clarify why the distance between financialization studies and mainstream social science is also overstated and counterproductive. This can be seen by returning to the misconceptions of three types of authority, or legitimate domination. In a seemingly innocuous footnote, Wolfgang Schluchter mentions a surprising turn of events in the organization of Weber's writings. A 1919 draft of *Economy and Society*, in the form of an address to the academic association of Vienna, contained a short but decisive mention by Max Weber of a *fourth type of legitimate domination*. Two citations of Wolfgang Schluchter indicate the importance of this observation:

144   *Conclusion*

Weber also proposed, in an address on the sociology of states, in October 1919 in Vienna, that the democratic principle of legitimacy was a fourth principle in his typology of authority.

And:

> He considered the implications in a discussion of the development of Western States. However, in the printing of *Economy and Society*, this question nonetheless was [mis]placed under the subtitle 'the estrangement from authority of charisma' [Der Herrschaftsfremde Umdeutung des Charisma].
>
> (Schluchter, 1988: 69, fn 238)

This is not simply an editorial artifact discovered by one of the editors of Weber's complete works (a formidable project still underway). Nor is this a minor matter of terminology or translation. The fact that Weber defined *four*, not three, types of legitimate domination (authority in Parsons; *herrschaft* in German), explicitly, in a major public academic forum, as a reaction to the dramatic unfolding events of the Russian Revolution and its implications for European states, is of great import. So, too, is the bizarre insertion of this problem, and text, into an unrelated corner of *Economy and Society* about the routinization of charisma.

The significance of this fourth type is clearly suggested by its title: 'The democratic principle of legitimation.' For whatever reason, despite its centrality in both this 1919 address and in Weber's draft introduction to *Economy and Society*, this fourth type (the democratic principle), never became an independent chapter or sub-section in Weber's published manuscripts. It was also completely ignored during the elaboration of modernization theory. The implication of this omission for interpretations of Max Weber, and rethinking the foundations of political sociology, are beyond the scope of this Conclusion.

However, this does serve to draw attention to a serious problem in recent studies of financialization in sociology and comparative political economy: The unnecessary distancing of these approaches from the mainstreams of social science. This makes the work of critical theories and approaches more difficult, and more marginal, than necessary.

Recent research on Max Weber supports this claim. Since Wolfgang Mommsen's *Max Weber and German Politics* was first published in 1958 (translated in 1985), scholars have recognized that the tension between charismatic leadership, direct popular appeals, and competitive electoral politics based on legal-rational norms is a central problem in Weber's political sociology (Mommsen, 1985). This tension is also at odds with ideologies of modernization that conceived tradition, charisma, and legal-rational authority as ideal types, but also, worse yet, in chronological order. This opened the door to manifold misinterpretations. The ideology of modernization depoliticized both the work of Max Weber and the question of democracy. Modernization theory was

Conclusion   145

built on Parsons' erroneous views of Weber's sociology of domination. Weber clearly stated, and wrote, that the democratic principle was a separate and far more problematic type of legitimate domination. Democratic principles are permanently problematic: They cannot be set into historical stone or attributed, completely, to any of the other three sources of legitimate domination (tradition, charisma, and rational-legal entities and institutions).

This is another example of how the historical–institutional method requires rereading the classics. Max Weber is not a role model – neither for liberalism nor for modernization theory in the US. Instead, the vast, complex, and problematic work of Max Weber provides new perspectives. Rereading the classics sharpens our questions. In this case, questions about the permanently problematic character of politics and the permanent challenges to all established orders produced by democratic principles. The message here, at the end of this study of financialization in the US, is that scholars of critical theory, critical sociology, and critical political economy need not marginalize themselves from the mainstreams of social science. To the contrary, the questions raised about financialization need to go mainstream. One challenge for financialization studies is to deepen critical perspectives. However, another challenge for financialization studies is to help bring the democratization of banking and finance back to the centers of social science and public debate.

A coda to the international literature on financialization

This study of the US was designed to address the variety, complexity, and diversity of claims about the political economy of financialization. As noted in the previous volume, since J.S. Mill, phenomena with too many variables and too few cases are seen to impede the use of statistical or experimental methods. Instead, the qualitative methods of comparing similarities and differences, conceptual analysis, and case study are required. The essentially contested concepts and opposing theoretical perspectives in political and social economy – and the transdisciplinary debates about households, finance, nonfinancial business, government, and the rest of the world – required far more consideration than expected. The massive amount of information in historical and contemporary sources on the US, and the rich diversity of academic and applied research on the US also required extra care, especially to deal with the biases, and realities, of American exceptionalism. At the end of the two volumes, readers will expect reflections of closure. However, since the beginning, the objective was not to synthesize financialization studies (Mader et al., 2020).

Instead, a select number of observations about recent (and overlooked) contributions to the burgeoning international literature on financialization must suffice. The following comments draw loosely from reading several influential books, articles, and working papers that have appeared since this study began in 2017. This provides the opportunity to check, one last time, the validity of inferences and the accuracy of the anomalies and provisos flagged in this study. The breadth of this study, in and of itself, surely resulted in errors. The

146 *Conclusion*

corollary is the first final comment. The attempt to explain the many complex relations within and across each social sector (households, finance, nonfinancial business, government, and the rest of the world) also seems, in and of itself, justified. Moreover, the lack of statistical matrices or dedicated software for the analysis of social networks are shortcomings of this study that, hopefully, will inspire others to pursue these approaches. The new literature of 'from whom to whom' that focuses on financial flows *within* the financial sector, in the US and abroad, is one of the most promising means to extend, and check, the findings herein about the long-term trends in the strategic management of financial portfolios by each US social sector and the manifold relations across social sector balance sheets.

A second observation is to recognize the limits to disaggregation in this study. The historical–institutional and balance-sheet approach herein dealt, primarily, with political economic aggregates on the macro and mezzo levels of analysis. This approach was vindicated by the ability to reveal, and begin to systematically unravel, serious errors of conceptual stretching, double-counting, and mis-aggregation that flaw economic approaches. However, disaggregation obviously begs the question of further disaggregation. If composition effects obtain at the macro level, then it follows that further composition effects may also exist on the mezzo level. Care was taken by paying attention to the traditional categories of US historical and official statistics; by increasing the number of observations back in time; by tracing broader trends in historical, institutional, and comparative perspective; and by exploiting the many official data sources on the US. This provided many insights, far more than was anticipated at the outset of this study. However, this study, like all studies, has limits, despite its large size. The hope here is that the findings herein may inspire further disaggregation. This may reveal further determinants, differences, and sources of variance on the regional, local, demographic, and organizational level, especially in terms of the dimensions of inequality, other than social class, that also remained beyond the scope of this study.

The opportunities for the latter are especially promising because of the new perspectives on power and micropolitics that have emerged over the last decades. This study has gone back to the classic modern foundations of political economy. However, this implies acceptance of the traditional, classic modern concepts such as social class and, by extension, the accompanying conceptions of how power, politics, and economic and social forces shape markets. New, micropolitical approaches to inclusion and exclusion have drawn attention to new, unrecognized types of violence, new identities, and different searches for recognition in the public sphere. This provides further challenges, and opportunities, to consider the questions raised in this book.

For example, *necropolitics* is perhaps the single most influential idea of critical theory in our times to come from the periphery (Mbembe, 2008). It appears as a keyword in Google Trends to peak in May 2020. In the past, before the COVID-19 pandemic, the concept of necropolitics remained on the margins of international social science. It was seen to apply only to postcolonial countries on the periphery. However, the political and electoral appeal of the blatant neo-conservative disdain for life at the center of the world system, especially in the two principal global financial centers (the US and UK), supports another intuition behind this study; that the concepts and theories about political economy on the periphery may provide much needed clarity about change at the center.

Researchers of the new micropolitics tend to trace their origins to the revolutionary ideas of Michel Foucault, and many other philosophers, literary critics, and social scientists from Europe. These new critical perspectives focus on the new relations between neoliberalism and social exclusion (Christiaens, 2019; Kotz, 2015; Allen, 2013). However, for our generation who read Franz Fanon and Herbert Marcuse in the 1970s and 1980s, these relations are not such a fundamental anomaly. To each generation, their own. However, with all due respect to the fundamental differences, and understandable preferences for intellectual distance, the same observation mentioned above about the unnecessary distancing of critical approaches from the mainstreams of social science applies here.

The first volume of this study contrasted the American belief that 'all good things go together,' with the popular expression from Brazil that 'all bad things go together.' A more systematic reading of recent contributions to critical studies of financialization and American political economy is required. However, with all due respect, this core problem of critical political economy also appears to apply to studies of financialization. The latter expression, that all bad things go together, is as false as the naïve American ideology that all good things go together. This study has traced vast amounts of data back in time and attempted to recover the original meanings of measures. This enabled the identification of core problems due to conceptual stretching, double-counting, mis-aggregation, and further confusions that arise from the mixing together of fundamentally different types of data, which in turn arises from accepting the terms of debate and data from secondary sources. Skepticism and pessimism are no substitutes for the more systematic critique of the concepts and categories of financial economics.

Specific mistakes ensue, including, ironically, in studies of financialization. For example, the exorbitant, murky financial claims of private and public entities are often accepted at face value. Face value is meant in a figurative sense because the literal meaning does not apply. The nominal values ascribed to financial derivatives are currently discounted, on average, by around *97 percent* (i.e. to *3 percent* of nominal values) by American monetary authorities such as the Office of the Comptroller of the Currency (OCC). The current director of the OCC, Charles Calomiris, can hardly be described as heterodox. The International Monetary Fund (IMF) did indeed publish a working paper, in 1998, that floated the idea of permitting banks and financial institutions to count the value of the nominal figures reported for their financial derivatives at 100 percent. However, that was 23 years ago. And the working paper in question failed to gain acceptance in any of the entities responsible for the regulation and supervision of banks and financial markets, in the US or abroad.

148 *Conclusion*

Further comparative issues arise for understanding the political and social economy of financialization. For example, the capture of public policy by corporate lobbies is central to explanations of financialization. However, this problem has two fundamentally different responses, one Madisonian, the other Eurocentric. The smaller, more centralized, and more hierarchical societies, polities, and governments of Europe may be far more amenable to and capable of regulation. The corporatism that obtains in small and midsize countries with open economies (compared to the contested pluralism and larger, more amorphous closed economy of the US), has long informed comparative political economy (Katzenstein, 1982).

However, since Article 51 of the *Federalist Papers* written by James Madison, a central idea in American politics runs in the opposite direction: That the only viable response to the downsides of lobbying is to promote and permit more lobbying. From this perspective, American exceptionalism implies a greater distance from the ideology of governance that is seen, correctly, to be at the center of financialization and neoliberalism. The critiques of governance stand. Part of the ideologies of financialization involve imposing corporate conceptions of governance in the sphere of politics. However, the critique misfires because it ignores the *greater ungovernability of the US*, a core, long-standing difference between the US and Europe.

This returns to the question of decentralization and the challenge laid down in this study to critical approaches, of all stripes, to elaborate viable policy agendas. In this respect, another example from a post-Keynesian classic is in order. Hyman Minsky's financial instability hypothesis has inspired a vast literature. This study has raised a warning flag by suggesting that post-Keynesian approaches, ironically, also accept at face value the endogenous mechanisms of private, and public, money creationism. However, the point here is to note a different, more positive, policy-related dimension of Minsky's work, and its reliance on *decentralization and democratization*. Minsky studied, critically, the centralization and consolidation of finance in New York City. However, in positive terms, he also proposed the decentralization of banking. Specifically, the creation of 100 local community development financial institutions as a response to the commission of a study by the Clinton administration in 1992 (Rosenthal, 2018; Minsky et al., 1992).

The public bank movement in the US has also emerged in local communities across the country to propose municipal banks and state government banks (Uğurlu and Epstein, 2021; Herndon and Paul, 2020; Marshall and Rochon, 2019; Hanna, 2018). These grass roots movements have proposed local public banks that differ, in the extreme, from the centralized finance agencies and large development banks (also described as special purpose banks), that remain at the heart of coordinated capitalist economies in Continental Europe and many emerging and developing countries, especially the largest such as the BRIC group of nations (Marois, 2021; Butzbach and Mettenheim, 2014; Mettenheim, 2010).

Decentralization matters because of the extreme centralization implied by industrial concentration, bids for oligarchic and authoritarian rule, and the continued ideological insistence on central bank independence. However, once again, this argument is far more mainstream in American political science than often supposed. After all, the *expansion of the scope of conflict* (Schattschneider, 1960), is a concept shared in the US by realists, liberals, and critical theorists. The expansion of the scope of conflict over monetary policymaking was explored in the previous volume. The point here is about the unfortunate point of departure in centralized polities.

Peter Haas described the capabilities of alternative paradigms in academia and public policy in terms of the scope and depth of epistemic communities (Haas, 1992). This concept indicates the amount of work to be done to begin to recover from the economic ideologies, and the extreme centralization produced by these ideologies, in the wake of neoconservative political reaction and financialization. It bears repeating: The Board of Governors of the Federal Reserve System held, during 2019, open public meetings hosted by each of the 12 regional Federal Reserve banks. Ironically, the record does not appear to include the presence of a single critical, or heterodox, or alternative social scientist.

Instead, local community leaders, teachers, labor union organizers, health care and social service workers, and staff from a wide variety of grass roots organizations spoke eloquently. A separate academic conference was held in September 2019, hosted by the Chicago Federal Reserve Bank. However, no alternative, heterodox, or critical political economist spoke, presented, or, apparently, participated in any of these 12 sessions. Indeed, the most discordant voice was William Isaac, the former chair of the Federal Deposit Insurance Corporation (FDIC). This absence is more than anecdotal. It indicates the incredible weight of economic ideologies and the mainstreaming forces of academic research and public policy debate. However, it also indicates the imposing scale of challenges to build alternative epistemic communities. In this respect, and with all due respect, the tendency of critical social scientists toward *self-marginalization* is also a contributing factor.

However, self-criticism is better demonstrated than demanded of others. Many of the questions raised in this book, and its preceding volume, have not been addressed sufficiently. And promising new avenues for research have emerged during the elaboration of this study. Pathbreaking research is now available in the study of the politics of accounting (Perry and Nölke, 2006); the question of labor and new contributions from Marxist approaches (Fine, 2013); new works in critical theory (Deutscher and Lafont, 2017); the elaboration of comparative frameworks for the study of financialization (Lapavitsas and Powell, 2013); better accounts of the relations between finance and the real economy (Bezemer and Hudson, 2016); and new conceptual, theoretical, and empirical considerations of financial exclusion and inclusion (Baradaran, 2015). Outside of academic research, the rise of the public bank movement, the agenda of

150 *Conclusion*

postal banking, and the resurgence of democratic socialism in the US are phenomena that also were excluded from this study.

The links between the political-economic problems addressed herein, and the unexpected vibrancy of the forces of opposition that emerged from the shadows of political reaction to step up, and scale up, to the macropolitical challenges of forming a national government in 2021 were not foretold here. In retrospect, that is unfortunate. The manifold challenges faced by new social reactions of self-defense against the commodification of life in the US have telescoped. Every week, new barriers and new trenches appeared to block change once again. During the frightful four years dominated by a grifter, a postmodern poser who adroitly played with the deepest fears and terrors of all, this study erred on the side of caution. The syndromes typical of second- and third-generation survivors of Nazi Germany, despite professional training in political science, make it impossible to write the names of political reaction. This book is a poor substitute for the proper honoring of the dead, maimed, and excluded from the past and present. The almost unbelievable scale of basic conceptual and theoretical errors unraveled in this book may, perhaps, be somewhat of a compensation.

References

Aglietta, Michel. (2015). *A theory of capitalist regulation.* London: Verso (1976, 1st edition).

Allen, Amy. (2013). 'Power and the subject,' in Timothy O'Leary, Jana Sawicki, and Chris Falzon (eds) *A companion to Foucault.* Chichester: Wiley-Blackwell, pp. 337–52.

Arendt, Hanna. (1963). 'The revolutionary tradition and its lost treasury,' in *On revolution.* London: Penguin, pp. 216–81.

Baradaran, Mehrsa. (2015). *How the other half banks: Exclusion, exploitation, and the threat to democracy.* Cambridge, MA: Harvard University Press.

Berberoglu, Berch. (ed). (2018). *The global rise of authoritarianism in the 21st century crisis of neoliberal globalization and the nationalist response.* London: Routledge.

Bezemer, Dirk and Michael Hudson. (2016). 'Finance is not the economy: Reviving the conceptual distinction.' *Journal of Economic Issues,* 50(3): 745–68.

Brown, Wendy., Peter E. Gordon, and Max Pensky. (2018). *Authoritarianism: Three inquiries in critical theory.* Chicago, IL: University of Chicago Press.

Bureau of Commerce. (1934). 'National income 1929–1932.' Washington, DC: Government Printing Office.

Burnham, Walter D. (1970). *Critical elections and the mainsprings of American politics.* New York: W.W. Norton.

Butzbach, Olivier and Kurt Mettenheim. (eds). (2014). *Alternative banking and financial crisis.* London: Routledge.

Christiaens, Tim. (2019). 'Financial neoliberalism and exclusion with and beyond Foucault.' *Theory, Culture, and Society,* 36(4): 95–116.

Deutsch, Karl. (1962). 'Social mobilization and political development.' *The American Political Science Review,* 55(3): 493–514.

Deutscher, Penelope and Cristina Lafont. (eds). (2017). *Critical theory in critical times: Transforming the global political and economic order.* New York: Columbia University Press.

Fine, Ben. (2013). 'Financialization from a Marxist perspective.' *International Journal of Political Economy*, 42(4): 47–66.

Friedrich, Carl J. and Zbigniew Brzezinski. (1956). *Totalitarian dictatorship and democracy.* Cambridge: Cambridge University Press.

Haas, Peter. (1992). 'Introduction: Epistemic communities and international policy coordination.' *International Organization*, 46(1): 1–35.

Hanna, Thomas M. (2018). *Our common wealth: The return of public ownership in the United States.* Manchester: Manchester University Press.

Herndon, Thomas and Mark Paul. (2020). 'A public banking option as a mode of regulation for household financial services in the US.' *Journal of Post Keynesian Economics*, 43(4): 576–607.

Huntington, Samuel. (1968). *Political order in changing societies.* New Haven, CT: Yale University Press.

Jones, Charles O. (2005). *The presidency in a separated system*, 2nd edition. Washington, DC: Brookings Institution Press.

Katzenstein, Peter J. (1985). *Small states in world markets: Industrial policy in Europe.* Ithaca, NY: Cornell University Press.

Key, Victor O. (1955). 'A theory of critical elections.' *Journal of Politics*, 17(1): 3–18.

Kotz, David. (2015). *The rise and fall of neoliberal capitalism.* Cambridge, MA: Harvard University Press.

Kuhn, Thomas S. (1962). *The structure of scientific revolutions.* Chicago, IL: University of Chicago Press.

Lapavitsas, Costas and Jeff Powell. (2013). 'Financialisation varied: A comparative analysis of advanced economies.' *Cambridge Journal of Regions, Economy and Society*, 6: 359–79.

Lenin, V.I. (1917). 'The dual power.' *Pravda.* No. 28, April 9. Available at: www.marxists.org/archive/lenin/works/1917/apr/09.htm.

Lindblom, Charles. (1959). 'The science of muddling through.' *Public Administration Review*, 19(2): 79–88.

Lukes, Steven. (2005). *Power, a radical view.* London: Palgrave Macmillan (1974, 1st edition).

Mader, Philip., Daniel Mertens, and Natascha van der Zwan. (eds). (2020). *The Routledge handbook of financialization.* London: Routledge.

Marois, Thomas. (2021). *Public banks: Decarbonisation, Financialisation and Democratisation.* Cambridge: Cambridge University Press.

Marshall, Wesley C. and Louis-Philippe Rochon. (2019). 'Public banking and post-Keynesian economic theory.' *International Journal of Political Economy*, 48(1): 60–75.

Mayhew, David R. (2005). *Divided we govern: Party control, lawmaking, and investigation, 1946–2002*, 2nd edition. New Haven, CT: Yale University Press.

Mbembe, Achille. (2008). 'Necropolitics,' in Stephen Morton and Stephen Bygrave (eds) *Foucault in an age of terror.* London: Palgrave Macmillan, pp. 152–82.

Mettenheim, Kurt. (2010). *Federal banking in Brazil: Policies and competitive advantages.* London: Routledge.

Mettenheim, Kurt. (ed) (1997). *Presidential institutions and democratic politics: Comparing regional and national contexts.* Baltimore, MD: Johns Hopkins University Press.

Minsky, Hyman P., Dimitri B. Papadimitriou, Ronnie J. Phillips, and L. Randall Wray. (1992). 'Community development banks.' Bard College Levy Economics Institute, Working Paper No. 83.

Mommsen, Wolfgang. (1985). *Max Weber and German politics, 1890–1920.* Chicago, IL: University of Chicago Press.

152 Conclusion

Perry, James and Andreas Nölke. (2006). 'The political economy of international accounting standards.' *Review of International Political Economy*, 13(4): 559–86.

Ramrattan, Lall and Michael Szenberg. (2019). *American exceptionalism: Economics, finance, political economy, and economic laws*. London: Palgrave Macmillan.

Remmer, Karen L. (1997). 'Theoretical decay and theoretical development: The resurgence of institutional analysis.' *World Politics*, 10(1): 34–61.

Rosenthal, Clifford N. (2018). *Democratizing finance: Origins of the community development financial institutions movement*. Victoria, BC: Friesen Press.

Schattschneider, Ernest E. (1960). *The semi-sovereign people: A realist's view of democracy in America*. New York: Holt, Rinehart and Winston.

Schluchter, Wolfgang. (1988). *Max Webers sicht des okzidentalen christentums*. Frankfurt: Suhrkamp.

Skocpol, Theda. (1992). *Protecting soldiers and mothers: The political origins of social policy in the United States*. Cambridge, MA: Harvard University Press.

Uğurlu, Esra N. and Gerald Epstein. (2021). 'The public banking movement in the United States: Networks, agenda, initiatives, and challenges.' University of Massachusetts Amherst Political Economy Research Institute, Working Paper No. 538.

Weber, Max. (1949). *The methodology of the social sciences*. New York: Free Press.

Index

Note: Page numbers in *italics* indicate figures and in **bold** indicate tables on the corresponding pages.

American economy, financialization of: Chicago Board Options Exchange volatility index 23, *24*; decomposition of consumption and production in NIPAs, 1929–2019 41–9, **42–4**, **48**; decomposition of drivers of GDP growth and 33–6, **34**; education advances and 28, *29*; GDP growth and 15–16, 17, 25–7, *26*; growth periods in the US and 14–15; introduction to 13–18; investment, consumption, manufacturing, and service industries in 16; investment and consumption in the NIPAs 1929–2019 and IMAs 1960–2019 *30–2*, 30–3; labor income shares and 16–17; labor productivity and 27–8, *28*; long-term perspectives on American political economy and *18*, 18–25, *21–2*, *24*; military expenditures and 29, *29*; National income and product accounts (NIPAs) and 3, 4–5, 16, 17; New York Stock Exchange (NYSE) and 15, *22*, 22–6, *24*; personal income data and 17; political economy of growth and 25–30, *26–9*; stock prices and 15; unemployment: 1948–2020 and 36–41, *37–40*; employment and industrial capacity in 17
American exceptionalism 14, 138–9, 142, 145
Americanization 23, 139
Arendt, H. 141

Baines, J. 113, 127
back to the future 2; recovery of concepts and 5, 10; traditional banking and 6

Bates, T. W. 121
Biden, J. 135
Bryce, J. 139
business enterprises 9–10

Calomiris, C. 147
capitalism: Americanization and 23, 139; golden age of 13; law of motion of 113
Chicago Board Options Exchange volatility index 23, *24*
Chicago Federal Reserve Bank national activity index (CFNAI) 27
Civil War 19, 20
composition effects 8; capital and 35; CFNAI and 27; consumption aggregates and 31, 90; disaggregation in historical institutionalism and 16; financialization, leverage, and social class 72; household debt and 103–5; long-term data on wages and prices and 20; NIPAs and 17; social sector balance sheets and 58; stock markets and 24
compounding financialization 3, 4, 9, 51, 55–6, 136; DFAs and 58, 65–8; Kuznets and 60; social classes, inequality and 82
conceptual analysis 18, 61, 145
conceptual stretching 4, 9; and inequality 56–7
Congressional Budget Office 63–5, *64*
COVID-19 pandemic 13, 15, 23, 135, 141, 146–7; household corporate equities holdings and 100; insurance policies and pension fund holdings and 101; unemployment and 39
Crouzet, N. 122

154 *Index*

Davis, L. 121, 127
debt: corporate 124–6, *124–6*; household 102–3, *103*, **104**, 104–5, **105**
decentralization 141, 148–9
deflation 19
democracy 141, 143–5
de Tocqueville, A. 139, 141
Deutsch, K. 142
Ding, Y. 122
disaggregation 9, 46; of capital 35; of DFAs 70; of household balance sheets 97–8; of home equity 106; and financialization 146
Distributional financial accounts (DFAs) 9, 55–8, 60–1, 82–4; financialization and inequality in US, 1989–2019 65–70, **66–7**
double counting, 4, and inequality, 58–9
Duménil, G. 114
Dutta, S. J. 113, 118

Eberly, J. 122
Economy and Society 143–4
education advances 28, *29*
endogenous money theory 1, 3, 14, 5, 55, 69, 101
Eurocentrism 140, 148

Fanon, F. 147
Federal Deposit Insurance Company (FDIC) Consumer finance surveys 57–8, 59, 103–7, **105**, *106*
Federalist Papers 148
Federal Reserve System 7, 37, 57, 102, 149
Fiebiger, B. 114–15, 119
financial crises, 2007–2008 14
financialization 1–10, 49–51; American economy (*see* American economy, financialization of); banking system and 5–8; broad definition of 28; centralization and 6; diversity of American political traditions and 139–40; evidence on consequences of 4, 8; Federal Reserve and 7; financial crisis of 2007–2008 and 1, 7; fiscal and financial ideologies in 6–7; household inequality (*see* household inequality, financialization of); international literature on 145–50; Max Weber and 139, 143–5; neocolonialism and 138–9; nonfinancial business (*see* nonfinancial corporations (NFCs), financialization

of); recent political events and 135–6, 137–8; separation of political powers and 141–2
financial payout ratios 116–17, *117*
Fordism 111
Foucault, M. 147

Gini coefficients 61–5, *62*, *64*
globalization 119
goodwill 122–3
Gouge, W. 56
government share of GDP, 1929–2020 92–5, *93–4*
Graham, J. R. 125
Gramsci, A. 139
Great Depression 14, 25–6, 56
gross domestic product (GDP) 15–16, 17; 1930s–2010s 41–7, **42–4**; decomposition of drivers of growth of 33–6, **34**; history of growth of 25–7, *26*; household balance-sheet data and 65–70, **66–7**; personal income, consumption, private investment, and government shares of, 1929–2020 92–5, *93–4*

Haas, P. 149
Hager, S. B. 113, 127
Harris, K. 135
Hein, E. 4, 13, 30, 112–13
historical institutional method 4, 18, 27, 37, 51, 55; balance sheet analysis and 4; DFAs and 72; financialization of US business and 111; macroeconomic indicators and 14–15; US banking and 5; US constitution of national income accounts and, 136; US households in DFAs and 98
home equity 105–6, *106*
household inequality, financialization of 136–7; balance-sheet data on 9, 55, 57–8, 65–70, **66–7**; balance sheets of US social classes and, 1989–2019 72–84, **73–80**; comparing ratios of financialization and leverage by US social class, 1989–2019 70–2, *71*; conclusions on 107–8; consumption categories 49, **50**; Distributional financial accounts (DFAs) and 55–8; Federal Deposit Insurance Company (FDIC) Consumer finance surveys 57–8, 59, 103–7, **105**, *106*; financialization and inequality in the

US DFAs, 1989–2019 65–70, **66–7**; Gini coefficients, taxes, and transfers, 1979–2016 61–5, *62, 64*; household debt, 1980–2020 102–3, *103*, **104**, 104–5, **105**; household financial portfolios in the Z1 financial accounts of the US 98–102, *99*; inequality in classic modern political economy and 59–61; introduction to 55–9; measures of wealth and 58–9; personal income, consumption, private investment, and government, 1929–2020 92–5, *93–4*; tendencies of wages and labor income shares from 1929–2020 in the NIPAs and 84–6, *85–6*; US household balance sheets in the IMAs, 1960s to 2010s 95–8, **96–7**; US personal income and its disposition in the US NIPAs, 1929–2019 86–92, **87–8, 91**
Huntington, S. 142

ideologies 2, 136–7, 149; American 142; modernization theory as 143
inflation 19–20, 101
insurance policies 101
Integrated macroeconomic accounts (IMAs) 13, 27, 55; investment and consumption in, 1960–2019 *30–2*, 30–3; US household balance sheets in, 1960s to 2010s 95–8, **96–7**
interest rates 19–20; corporate bond 1800–2019 *19, 21*; financialization and decline of 3; government debt and 15, 60; monetarism and 7; real for corporate financial income and payout ratios *115*; rentier class and 113; portfolio income and 114
Isaac, W. 149

Jackson, A. 56
Johnson, L. 19

Knafo, S. 113, 118
Korean War 20, 29, 85
Krippner, G. R. 113–15, 117–19, 121
Kuznets, S. 14, 17, 62–3, 136; on economic determinants of inequality and political factors that may reverse it 59–60; on extreme inequality of the US in the early 1930s 56–7

labor productivity 27–8, *28*
Lazonick, W. 124

Leary, M. T. 125
Lenin, V. 141
leverage and financialization by social class 70–2, *71*
Lévy, D. 114
Lindblom, C. 140
loading on the dependent variable 4, 16, 18; and inequality 60; use of NIPAs to avoid, 92, 94

Madison, J. 148
Marcuse, H. 147
Max Weber and German Politics 144
Methodology of the Social Sciences, The 143
Mexican-American war 20
military expenditures 29, *29*
Mill, J. S. 145
modernization theory 144–5
Mommsen, W. 144
monetary policies 21–2
Musk, E. 135
mutual funds 101

National income and product accounts (NIPAs) 3–5, 13, 16–17, 27, 55–6, 136; investment and consumption in, 1929–2019 *30–2*, 30–3; tendencies of wages and labor income shares from 1929–2020 in 84–6, *85–6*; US personal income and its disposition in the US, 1929–2019 86–92, **87–8, 91**
necropolitics 146–7
neocolonialism 138–9
New Deal programs 19, 25, 30, 33, 36, 84
New York Stock Exchange (NYSE) 15, 22, *22*, 22–6, *24*
nonfinancial corporations (NFCs), financialization of 9–10, 137; conclusions on 129–30; introduction to 111–14; profits-without-investment puzzle and 112; rise of debt and 124–6, *124–6*; rise of financial assets and *120*, 120–3; rise of financial income and 114–20, **115**, *115–18*; shareholder primacy narrative 112–13; *versus* unincorporated business firms 126–9, *127–8*

Orhangazi, Ö. 114–16

pension funds 101
personal consumption, 1929–2019 90–2, **91**

156 Index

personal income: consumption, private investment, and government, 1929–2020 92–5, *93–4*; in the NIPAs, 1929–2019 86–90, **87–8**

pluralism 1–2, 6, 10; critical political economy and 55; US traditions and 139–40

Polanyi, K. 1–2

political development theory 142

political economy, US 139–43; democracy and 141, 143–5; of financialization and growth in 25–30, *26–9*; inequality in classic modern 59–61; long-term perspectives on *18*, 18–25, *21–2, 24*; Max Weber and 139, 143–5; recent events and 135–6, 137–8

Political Order in Changing Societies 142

prices 19–21, *21*

private investment, 1929–2020 92–5, *93–4*

Rabinovich, J. 119, 121–2, 123

representative government 141

Roberts, M. R. 125

savings and investment rates: 1930–2010s 47–9, **48**; political factors and 56–7

savings deposits 100–1

Schluchter, W. 143–4

Schwartz, H. M. 118, 122

separation of powers, 2, 139–40

social class: financialization of inequality and balance sheets of US, 1989–2019 72–84, **73–80**; ratios of financialization and leverage by, 1989–2019 70–2, *71*

taxes 61–5, *62, 64*

Tesla, Inc. 135

Thompson, E. P. 1–2

time deposits 100–1

totalitarian centralization 141

trade receivable assets 118, *118*

transfers, social policy 61–5, *62, 64*

Trump, D. 135

unemployment 17; 1948–2020 36–41, *37–40*

unincorporated business firms 126–9, *127–8*

US constitution of national income accounts, 2, 136

van Buren, M. 56

Veblen, T. 122

Vietnam War 19, 20, 29, 85

Volcker, P. 119

wage rates 19–20

War of 1812 20

wealth: capitalization of 60, 82; measures of 58–9

Weber, M. 139, 143–5

Welfare States 62, 65, 140

World War II 14, 85

Z1 Reports 98–102, *99*

Printed in the United States
by Baker & Taylor Publisher Services